Grantlee Kieza OAM was Australia's leading boxing journalist for more than 40 years, and in 2018 was inducted into the Australian Boxing Hall of Fame for his writing and work as a cornerman for some of Australia's greatest fighters. He was beside trainer Johnny Lewis for all three of Jeff Fenech's world championship triumphs and was also in the corner for other greats including Jeff Harding, Lovemore Ndou, and Aussie Joe Bugner. He held senior editorial positions at *The Daily Telegraph*, *The Sunday Telegraph* and *The Courier-Mail* for many years – and interviewed some of history's greatest champs from as far back as the 1920s. He was awarded the Medal of the Order of Australia for his writing, as well as three Queensland Media Awards and two Australian Sports Commission Awards. He was a finalist in the Walkley Awards and for the Harry Gordon Award for Australian sports journalist of the year.

Grantlee Kieza with Jeff Fenech, Jeff Horn, and the WBO welterweight title belt Horn took from Manny Pacquiao a few days later before more than 50,000 people at Suncorp Stadium. *Darren Edwards*

T0267185

GRANTLEE KIEZA

KNOCKOUT

GREAT
AUSTRALIAN
BOXING
STORIES

ABC
BOOKS

Aboriginal and Torres Strait Islander readers are respectfully advised this book contains names and descriptions of people now deceased.

 The ABC 'Wave' device is a trademark of the Australian Broadcasting Corporation and is used under licence by HarperCollins*Publishers* Australia.

HarperCollins*Publishers*
Australia • Brazil • Canada • France • Germany • Holland • India
Italy • Japan • Mexico • New Zealand • Poland • Spain • Sweden
Switzerland • United Kingdom • United States of America

HarperCollins acknowledges the Traditional Custodians
of the land upon which we live and work, and pays respect
to Elders past and present.

First published in Australia in 2023
by HarperCollins*Publishers* Australia Pty Limited
Gadigal Country
Level 19, 201 Elizabeth Street, Sydney NSW 2000
ABN 36 009 913 517
harpercollins.com.au

A catalogue record for this book is available from the National Library of Australia

ISBN 978 0 7333 4260 8 (paperback)
ISBN 978 1 4607 1542 0 (ebook)

Cover design by Louisa Maggio, HarperCollins Design Studio
Cover images: Lionel Rose by Bettmann / Getty Images; Jeff Fenech by Ken Levine / Getty Images
Back cover image: Author's private collection
Typeset in ITC Bookman Std by Kirby Jones
Printed and bound by CPI Group (UK) Ltd, Croydon, CR0 4YY

For Angelo Di Carlo,
a great friend to the fight game and to me

Contents

The Later Rounds

INTRODUCTION

Taking on Mike Tyson and the World's Greatest Fighters

Mike Tyson, the most feared boxer in the world, grabbed the front of my shirt and hurled me towards a wall. His face tattoo scrunched into a smudge around his fierce, burning eyes as he bared his teeth and let out a loud, guttural snarl. Like so many of Tyson's terrified opponents, I limply tried to cover up, bony elbows in front of my face. But Tyson was too fast. He pivoted low, squatting down on his tree-trunk thighs, then, in an instant, he swivelled into a left hook that rocketed towards my chin. Over the years I'd sat down to eat with world heavyweight champs from Adolf Hitler's hero Max Schmeling to Vladimir Putin's nemesis Vitali Klitschko, but now I was being force-fed a knuckle sandwich by the most ferocious of them all. My life flashed before my eyes.

Reporting on boxing had been a big part of that life from the time I covered my first professional fight at Brisbane's old Festival Hall in 1980 on a night Tony Mundine beat Steve Aczel.

Eighteen months later I was writing for *The Daily Telegraph* in Sydney and doing boxing training of my own at the inner-city Newtown Police Boys Club. It was there I met the young amateur fighter Jeff Fenech.

Jeff had been a juvenile delinquent and reluctant guest of a boy's home, but he had a dream to fight at the Los Angeles Olympics under the guidance of his coach, Johnny Lewis, who lived in the Erskineville public housing flats and worked as a signwriter for the local council.

Johnny asked me to help him with his fighters in the gym and work in their corners as a second on fight night, and for the next decade, as Fenech battered all comers from around the world, packing out major stadiums in Brisbane, Sydney and Melbourne, I was in his corner.

Fenech even helped me sell tickets when I decided to have a crack at promoting fights as well in the early 1980s. One of the bouts, at Griffith in the New South Wales Riverina and featuring the former Commonwealth champ Jeff Malcolm, was covered by a young local newspaper reporter named Michael McCormack, who went on to become Australia's Deputy Prime Minister.

I ended up also working the corner for some of the biggest fights ever involving Australians, including Lovemore Ndou's incredibly brave effort in going 12 rounds with the Mexican Canelo Alvarez at a baseball stadium in Veracruz in 2010, and Bob Mirovic taking on the 213-centimetre-tall Russian Nikolai Valuev in Germany.

Fenech's success resurrected boxing in Australia to the levels it had enjoyed from the 1930s to the 1950s, when it rivalled the major football codes for popularity, with stars such as Jimmy Carruthers, Vic Patrick, George Barnes, Fred Henneberry, Tommy Burns and Jack Hassen, all of whom I interviewed over the years.

In 1989 I was in Atlantic City, New Jersey, to see another Johnny Lewis fighter, Jeff Harding, become world light-heavyweight champion. The fight's co-promoter was a big-noting real estate spruiker named Donald Trump.

Two of the biggest fights I covered were in England. In 1987 I was in Aussie Joe Bugner's corner when he fought future world champ Frank Bruno before 37,000 people at White Hart Lane, the home ground of the Tottenham Hotspurs football team, and in 2005 I watched Ricky Hatton's swarming pressure overcome Kostya Tszyu's power in Manchester.

A week later I was in Washington DC doing battle with Tyson. Thankfully, 'Iron Mike' was just playing around, and he put the brakes on his left hook before it hit me in the head. Jeff Fenech took some photos of us shaping up together.

At the time Fenech was training Tyson for a comeback fight against an Irish behemoth named Kevin McBride.

Muhammad Ali was in Tyson's dressing-room that night and he gave me a sad little wave and a half-smile of regret as he slowly shuffled out of Washington DC's MCI Centre later that evening, hanging onto his ex-wife Veronica Porché.

A dozen years later I was in another dressing-room, this time at Suncorp Stadium where Jeff Horn had just defied the odds and logic to beat Manny Pacquiao, one of the most celebrated boxers of all time. Horn was lying on a massage table in his blood-splattered boxing trunks and boots, as still as a dead man. His brother Ben gently held a plastic bag full of ice against the torn and tattered face of the new world welterweight champion.

Prepared brilliantly by the coaches Glenn Rushton and Dundee Kim, Horn had just won the biggest fight in Australian history before more than 51,000 people at Suncorp and a television audience estimated to be 500 million.

That afternoon I shook the humble hero's hand and told him his victory was the most extraordinary thing I had seen in a lifetime of covering boxing. A mild-mannered schoolteacher who didn't like fighting had just beaten one of the most savage sluggers in history.

It was proof that in the mad, chaotic, mesmerising sport of boxing anything can happen. Anything.

Grantlee Kieza
May 2023

HITS AND MEMORIES

Jai Opetaia: The Toughest Man In the World

Australia's iconic boxing champion of the 1940s, Vic Patrick, once told me that even if you were just a sparring partner or prelim fighter it still took a lot of heart to lace on a glove. Jai Opetaia must have a heart the size of a watermelon. On 2 July 2022, he defied the agony and handicap of a badly broken jaw to topple the rugged Latvian Mairis Briedis for the world cruiserweight title.

Opetaia finished the fight with his jaw swinging like a pendulum in a high wind. The injury was so severe, he couldn't even grit his teeth to cope with the excruciating pain.

Having been inspired to pursue greatness in his sport by his Socceroo cousin Tim Cahill, Opetaia overcame hand and rib surgeries, a bad case of the flu and then the death of his grandmother in fight week before punching on through almost unimaginable agony as Briedis teed off with heavy shots on Opetaia's pulverised face.

Opetaia's world title win at the Gold Coast Convention Centre was an astonishing feat of courage, a performance that drew comparisons with South Sydney Rabbitohs hardman John

Sattler winning the 1970 grand final after his jaw was broken in the opening minutes.

It wasn't until two weeks after surgery following his win that the 27-year-old fighter could even move his mouth enough to talk about how the crushing fists of his opponent broke his jaw on both sides.

Opetaia told Sydney's *Sun-Herald* that by the end of the fight his jaw wasn't even connected to his skull.

'The will to win was a lot stronger than the pain,' he explained. 'I didn't even second-guess it. I was willing to die in that ring.'

Opetaia's jaw was first broken on the left side by an uppercut in the second or third round. He tried to bite his bottom jaw into his mouthguard to make it more solid, but the left side of his jaw was displaced.

Then Briedis broke the other side of his jaw.

'Now that I look back on it, it really makes my stomach curl,' Opetaia said.

Still, the young, superbly conditioned southpaw held tough and landed more punches on Briedis than Briedis landed on him.

Knowing he was trailing on the scorecards, Briedis attacked relentlessly in the second half of the fight, but Opetaia boxed superbly, despite his injuries, and took a unanimous points decision.

Opetaia underwent surgery on his jaw at the Gold Coast University Hospital and recovered in the same hospital room where he'd been ten weeks earlier after surgery on ribs torn off the cartilage during sparring.

His victory was also an astounding triumph for his new trainer, Mark Wilson, who has worked with many of Australia's leading amateur boxers, including heavyweight sensation Justis Huni.

Wilson had been asked to come on board as Opetaia's coach six months before the world title win. The pair had worked closely together during Opetaia's amateur days in the lead-up to his appearance at the London Olympics, not long after his 17th birthday.

Wilson is very much an old-school trainer, having learned boxing in his western Queensland hometown of Cunnamulla from 'Bronco' Johnson, whose son Billy was a renowned rugby league hooker and a champion boxer.

I'd promoted Billy's last professional fight in 1984, on a card at Belmore Sports Ground in the days when he was the Bulldogs' first-grade hooker.

Wilson had little time to celebrate in the aftermath of the pulsating bout.

He had breakfast with his family and then drove 1000 kilometres west back to Cunnamulla to honour his pledge to be a guest speaker at a junior rugby league carnival.

Jeff Horn: School Teacher Sets Lesson in Courage

Jai Opetaia's world title victory came five years to the day after Jeff Horn's monumental upset of Manny Pacquiao for the World Boxing Organization (WBO) welterweight title (66 kg) on 2 July 2017. Both fights were promoted by Dean Lonergan, a former New Zealand representative rugby league player who saw the opportunity to make boxing a stadium sport in Queensland with the right bouts.

Horn and Opetaia had been teammates at the London Olympics, where Horn was the best-performing Australian, making it into the quarter-finals. The Australian men's team at those Games was an outstanding line-up that also included Ibrahim Balla, Cameron Hammond, Damien Hooper, Luke Jackson, Johan Linde, Jesse Ross, Billy Ward and Jackson Woods.

Against Pacquiao, Horn not only won his own personal gold medal bout but created a piece of stunning history before the biggest crowd ever for an Australian boxing contest.

In the late afternoon sun, before more than 51,000 roaring fans at Suncorp Stadium, Horn showed that nice guys can finish first.

I'd first met him three years earlier, when, together with photographer Peter Wallis, I profiled 'The Fighting Schoolteacher' for a newspaper article. Peter captured some wonderful photos of Jeff working as a relief teacher at the Pallara State School in Sydney's south-west. He was surrounded by eager young students, including one girl who donned a pair of boxing gloves for the picture and proceeded to land a series of mean left hooks on her patient schoolmaster.

Jeff was one of the most remarkable sportsmen I'd ever met in 40 years of covering sports around the world, a decent and polite young guy who, despite his good nature, made his living as a schoolteacher before finding a more lucrative career in the toughest and most brutal sport of all.

At the time of the Pacquiao fight, Horn's ailing grandfather Ray Horn was 89 and battling the flu. There were grave fears he'd be too crook to be ringside but he made it and was slumped in a chair next to me, the hood of a Jeff Horn souvenir tracksuit pulled over his bare scalp to protect it from the savage Brisbane sun.

We were right behind Horn's corner, and even though Ray was almost blind and pretty deaf, he broke into a huge grin when he heard the challenger's theme song, 'Seven Nation Army', pumping from the loudspeakers. He knew that 'young Jeff', as he called him, would soon be starring in Australia's biggest-ever fight.

Marching to history, Horn stopped briefly on his way to the ring to touch fists with the old man.

On the night before the fight, Manny Pacquiao had led a Bible class in Brisbane, where he'd prayed for Horn's safety as he has done for all his opponents in recent years.

Pacquiao should have been more worried about his own safety as Horn showed that he was a much more dangerous opponent than Pacquiao expected. The Filipino's camp had claimed that, given the champ's experience and reputation, he could knock

Horn out any time he wanted. Pacquiao tried and tried in the early rounds, only to hit air more than target.

In Round 6 Pacquiao suffered a bad cut on the right side of his head, but the ringside doctor let the fight continue.

By Round 7 the left side of Pacquiao's scalp was gushing blood and Horn had bruises and bumps all over his forehead from the head clashes. At the end of the round Horn's father, Jeff Sr, a small man with a huge smile, was almost bursting with pride and expectation as he came over to Ray. 'Dad,' he said, 'Jeff is about to become the welterweight champion of the world!'

But in Round 8, Horn hit a roadblock, hard. Pacquiao pushed Horn over but the American referee, Mark Nelson, ruled a slip. Horn finished the round with the right side of his face badly swollen.

Then Pacquiao surged in the ninth, as his vaunted left hand (and plenty of rights too) found the target.

Horn was rocked repeatedly, his legs wobbled and he staggered.

The referee's shirt was spattered with blood. 'You've had enough,' he told Horn. 'Show me something in this round or I'm stopping the fight.'

But Horn was not about to quit. He gained the upper hand in Round 10, and while Pacquiao still looked dangerous, Horn was back to using footwork to dodge shots.

In Round 11, the referee warned The Fighting Schoolteacher for pushing Pacquiao in the throat with his elbow in a clinch, but at that point Horn didn't care what he did for victory.

The pair slugged it out in the 12th and final round, but Horn was getting the better of it.

Horn's wife, Jo, pregnant with their first child, was cheering louder than anyone as he roared towards victory. His mother, Liza, pumped her fists towards the heavens and his dad couldn't wipe the smile off his face.

* * *

At the end of the bloodbath Australia had a new sporting hero.

Liza, who recalled having to wrap her arms around her son many times after bullies attacked him at school, exclaimed: 'I'm just overcome. I'm so proud. I know how hard he has worked for this. It's hard to believe this is the same boy who was picked on at school.'

'This has been a remarkable journey,' Horn's father told me, 'and it just shows what anyone can achieve with determination and a plan.'

Later, in Horn's dressing-room, Jo sat quietly with her battered husband, alongside me and the few members of his inner circle, while Dr Ben Manion inserted seven stitches in blue thread over the right eye of the new world champ.

Eleven years earlier Jo had fallen in love with a shy, introverted and bookish teenager at MacGregor High in Brisbane's south. She always calls him Jeffrey.

He was a bit of a nerd then, she recalled, a nerd who had taken up boxing because of bullying at high school.

Now her husband had just beaten one of the most ferocious boxers of all time in an epic brawl, one of Australia's greatest ever sporting events.

'He's still a bit of a nerd but now Jeffrey's the world champion,' she said proudly that afternoon, still shaking her head at the enormity of the occasion. 'Wow. This has just been the most amazing day. An amazing day.'

After the fight, grandad Ray Horn was embraced by Queensland Sports Minister Kate Jones, who had tears in her eyes.

Ray's eyes were misty with a mix of pride and joy as he declared that seeing Horn win the world title was one of the best days of his long life. He'd once carried the bag of the Australian champ Tommy Burns in Brisbane when he was a kid. This was much better. 'Seeing Jeff become world champ is one of the things that's kept me going these last few years,' he told me. 'He's always been such a lovely young bloke and I've always wished the very best for him. Nothing will top what he did today.'

George Kambosos: The Spartan Warrior

One of Manny Pacquiao's main sparring partners for the Horn fight was a battling Sydney professional named George Kambosos Jr. George had boxed in virtual obscurity for many years, funding his career with meat raffles, despite scoring good wins over top Aussies such as Brandon Ogilvie and Qamil Balla.

Kambosos sparred 45 rounds with Pacquiao in the Philippines in the weeks leading up to the Horn fight and talked up Pacquiao's chances at full volume, predicting Horn would not last six rounds.

He ended up with egg on his face that time, but Kambosos covered himself in glory four years later at boxing's most famous arena, Madison Square Garden in New York, where he scored a stunning upset against the previously unbeaten hometown star Teofimo López for the world lightweight title.

A 7–1 underdog, 'Ferocious' Kambosos dropped Lopez in the process and then climbed off the canvas himself to win a nail-biting decision.

Lopez was a feared knockout puncher who was coming off an upset of his own against the Ukrainian wizard and two-time Olympic gold medallist Vasiliy Lomachenko.

But Kambosos asserted himself early, decking Lopez with a perfect right-hand counter in Round 1 to announce his arrival as a genuine world beater in the lightweight (135 lb or 61 kg) division.

'I felt Lopez was a bully,' Kambosos told the podcaster Joe Rogan. 'He bullied all his past opponents but I've come from being bullied. I was an overweight kid at a young age, and I'd been bullied all my life. I was 135 pounds (61 kg) at ten years of age until I fell into boxing. I knew straight away how to stand up to this guy.'

Bloody but unbowed Kambosos had to climb from the canvas in Round 10 to seal the points decision.

Later he told the *Bleacher Report*: 'Any other lightweight in the world would not have lasted. I got up. I showed the heart that I have. I'm a warrior. I'm a spartan warrior. I'm cut from a different cloth. There really is no quit, there is no retreat or surrender in my head.'

Kambosos was born in Sydney in 1993, but his paternal grandparents had moved there from the Greek town of Sparta. Kambosos has the Spartan war cry 'Never Retreat, Never Surrender' tattooed on his back.

Lionel Rose Inspires a Nation

In all the extraordinary triumphs of Australian boxers, there has never been a performance to top the victory by 19-year-old Gunditjmara man Lionel Rose against Japan's world bantamweight champ Fighting Harada in Tokyo on 27 February 1968.

Rose had spent his early years in a dirt-floor shack made from strips of bark, among a handful of similar humpies in an Aboriginal settlement called Jacksons Track in the bush of Victoria's Gippsland.

There was no running water, no electricity and certainly no money. Kerosene lamps, candles or the flickering light from his mother's cooking fire inside an old oil drum illuminated the ragged home at night. Lionel grew up eating possums, rabbits and wallabies. He and his siblings cleaned their teeth with charcoal and slept on chaff bags.

Despite his humble start in life, he wielded the aristocratic name Lionel Edmund Rose, a moniker, one American writer said, that was more suited to a pukka colonel from a Rudyard Kipling story than a prize-fighter.

Now Rose was facing a formidable, all-action champion in front of a hostile crowd in Tokyo's Nippon Budokan Hall – World War II was still fresh in the minds of boxing fans around the world. By the end of the fight he'd scored an astonishing victory, repelling the kamikaze attacks of the savage world champion with superb footwork and hand speed.

After his monumental win by 15-round points decision, Rose returned to Melbourne on the last day of summer, a broiling, breezy Thursday. The little teenage boxer seated towards the back of the DC-9 was dressed in a freshly pressed suit with tie and pocket handkerchief. His world had changed forever.

In a nation that prided itself on punching above its weight at sport, this shy, modest 53-kilogram 19-year-old had notched up a victory so remarkable he would soon be voted Australian of the Year and receive one of the Queen's most prized awards – a Member of the Most Excellent Order of the British Empire (MBE).

They were impressive accolades for a young Indigenous man in a country that had only just included its first people in its census and was not noted for honouring them.

As the DC-9 began its descent, Lionel remembered the words of George Bracken, another Aboriginal fighter who was his inspiration. 'Boxing is one of the few places where an Aborigine can be treated as an equal,' Bracken had told him, again and again. 'Because with our people, we all started life behind the eight ball.'

The DC-9 touched down with a screech of tyres and a smell of smoking rubber. Lionel saw an unusually large crowd surrounding the airport terminal. Australians of all ages and races were waving and cheering and holding up placards. The sight reminded him of the photos he'd seen of crowds awaiting rock stars from America and England.

Lionel turned to the flight attendant. 'Excuse me, miss,' he said. 'What are all the people doing here? You got The Beatles up the front or something?'

'No,' she replied, surprised. 'Those people are here to see you.'

The reception for Australia's first Indigenous world champion was unlike anything ever seen in this country. It was a seminal moment in the nation's history and in our changing attitude towards Indigenous people, all brought about by the bravery and skill of a young boxer from a disadvantaged background.

An estimated 250,000 people lined the route from the airport to Melbourne Town Hall. Nobody – not The Beatles, the Queen or US president Lyndon Johnson – had ever drawn a cheering crowd like the one Lionel drew that day. More than a century and a half after Australia's first recorded prize fight between two convicts in Sydney, boxing had scaled its greatest height.

Not too many years before, Lionel had sparred with rags on his hands because he couldn't afford gloves, learning his craft in a ring his father made from fencing wire stretched between saplings. Now, a fleet of open-top limousines ferried him and his team to the town hall.

It was less than a decade since Lionel and his grandmother, Adelaide Rose, then almost 70, hitchhiked from Jacksons Track to Melbourne so the little boy could see George Bracken win a fight.

Few fighters I have known were as inspiring as Lionel Rose: humble, gracious, funny and so unaffected by his success that his favourite pastime in later life was a slow walk to the TAB to place small wagers on even slower horses.

Boxing gave him a platform and a status he might otherwise never have known.

Kostya Tszyu's Last Hurrah

One of the most brutal fights I ever covered was yet another shock result: local hero Ricky Hatton's 2005 stoppage of Australia's adopted Russian import Kostya Tszyu after 11 rounds at England's Manchester Arena.

It was a toe-to-toe brawl that featured several borderline low blows by Tszyu in Round nine, and then a blatant full-blooded smash to the groin from Hatton that put Tszyu on his knees.

'Well, it's a fight,' an unapologetic Hatton explained to me later, 'it's not a tickling contest.'

Hatton conceded, though, that he felt genuine sorrow after handing out a savage beating to Tszyu before 22,000 fans that ended the pigtailed star's career.

'Of course, no one likes to see a great champion hurt and stopped,' Hatton said.

'But I'm sure Kostya would rather go out on his shield like he did tonight. If I can achieve half of what Kostya has done in his career I'll be a very proud man.'

Tszyu was taken to hospital immediately after the fight with a suspected broken jaw. He was also urinating blood, but he was later cleared of any serious damage.

Yet despite the beating he'd suffered and the enormous disappointment he felt after 27 years in the fight game, Tszyu's graciousness in defeat earned him the hostile crowd's respect.

'I am a proud man,' Tszyu told them after Hatton's hand was raised in victory, 'but I lost to the better fighter. I planned lots of things, but Ricky was better than me in every way tonight.'

When Tszyu landed in England two weeks before the fight he'd demanded the superstar treatment. He arrived at the MEN Arena in an enormous stretch limousine surrounded by 80 bodyguards, hired in case the crowd went berserk when Tszyu iced their hometown hero as most experts and bookies predicted.

But when Tszyu was being mugged in the 10th and 11th Rounds, none of the tattooed musclemen hired to protect him could offer any assistance.

Instead, it was Tszyu's veteran trainer Johnny Lewis who surveyed the cut under Kostya's left eye, the huge swelling on both cheekbones and the weariness in the legs of the 35-year-old war machine. Johnny told British referee Dave Parris that his boy was done.

'Kostya needed a knockout to win,' Lewis said, 'and he didn't have a knockout in him.'

Tszyu received $5.4 million for the fight, while Hatton, who made $3 million, created a magic moment for British fight fans equivalent to Randolph Turpin's shock victory over middleweight great Sugar Ray Robinson in 1951.

Hatton had earned the nickname 'Ricky Fatton' because of his heavy appearance between fights, but he lost more than 20 kilograms to make the junior-welterweight limit of 63.5 kilograms for the epic battle.

He said he couldn't wait to get reacquainted with two of his oldest friends, 'Mr Guinness and Mr Dom Perignon' after shunning their products while training.

'I knew it would take the greatest performance of my life, but I always believed I could stop Kostya,' Hatton said.

'Kostya is 35 and he had peaked. I'm 26 and just hitting my best now.'

From the outset, the Englishman, fighting like his hero Jeff Fenech, had elected to take the fight to the heavier-hitting Tszyu and wear him down.

He had immediate success, but the Tszyu camp believed Hatton would eventually run out of gas. He didn't.

'You have to have balls of steel – a lot of bottle and courage to fight Kostya Tszyu like that,' Hatton said, 'to take him head on and try to get inside his powerful punches.

'When my corner told me that he wasn't coming out for the last round I was so happy that I almost shot my bolt.'

Kostya learned pretty quickly that fame usually doesn't last in boxing.

I interviewed the mighty heavyweight Smokin' Joe Frazier several times, the first when he arrived in Sydney in July 2005 as a guest at the Sir Roden Cutler Medal dinner.

It had been 30 years since Frazier's first visit to Australia, when he'd knocked out another former heavyweight champ Jimmy Ellis at the Junction Oval in St Kilda.

Frazier's win earned him a third fight with Muhammad Ali in the 'Thrilla in Manilla', a fight so savage both men felt that they were close to death at the end.

Hard fights took their toll. When I first met Frazier, he seemed a lot older than his 61 years. His eyes were languid and he told me he didn't follow boxing closely anymore.

I was at the dinner with Kostya, who had just lost his world title to Ricky Hatton. After introducing myself to Joe as a sportswriter, I introduced him to the pigtailed former world champ.

Joe had no idea who Tszyu was. He asked perhaps the greatest junior-welterweight of all time: 'You a sportswriter, too?'

Tim and Nikita Tszyu: The Sons Also Rise

Most great fighters grow up poor and hungry in the school of hard knocks but Kostya's fighting sons Tim and Nikita Tszyu, Australia's latest boxing sensations, went to one of Sydney's most expensive private schools – Newington College – and grew up in a mansion with their father's Bentley in the garage.

'But my dad never gave me anything for free,' Tim once told me. 'He was so focused – like an army sergeant. With or without money everything had to be precise, had to be on point, no arguments. When you have a father like that it's actually quite a tough upbringing. Life with my father wasn't easy. It was actually quite hard. He made me work. He made me hungry for success.'

I remember Tim and his younger brother Nikita as small boys swinging from the top rope of the boxing ring in Kostya's gym as though they were on monkey bars in the playground.

'My earliest memories of boxing are going to that gym,' Tim told me. 'At a very young age I was training with my uncle (Igor Golubev) and I'm still training with him now. From a young age

I was always put in with the big boys who could fight, so I was always challenged. I love challenges and I love big tasks. That's what motivates me.'

Tim grew up studying fighters and fighting. Apart from his father, the best boxer he ever saw was Roy Jones Jr. 'I loved his style growing up,' he said. 'Mike Tyson as well, Lennox Lewis, that great rivalry. I'm a big fan of Floyd Mayweather, too. I like the way Floyd fights. I like the way he approaches boxing. Lately I've taken a liking to GGG (Gennady Golovkin) and it's a goal of mine to fight him as well. I try to learn from those guys, but I don't really try to copy their style.'

In 33 amateur fights, Tim lost only once, against the Rio Olympian Daniel Lewis, and he won the Golden Gloves at Caboolture in Queensland three times. Younger brother Nikita was also a standout amateur before taking a long break from boxing to study architecture.

Tim admitted that it hurt, when after years of extolling the importance of family and his way of life in Australia, Kostya left both to start a new family back in his native Russia.

'My dad found new goals and as a man I understand what he did. I never took it to heart,' Tim explained.

'We are still friends and that's all that matters.'

In 2017 Tszyu posed for a photo with Jeff Horn for a newspaper article I was writing in the lead-up to the Horn-Pacquiao fight.

Tim was only a novice pro at the time but ambitious.

'Watching the Pacquiao fight convinced me I could beat Horn,' Tim said. 'I was in the crowd at Suncorp Stadium that day and as soon as Horn won I told my manager [Glen Jennings] that I believed I could beat him. It became my goal, and I worked my way to getting the fight.'

Tim believed that after Horn beat Pacquiao, the Australian's hunger had waned, and so it proved to be when they fought in Townsville in August 2020.

Tim sparred with Manny Pacquiao for three weeks in Manila before stopping Horn in eight rounds, with Horn on the canvas in Rounds 3 and 6.

Two years later Nikita Tszyu outpointed Horn's brother Ben at the Hordern Pavilion in Sydney.

Nikita Tszyu said he followed his father's example in toughening his hands by punching them every day into a bowl containing ball bearings, and that he and Tim had engaged in so many fights against each other as youngsters, often bareknuckle, that he couldn't keep score.

On 12 March 2023, Tim scored a ninth-round stoppage of Detroit's lanky former world champ Tony Harrison at the Qudos Bank Arena in Sydney, winning the vacant WBO interim junior-middleweight title.

Who Wins: Jeff Fenech versus Kostya Tszyu?

Most of what I know about boxing I learned from two great mentors – Johnny Lewis and Ray Wheatley.

For years, Ray was Australia's most influential official on the world stage, organising many world title fights for Australians through the New Jersey-based International Boxing Federation (IBF). He was also the most successful publisher of boxing magazines ever in Australia, his *World of Boxing*, *Title Fight* and *Australian Boxing Legends* magazines running for 30 years. He bashed me up sparring a few times, too.

Johnny is this country's most successful fight trainer, taking six boxers to world championships: Jeff Fenech, Jeff Harding, Kostya Tszyu, Gairy St Clair, Billy Dib and the American Virgil Hill. His most recent star was the Tokyo Olympic bronze medallist Harry Garside, who uses ballet as part of his training and wore nail polish during his Olympic campaign, citing his desire to defy gender stereotypes. I was lucky enough to be Johnny's offsider in all of Fenech's world title wins and in many bouts featuring Harding and other Lewis fighters, including Aussie Joe Bugner, Peter Mitrevski, Shane Knox and Pat Hailwood.

For much of his career Johnny was a humble Erskineville signwriter who coached amateur boxers after work. In 2016, he was inducted into New York's International Boxing Hall of Fame. Sadly, the news of his award came in the same week as the passing of his much-loved mother, Marge.

'Mum would have been so proud,' he said, 'but I know she is in heaven smiling down on me. She probably got the news of the award before I did.

'I have had a wonderful time in boxing. It is a great sport and as I always say the secret to being a good trainer is having good fighters who work hard. I certainly had the very best.'

Thirty-five years earlier, back in 1981, Johnny had begun training a wild young tearaway named Jeff Fenech at the Newtown Police Youth Club. He asked me to help out in Fenech's corner.

It was a wild ride unlike any ever in Australian boxing. Within eight years Fenech had become the most successful fighter in Australian history, winning three world titles while still undefeated and knocking out the 1984 Olympic gold medallist Steve McCrory.

Fenech's success brought other champions to Lewis's door, first light-heavyweight (79 kg) Jeff Harding and then Kostya Tszyu, who dominated the junior-welterweight division for a decade, destroying one champion after another.

One of the constant questions Johnny was asked was who was the better fighter, Fenech or Tszyu?

'Jeff Fenech,' Johnny said without hesitation. 'What Jeff did in boxing, I don't know if we'll ever see that equalled again. Jeff only had twenty-eight amateur fights and half of those were in Police Boys Clubs, yet he still won a medal at the World Cup and with fairer judging could have won the Olympic gold medal in 1984. As it was, he knocked out the gold medallist, Steve McCrory, two years later to retain his world bantamweight title.

'Kostya had a huge start on Jeff. When he turned pro, Kostya already had something like 300 amateur fights against the best in the world, other Russians, Cubans, Americans and East Germans. Jeff trained with such intensity; he would do more work in an hour in the gym than Kostya would do in two. He would fight or spar anyone – even trade punches with another of my world champs, Jeff Harding, who was 20 kilograms heavier – whereas Kostya wouldn't move out of his division [junior-welterweight]. Jeff could fight all night and never get tired, and Jeff Harding was like that, too. Kostya had a tendency to tire and sometimes he tired early. Kostya was very fortunate that he had a great punch in both hands.'

Johnny was a long-time committee man at the Newtown Jets rugby league club and later a trainer for the Australian rugby league team. On one occasion in 1985, Johnny and I were guests of the Queensland rugby league team for a State of Origin match at Brisbane's old Lang Park before it was rebuilt as Suncorp Stadium.

Jeff Fenech was up from Sydney to fight a tough, wiry bantamweight from England named John Farrell at Brisbane's Festival Hall three days after the State of Origin, so he came along. On the night, Queensland beat the Blues 20–6, but much of the action that evening was outside the ground.

Johnny had made the mistake of wearing a Blues hat to the game. As we walked out of the stadium one of the Queensland fans, celebrating with a can in his hand, crash tackled him onto the concrete footpath, tearing all the skin off Johnny's hands.

Jeff quickly decked the assailant with a short left hook. As Johnny struggled to get up off the concrete, Fenech hovered over his attacker, fist cocked for another swing.

Then we heard a booming voice: 'Jeff, don't hit him, please don't hit him.' It was the great John Sattler, the man who won a grand final for the Rabbitohs despite a broken jaw. He was charging at us like he was about to bulldoze us out of the way to score a try.

We thought 'Satts' was running in to save the life of Johnny's assailant, but instead he kicked the culprit up the backside so hard he almost launched him into orbit. The poor bloke is probably still walking around bow-legged.

Tommy Raudonikis and the Mile-High Club

Johnny Lewis became friends with the great Newtown Jets halfback Tommy Raudonikis as well as the club's wealthy backer, John Singleton.

In 1982, Tommy and Johnny had to fly to Griffith in country New South Wales on a promotional visit for 'Singo' along with Paul Ferreri, who was a slick Commonwealth bantamweight boxing champion and a dapper dresser. They would be travelling in a tiny four-seater plane with a trainee pilot at the controls.

Johnny admits he has a heart the size of a pea and was shaking even before they took off. 'Tommy had got on the plane straight from a Newtown game at Henson Park,' Johnny said. 'He didn't have time to shower and he was covered in so much dirt he looked like one of those New Guinea mud men. He'd forgotten to put his teeth back in after the game and was also carrying a carton of beer.'

Paul Ferreri was from Melbourne and had no idea who this weird-looking bloke all covered in dirt and mud was.

They were somewhere over the Blue Mountains and Tommy had already sunk half a dozen cans and was busting for a leak when he realised there was no dunny on the plane. He decided to improvise by relieving himself into an empty Toohey's can but he missed the mark and instead sprayed all over Paul Ferreri's new, neatly pressed clothes.

Johnny had to jump between them to stop Round 1. Then, with the little plane rocking all over the place due to turbulence, Tommy decided to light up a smoke. Before long, his ash had ignited the shag pile carpet on the walls of the cabin. Now the plane was on fire, 3000 metres in the air. Desperately, Johnny used the contents of one of Tommy's beer cans to extinguish the flames.

Johnny's great success rate in boxing has been compared to Wayne Bennett's in rugby league. The two became good friends. Johnny met Wayne through Bennett's players, who were on Australian rugby league teams when Johnny was the national side's fitness trainer. They included Kerrod and Kevvie Walters, Steve Renouf and Gary Belcher.

In 1992, Johnny was in Bismarck, North Dakota, with his boxer, the hometown star Virgil Hill for a world title fight. Virgil was getting on the scales when Johnny got a long-distance call from Wayne at the Sydney Football Stadium. Wayne was ringing to thank Johnny for the help he gave Wayne's Broncos players in beating St George in the grand final.

With so much success in the sport, what's Johnny's best memory from the fight game?

'With each of my fighters there's something that sticks out,' he told me. 'But I'd have to say number one was getting Jeff Fenech to the Olympics in 1984. We were both broke and there was no prize money, just the joy of succeeding from all the hard work he put in. Personally, I'd been on a bit of a downer at the time because Newtown had been put out of the New South Wales rugby league competition at the end of 1983.

'I was still working as a signwriter then and I was lucky that I could pour my sporting interest into training this young amateur kid with an unbelievable hunger to succeed. It took my mind off the death of my football team. I'd followed Newtown ever since I could walk across the road from the council flats to Erskineville Oval, watching their great players such as Gordon Clifford, Henry Holloway, Dick Poole, Frank Farrington.'

And what was his worst memory from boxing?

'Any time a fighter gets hurt. It's a tough sport. You can't get away from that. I remember a really good little boxer from America named Chuck Wilburn came to Sydney to fight Brisbane's Hector Thompson in 1976. He trained at Ern McQuillan's gym in Newtown. I used to drive Chuck home to the place he was staying. I got to know him well.

'Chuck was going strong in the fight, but Hector wore him down and Chuck tired badly and finally collapsed in the last round. When you see the stretcher come out at the fights it leaves you with a rotten feeling in the gut.

'I went to the hospital to see if Chuck was okay. I waited for hours to make sure he was all right but in the morning the doctors came out and said Chuck had passed away. A young family man gone just like that.'

Vic Patrick and the Glory Days of the 1940s

In 2005, shortly before his passing, I gave the great 1940s lightweight Vic Patrick the chance to finally test his punches against a world champion 60 years after he peaked as a lightweight boxer.

Vic was closing in on 85 and, in the championship rounds of life, was suffering from low blood pressure and the hole in his heart left by Nancy, his childhood sweetheart and late wife of 54 years.

But the sparkle was still there in his eyes and his handshake was as firm and commanding as it was in the days when he won the nation's admiration as our greatest fighter during Australian boxing's golden age.

I'd arranged for Vic to catch up with another shock-punching Vic – Vic Darchinyan. In a fight of see-sawing savagery, Darchinyan, trained by Jeff Fenech, knocked out IBF flyweight champ Irene Pacheco in Hollywood, Florida, with a barrage of big left hands in December 2004.

The new Vic visited the old Vic at his unit above the Parramatta River in Sydney's Drummoyne, to show him just how he did it, and the pair compared knockout notes.

Like Vic Patrick, Vic Darchinyan fought as a small, compact southpaw who attacked his opponents with all the venom of cartoon villain Yosemite Sam, marching forward with a determined scowl, his right arm working as a range finder and the big straight left coming over the top like a battering ram.

Unlike Darchinyan, Patrick never got to fight for a world title. He was such a big drawcard at Sydney Stadium, regularly drawing capacity crowds of 14,000, that promoters didn't want to risk losing the craggy faced sinewy little destroyer to America.

One of ten children born to an illiterate Italian fisherman, Vic Patrick was christened Victor Patrick Lucca in 1920. His education started in a one-teacher school in Spencer on New South Wales' Hawkesbury River. At 12 he got his first full-time job, getting his feet and hands cut to shreds carting oyster shells.

'It made me strong and tough,' Patrick said. 'Often we'd be out of bed at 4 a.m., getting around in the cold mud of the river. The little baby oysters were so thin they were like razor blades.

'You'd be picking them up and there would be myriads of cuts up and down your arms. When we woke in the mornings and spread out our fingers they'd open up and bleed.'

When he was 18, Patrick moved in with a married sister in Sydney's Newtown and got a job at the Bonds clothing factory earning 36 shillings a week. But after he paid a pound board and bought some clothes his pockets were empty.

He was playing penny poker one night under the streetlights in Newtown when he heard a fellow named Tiger Edwards say that a preliminary boxer could earn a pound for fighting four rounds.

'That was more than half a week's pay so I was keen to have a go,' he said.

His first fight was in 1940 at Sydney's Carlton Stadium. It was the height of World War II and an Italian surname wouldn't do, so the kid known as Patsy Lucca used the fighting name 'Vic Patrick'.

'I fought a chap named Les Shocker and I shocked him all right,' Vic told me. 'I knocked him out in the first round. My trainer, Ern McQuillan, got me the fight on short notice and he was taking a whole group of us to the fights in his big old Buick.

'He couldn't fit everyone in the car so a couple of us younger blokes had to get in the boot.

'When we got near the stadium, Ern's car ran out of petrol and we had to all get out and push.

'I got a pound for winning the fight and Ern took his 25 per cent cut – which was five bob – and then he charged me another two bob for car-fare.'

Vic earned £2 for his debut at Sydney Stadium in 1940 the night the ageless American Archie Moore beat Australia's fiery middleweight Fred Henneberry in the main event.

Vic soon established himself as a box office bonanza for his promoter, John Wren and Stadiums Limited, who would take 50 per cent of the gate, leaving Patrick and his opponent to split the other 50 per cent.

After two years as a pro, Vic had his nose broken in the first round against the former world champ Tod Morgan for the Australian lightweight title but was so well conditioned that he ignored the blood cascading down his throat for the next fourteen rounds to win on points.

'Morgan was an American living in Australia and he had once held the world title,' Patrick told me. 'He was as cunning as a fox with two tails and he could hit like hell from all angles.'

Patrick had ideas about training that would stun today's sports scientists. 'I smoked like a chimney, big fat cigars and Craven A's,' he recalled. 'And I liked drinking beer and eating oysters. I believed hitting the bag in the gym and sparring good fighters sharpened you more than running around a track.

'At Ern McQuillan's gym Ron Richards and I used to hit a punching ball that was filled with corn. Geez it made you hit hard.

'I never ran a yard of roadwork in my life, either. After all, you'd never see a horse kicking a bag in preparation for a Melbourne Cup.'

On the night of Vic's greatest triumph, when he defended the Australian welterweight title against Tommy Burns, he arrived at Sydney Stadium in a 1927 Chev Tourer and immediately burst into tears. It wasn't that the emotion of the occasion had got to him, even though the battle had been ballyhooed for years. Patrick, a canny businessman all his life, was crying because of all the money going to waste.

Tickets cost half a week's wages and the promoters could have sold 50,000, such was the excitement about the 1946 battle between the craggy-faced, hard-punching Patrick and the handsome movie star Geoff Murphy, who had adopted the fighting alias of Tommy Burns in honour of the old heavyweight champ.

Patrick told me that while there were 14,000 people jammed into the 'old tin shed of Sydney Stadium, there were another 5000 out the front who had queued up but couldn't get tickets'.

'I literally cried at all the money walking out the door,' he told me. 'Thousands of people all with two guineas for my pocket being turned away.

'It was a fight that captivated Australia. Burns had a great left hook and he really hurt me in the seventh. But in the ninth, I got him on the ropes and saw his beautiful chin looking at me and clobbered him with two uppercuts and stopped him.

'It was a great moment in my career.'

Patrick and Burns were each paid £2350 for the fight, but a bout with Welshman Ronnie James, who would become the father-in-law of rugby league star Johnny Raper, fell through.

'I cried over that one too,' Patrick recalled. 'We were going to fight for the British Empire lightweight title and I was supposed to get 6000 quid, which in those days was enough to buy three houses in Double Bay.

'But Ronnie couldn't make the weight so I missed out. But I can't complain. I had a fantastic career'.

Patrick was such a devastating puncher that he usually had to fight bigger men to get fights and even though he weighed just 61 kilograms he battled 72-kilogram middleweights.

His main sparring partner was the much bigger Ron Richards.

Working the Corner for Jeff Fenech

Australia's most successful boxer, Jeff Fenech, won three world titles at different weights in the ring and was awarded a fourth in 2022 by a recount, 31 long years after a controversial decision that ruled his fight with Ghana's Azumah Nelson in Las Vegas a draw. That decision robbed Jeff of the World Boxing Council (WBC) junior-lightweight title.

The one-time street urchin I dubbed the Marrickville Mauler was the poster boy for toughness. I was in Fenech's corner alongside trainer Johnny Lewis when he won the IBF bantamweight title in 1985, the WBC super-bantamweight title in 1987 and the WBC featherweight title in 1988.

Super-fit, always throwing punches, Fenech won a museum full of belts and fought a trilogy with Nelson that spanned 17 years.

In 2002, he became the first Australian of the post World War II era to be inducted into the International Boxing Hall of Fame in Canastota, New York.

For nearly two decades Fenech symbolised the fighting spirit of this country, a scrawny battler who become an irresistible, indestructible boxing champion, unbeaten in his first 27 pro fights.

Johnny Lewis moulded Fenech into a ruthless fighting machine with the same loving attention to detail that the sculptor Rodin moulded The Thinker.

Fenech's fighting style throughout his career was simple. He would start hitting opponents from the first bell and would keep hitting them without respite until the final bell or until such time as they collapsed at his feet from exhaustion and pain. There have been more scientific boxers, harder punchers and more flamboyant showmen inside the ring, but for sheer tenacity and unstinting courage few boxers have done what he did. And all with brittle hands and asthma.

Everyone can learn much from his journey from a little flat in Livingstone Road, Marrickville, to becoming one of the great personalities this country has produced.

Hard work and determination go a long way in this world.

On the night after Fenech's Round 14 knockout over American Olympic gold medallist Steve McCrory at the Sydney Entertainment Centre in 1986, I was with him and some friends at his still unfinished house in Erskineville, just around the corner from the boxing gym that had set him on his course to become one of the biggest sports stars in Australia.

Lying on the floor of the unfurnished bedroom, Fenech was buried under a pile of blankets, the telephone grafted to his ear. Standing by his bedside like he was some great general wounded in battle were a few close friends: Joe Aquilina, who first met Fenech as his sponsor but soon became like a brother; the Souths rugby league hardman Mario Fenech; and Peter Mitrevski, a three-time Australian champion who was Fenech's main sparring partner.

'Of course, I'm talking funny,' Fenech said into the phone.

'I just got my head bashed in, remember? I've still got brain damage.'

Fenech actually had a cold, which compounded his many woes. The flippancy was a translucent screen over an awful truth: for the first time in a fight, Fenech had come away looking like a loser. Both of his eyes were swollen to slits. One side of his face was red and distorted; the other side was purple. His jaw was swollen dramatically, as though he'd contracted the mumps. Worst of all, his left hand had finally and completely betrayed him. Now his fist was black and swollen with pain, which had soured what should have been the sweetest and most satisfying victory in his time of fighting.

For 14 rounds against McCrory, Fenech had gritted his teeth and pushed the agony of his hand damage into the darkest corner of his mind as he retained his IBF bantamweight title.

He had bludgeoned the American around the ring until Paul Moore, the referee and former Australian welterweight champion, had no alternative but to drag him away from an opponent whose resistance had wilted long before his hopes of at least seeing out the distance.

When the fight was over and Fenech, the boxer capable of so much animal-like ferocity, no longer had to behave like a beast, all of his defensive mechanisms collapsed. Unashamed, he wept with pain, blubbering like a five-year-old who had scraped his knees on playground concrete.

From the time he won his first Australian amateur title in Melbourne three years earlier, Fenech's left hand had conspired against him with the right. The left was always the real troublemaker. His hands have been misshapen since birth, and he became a world boxing champion incapable of making a true fist. When he closed his fingers together, the index finger of each hand would poke out from the others in a point. When he landed with a punch – and his left jab was always the most frequent form of attack – most of the blow's force was taken on the pointed index finger, leaving his knuckles bruised and swollen.

After Fenech had stopped McCrory in a fight that had been mostly one sided, his left index finger swelled to the size and colour of a plump barbecued sausage. He spent the time usually allotted for jubilation in his dressing-room crying and moaning. At the post-fight party in ante-room at the Sydney Entertainment Centre, he was propped against the bar like a drunk, too tired to move and barely able to speak. He muttered muffled farewells to friends and well-wishers through fat lips, his face already adopting the distorted contours it would bear for the next week or two.

Old McQuillan, Vic Patrick's trainer, once told me that it wasn't speed, toughness, fitness or nous that made a great fighter. 'The most important thing a fighter must have is guts,' Ern said. 'If ya haven't got guts, you shouldn't be in the bloody business.'

No fighter ever had more guts than Jeff Fenech.

Joe Bugner Fought Muhammad Ali, Joe Frazier, Elvis Presley and Frank Bruno

In 1987, I was sitting in the back of a Bentley S3 limousine wedged between a two-metre tall, 130-kilogram bodyguard and the much smaller but far more dangerous Fenech. Facing me was Johnny Lewis, the heavyweight fighter Aussie Joe Bugner and his Queensland-born wife, Marlene, a glamorous former newspaper journalist.

A motorcycle cop, his siren blaring, led us through the thick north London traffic from our hotel at Regent's Park to White Hart Lane, the home ground of the Tottenham Hotspurs Football Club. It was a bitterly cold Saturday night as Bugner got ready to fight England's most popular sportsman, Frank Bruno, in what was until then the richest fight ever staged in the United Kingdom.

Big Joe, 193 centimetres tall and 110 kilograms, had already fought Muhammad Ali twice as well as other leading international heavyweights including Joe Frazier, Ron Lyle,

Greg Page, Ernie Shavers, Jimmy Ellis, Henry Cooper, David Bey, James Tillis and Chuck Wepner, the journeyman Sylvester Stallone used as the model for his celluloid hero 'Rocky'. Bugner had once even gone toe to toe with 'The King' – Elvis Presley.

I would be working as Bugner's cornerman for the Bugner–Bruno clash, a fight that had been put together during volatile times around the world. A freak hurricane, with winds hitting 200 kilometres per hour, had just ravaged the south of England, killing 23 people. The world's stock markets had crashed, with a 25 per cent drop in Australia on one day.

Bruno was the great British sports hero of his time while Bugner was the most reviled. Born in Hungary, Bugner grew up in the UK as an unwelcome refugee, and the fighting public had treated him with disdain ever since he beat Henry Cooper, British boxing's then favourite hero, in 1971 at Wembley Arena. It was sport's equivalent of shooting Bambi. On that one night, in a close decision over 15 rounds, Bugner won the British, Commonwealth and European titles.

Bugner was still only 21, but the win saw him rated as one of the best heavyweights in the world during a golden age of the division. 'Henry was a demi-god in Britain and the British press never forgave me for beating him,' Bugner said.

Now that he was living in Sydney and billing himself as 'Aussie Joe', the Poms hated him even more.

Bruno was being paid £400,000 and Bugner £250,000. The winner would face Mike Tyson for the world heavyweight title.

In his heyday, Bugner had fought the best boxers in the world, twice going the distance with Muhammad Ali, the second time for the world heavyweight title in Kuala Lumpur, Malaysia 1975.

Many people say Ali was the greatest athlete in history. I asked Joe what it was like to punch him in the face.

'Very difficult,' Joe told me. 'Ali was so fast and evasive. He was hard to nail with more than one punch at a time, but I did manage to get my left jab going in both fights and I connected with plenty of shots. I'm proud of the fact that I'm the only man in history to go the distance with both Ali and his great rival Joe Frazier.'

Ali talked himself up better than any athlete in history. He even called himself 'The Greatest'. Was he really that good or was his reputation inflated by the hype?

'He was that good,' Bugner said. 'To me he was like football's Georgie Best, a great natural talent with charisma. He had two great weapons. He was utterly fearless, no matter what happened in a fight, and he was able to dominate opponents psychologically as much as physically. His speed for a big man was quite incredible. He was the greatest heavyweight of all time, in my opinion. He was bigger than the sport of boxing, too. He marketed his own fights and himself unlike any athlete in history.'

Bugner had first laid eyes on Ali when he came to London in 1963 to fight the revered Henry Cooper.

'Ali was still known as Cassius Clay then,' Bugner said. 'The fight was a huge outdoor event at Wembley Stadium. Ali was very brash and winning easily – poking his tongue out and making it look easy. But Cooper landed a big left hook and dropped him at the end of the fourth round just as the bell rang. In my opinion it was a very, very lucky punch. Ali was badly dazed. Angelo Dundee, Ali's trainer, opened a rip in the glove and asked for the glove to be replaced. That took about ten minutes, which Ali needed to recover. Ali came out in the next round and cut Cooper to shreds.

'The next year, Ali won the world title in an upset against Sonny Liston, a fighter I later sparred with, a big powerful guy who terrified everyone. But Ali gave him a boxing lesson. Then Ali came back to England in 1966 and stopped Cooper again at Arsenal's Stadium in London. Both the Cooper fights were huge news in England. At the time, I was a schoolboy more interested in athletics than boxing. I was England's national junior discus champion at 14. Track and field was my first love, but I was also doing boxing training at the Bedford Boys Club and my coach thought I showed a lot of promise.'

Bugner had left the Hungarian town of Szoreg when he was six. 'The Russians moved in and my mum, Margaret, moved us out. She was a single parent and she left the country with five children. She put us on a bus for a while and then we walked through the night across the border to a refugee camp in Yugoslavia. We ended up in England in 1957.

'I always loved athletics more than boxing. When I was little, my hero was the actor Steve Reeves, who played Hercules and carried a discus. I had dreams of going to the Olympics until boxing arrived. At school one of the teachers said we were going to do some boxing and I didn't want any part of it. But I said I'd have a go. In the first round, I got a bloody nose and I hated it. But I got better and better. I had 14 amateur fights and won 11.'

What made Bugner fight if he didn't really like it?

'I loved the excitement. It really is a great thrill to be going out there to fight Muhammad Ali or Joe Frazier and the crowd is cheering and the world is watching on TV. The adrenaline is racing through your body at 100 miles an hour. It's a different excitement to any other sport. You're in the ring totally exposed, nowhere to hide, just you and the other bloke, who is trying to tear your head off.'

At 17 Joe turned professional, and it was a disaster. 'I fought a big bus driver from Birmingham named Paul Brown at the Anglo American Sporting Club in Mayfair, London. I was too busy looking for the movie stars Stanley Baker and Oliver Reed, who I heard were in the crowd. Paul hit me with a big haymaker and it was goodnight. He stopped me in Round 3.'

But the lanky teenager was determined to prove himself. 'I fought Paul again twice the next year, 1968, and I knocked him out both times. I lost only once – on points – in my next 33 fights.'

There were rumours that Bugner never hit anyone really hard again, though, after Ulric Regis died following their bout at Shoreditch in London in 1969. 'It was the worst night of my life,' Bugner said. 'It haunted me and it was something that took many years for me to overcome. In the end I had to learn to live with it. Perhaps, because of it, I unconsciously held off my opponents. Ulric was a good heavyweight from Trinidad. He was out on his feet and the referee should have stopped the fight, but I won on points over eight rounds. A few hours after the fight Ulric collapsed. He died a few days later after surgery for a clot on the brain. The verdict was accidental death. I know it was not my fault, but it still shook me up for a long time.'

Bugner first met Muhammad Ali that same year, 1969, in New York. 'I was 19 years old and Ali was attempting a comeback after being banned from boxing for three years for refusing to join the American army,' Bugner said.

'I'd been boxing as a professional since 1967 and was seen as a rising star in Britain. My managers took me to America to train with some of the greats. Ali offered me $10,000 – which was a small fortune in those days – to spar with him.

'I first met him in a coffee shop at Loews Midtown Hotel in Manhattan while I was having breakfast. There were 200 people surrounding him as soon as he walked in. The first thing he says is, "So you're this white boy thinks he can whup me? You caaan't whup me. Man, you soooo ugly. Your mamma must have been sad when she had you."

'I said, "Muhammad, if you think I'm ugly you haven't seen my sister." That stunned him. For the first time in his life he was speechless.'

In their first sparring session they did five rounds at Gil Clancy's gym in Lower Manhattan. Clancy had helped make Emile Griffith a great world champion.

Bugner felt like he had butterflies racing around his stomach. 'Ali was already this great figure in sporting history and I was this big lanky teenager. He was a legend, my idol. There was a big crowd watching and once again Ali wanted to put on a show.

I had one tactic only against him and that was not to let him beat the crap out of me. I was taller than him and had a longer reach so I kept sticking my left jab at him and then covering up when he attacked. I landed plenty of jabs and a few rights. Sparring the master was an education. After the sparring finished Ali told me I hadn't given him a black eye but a "white eye".

The pair formed a lifelong friendship even though they would go on to fight twice. 'Ali and I both liked to joke around. He would hire me as a sparring partner for different fights. I learned so much from him in sparring and all the time I was making my own career as a fighter in England. His jab was the main thing I tried to copy. Fast and snappy, a great weapon in both attack and defence. We must have done 200 rounds over the years.'

As a teenager Bugner also sparred the monstrous Sonny Liston in Newark, New Jersey. 'Liston was getting ready to fight the big brawler Chuck Wepner. Sonny was one of the most intimidating heavyweights of all time, but I liked him. Wepner went nine rounds with Sonny, but they brought him to Wembley for his next fight and I stopped Wepner in three. Then in 1975 Wepner managed to drop Ali before losing to him in a world title fight. Sylvester Stallone wrote the movie *Rocky* based on that fight.'

In February 1973, Ali and Bugner had their first bout over twelve rounds in Las Vegas. Frank Sinatra and Sammy Davis Jr were ringside and Bugner warmed up with a fight against Elvis Presley. 'Elvis was performing in Las Vegas then,' Bugner said. 'Ali was no longer the world champ but was angling to get another fight with the titleholder, Joe Frazier. Elvis had given him a beautiful robe with the words 'People's Choice' in gemstones on the back.

'Before the fight, Elvis invited about 50 or so people to his hotel suite for a party. I was on my best behaviour but I said to him, "Excuse me, Elvis, that's a beautiful robe you gave Ali. I'd love one too because as you know I'm the only one in the fight who is actually a champion." At the time I was the European heavyweight champion and I had just defended my title. But Elvis turns around and says, "Man, you're no champion!" Just like that. He tried to humiliate me. I told Elvis to get stuffed and I walked out.

'Did Elvis tell everyone: "Joe Bugner has left the building?" No, but his bodyguard, a guy they called Big Red [Red West], comes over and says, "Hey, man, whatya doin' – no one speaks to the King like that." I said: "Tell the King he's a dickhead."'

So fight night with Ali arrived. Bugner was 22 and facing the man he reckoned was the greatest athlete of all time. He must have been petrified.

'I was actually very confident,' Bugner told me. 'I was only young but already very experienced. By that stage I'd had 48 professional fights and had beaten Henry Cooper and the best in Europe. I'd also sparred with Ali many times so I felt I knew what to do to beat him. If you watch the fight, you see that I came out very aggressively and rocked him in the first round with my right hand. My jab worked well too, but Ali was just sharper and faster and he was able to pick me off. He won on points over 12 rounds. Still, I gained a lot of credit for giving him a good fight.'

What was the toughest thing about Ali to overcome?

'Ali had speed, great technical skills and of course the confidence to impose his will. I tried to out-jab him. I felt I knew Ali inside out from sparring him. My left jab was my best punch and I knew it gave Ali trouble. I had the reach advantage but once he got his distance he would counter with his own left hand and bring out combinations of punches from nowhere. I caught him with a beautiful right hand and he said, "Damn, good punch, white boy, do it again!" Now, I was only 22 and pretty naive. When I tried the same punch again he was ready and caught me with four solid punches to the jaw.'

Ali won on points.

Sammy Davis Jr jumped into the ring to hug Ali straight after the fight, but Frank Sinatra later told Bugner that he thought Ali had lost.

Bugner went straight from the frying pan to the fire. After losing to Ali, his next fight was against Joe Frazier, who had just been deposed as world heavyweight champ by the monstrous George Foreman.

'Frazier and I had 18,000 people at Earls Court in London,' Bugner said, 'and we went flat out for 12 rounds. It was brutal and we both hurt. In the end, Frazier scored a very close decision, though George Foreman, who was part of the TV commentary team, thought I won.

'Frazier was the best fighter I ever faced. Ali was much more gifted and a much better boxer technically, but Frazier was a real fighter – strong, tough, fit. Non-stop aggression, and I proved that I had the chin to stay with one of the toughest men who ever lived.

'I boxed Ali in February of 1973 and the Frazier fight was in July. Fighting two of the great fighters of that era in a five-month period – that was really something.

'Let me tell you I was pretty scared to fight Frazier. I had read about his bouts, his notoriety, his ability to smash fighters not always in the first three or four rounds but towards the end of the fight because his stamina must have been awesome. Many of the fans who were there that night at the fight in London were Australians. Frazier was only 5 feet, 11 inches [180 cm] but until he was stunned by Foreman, he seemed invincible and he was trying to prove that his only loss was a glitch and that he was still the world's best.

'He hit me with a beautiful right cross in Round 10 and down I go. He thought I was going to stay down but he did not realise I had an iron jaw. After a count of three or four I got up and instinctively threw a hard right hand that caught him flush. I thought I could stop him but then the bell rang.'

Frazier wasn't the heaviest puncher Bugner faced, though. 'He hit hard but for one punch, the biggest hitter was Earnie Shavers. He dropped me in Dallas in 1982, then cut my eye with a headbutt. Ron Lyle in 1977 in Caesars Palace was my toughest fight. Ron was a convicted killer. I fought him to a split decision but ended up in hospital with bleeding kidneys.'

In October 1974, Ali spectacularly stopped George Foreman in Zaire in what was billed 'The Rumble in the Jungle', and he regained the world title. Two weeks later, Bugner won a clearcut decision over Ali's friend and former champion Jimmy Ellis.

Bugner won eight fights straight between 1973 and 1975, and Ali agreed to a rematch. The fight would not be in England, however, but at a football stadium in Malaysia, because promoter Don King wanted a title fight before a big Muslim audience.

'It was in broad daylight, and coming from England I found the heat and humidity in Malaysia overpowering,' Bugner said. 'I went to Malaysia four or five weeks before the fight. It was hell for the first two weeks. I had diarrhoea and all the other sicknesses that you could think of in a country with tropical conditions. Ali arrived there ten days before the fight and he looked in those days magical. I knew Ali had taken me seriously because I was young and improving.'

'I don't know whose plan it was to unsettle me but I got a death threat just before the fight. I had all these commandos guarding me from a potential sniper attack but I'm 6 feet, 4 [193 cm] and they were all 5 feet, 2 [155 cm]. It wasn't a lot of protection. I was very fit but Ali handled the heat better than me. He fought with his hands low but only when he was out of punching range. His radar worked very well and he was able to slip punches and counter when he got in range. When I set myself to punch, Ali seemed to know what was coming and he responded in a flash. In the later rounds Ali still had the fitness to dance around me and stay out of any trouble.'

Lionel Rose beat a Japanese fighter on the undercard, but Bugner's performance was not memorable, and after the fight the British boxing commentator Reg Gutteridge wrote that in 106°F

(41°C) heat, Bugner was the only person who froze. Another used the old line that Bugner had the body of a Greek statue but fewer moves.

'After the fight some guys from the British press asked me to pose with a drink in the swimming pool to show the heat of the place. Instead, they all wrote that I'd treated the fight like a holiday and wouldn't have a go. I was really stitched up.'

The friendship between Ali and Bugner endured and the pair toured Australia in 1979 boxing exhibition bouts.

Bugner lived in Beverly Hills for ten years from 1975. His neighbours included the actor Dean Martin and the singer Tom Jones, who was best man at Bugner's wedding to Marlene, his second wife.

'Ali had a house in Hancock Park not far from me. Two of my kids went to the same school as Ali's daughter Laila and I met my wife at Joan Collins's house.

'I spent some time with Ali at the Sydney Olympics. The Parkinson's disease had ravaged him by then but he was still too sharp for me. I said to him: "Muhammad, damn you're lookin' good" and he whispers, "Joe Bugner, I wish I could say the same." I gave him a kiss and he froze and said: "Don't do that again." I said, "Muhammad, it's a common custom for Europeans." And he says, "Man, we ain't in Europe".'

The Bugner–Bruno fight would be one of the biggest bouts I ever covered, and Joe one of the greatest characters I ever met. But more of that later ...

Women Take Over the World

The rise in popularity of women's boxing in the 21st century gave Australia's female fighters the chance to show they were every bit as rugged and courageous as their male counterparts.

On a day of tear-jerking emotion, Skye Nicolson won 2018 Commonwealth Games gold in memory of her two boxing brothers who died before she was born. The 22-year-old from Yatala, just a short drive from the Games venue on the Gold Coast, outpointed Northern Ireland's Michaela Walsh 3–2 in a desperately close battle to top the winners podium in the 57-kilogram division, capping Australia's best-ever boxing performance at a Commonwealth Games.

The Australian team finished the Gold Coast Games with three gold medals, two silver and three bronze.

After her final triumph, Skye threw her arms heavenward and leaped about the ring in celebration. She dedicated her gold medal to her brothers Jamie, a Barcelona Olympian and Commonwealth Games bronze medallist, and ten-year-old Gavin, who were both killed in a car accident on the Pacific Highway at Helensvale in 1994 while on their way to boxing training at Nerang.

Skye was born the next year as her parents, Allan, who was 45 at the time and Pat, who was 42, tried to heal their broken hearts with new life.

While she never met the two boys, their memory has shaped Skye's life. Her parents established a boxing club in their backyard in their memory and Skye began training there just for fun when she was 12.

The youngster with the model looks and catwalk grace had sparred with Walsh at the Australian Institute of Sport in Canberra in the lead-up to the gold medal showdown and was always confident she had her opponent's measure.

Two years earlier, Skye had emulated brother Jamie with a bronze medal at the world championships in Kazakhstan. Jamie had done it in Moscow in 1989 when the Australian coach Johnny Lewis was introduced to a baby-faced Russian named Kostya Tszyu who he eventually turned into one of the all-time greats.

Skye looks like Jamie and fights like Jamie, with an elusive southpaw style of quick punches and darting movements. At 57 kilograms, she's also in the same weight division. She was initially trained by her father and older brother, both named Allan Nicolson, but for the three years preceding the Commonwealth Games she was coached by Gold Coast barrister Wayne Tolton, with her family assisting.

In one of the most courageous displays at the Games, Australia's Anja Stridsman also took gold, fighting with an Achilles tendon in her knee donated from a cadaver.

The 31-year-old boxed brilliantly to win a unanimous 5–0 decision over England's Paige Murney for the 60-kilogram women's gold medal in her first tournament since a knee injury threatened to end her career.

In her three fights on the Gold Coast, Stridsman never lost a round, a testament to the brilliant coaching of Joel Keegan on the New South Wales Central Coast and to the work by national coaches Kevin Smith and Shara Romer.

Stridsman migrated to Australia from Sweden 11 years earlier for study and took up boxing in 2010 just to get fit. Two months before the Commonwealth Games trials in 2017, she tore her anterior cruciate ligament in a fight in Poland.

Even though Stridsman could barely walk, she and Keegan continued to train together. Stridsman won the national title in Sydney in November, all the while fearing that her leg would collapse on her at any time. She then paid $13,500 to have surgery to replace her damaged knee tendon.

Melbourne's Harry Garside also won gold as a prelude to Olympic success. Victorian heavyweight Jason Whateley and Perth's 75-kilogram fighter Caitlin Parker took silver, while Taylah Robertson, Kaye Scott and Clay Waterman won bronze.

Shannon O'Connell embraced guerrilla tactics in her challenge for fellow Aussie Ebanie Bridges's world bantamweight title in Leeds, England, in December 2022.

At the time, Shannon, who had been fighting her whole life, was almost 40 and a mother of three.

During the weigh-in, Ebanie, the self-styled blonde bomber, stripped down to barely-there lingerie, and promoted her OnlyFans site. At the time she was also selling her sweaty socks online.

Shannon played rough with a hard edge, as she has done all her life. Her father was killed when she was only two. Her mum was taken by a heroin overdose. The tragedies would have destroyed a lesser mortal but instead they made her stronger.

I interviewed Shannon at length in 2016. She was walking slowly from a house in Wynnum, on Brisbane's southern bayside, where a tattoo artist had spent three hours decorating her right arm. She had just had the image of her late father – firm jaw and button nose, just like hers – etched permanently into her epidermis, and it had been a traumatic experience.

Shannon was just an infant when 25-year-old Kevin O'Connell, an Adelaide electrician who rode speedway motorcycles in his spare time, became the first fatality at Speedway City on Adelaide's rural outskirts the day before Australia Day 1985. Sliding across the treacherous clay surface, he hit an unprotected concrete wall and was killed instantly.

Shannon has no real recollection of her lifelong hero, only fragments of family folklore and snatches of memory. She's heard so many stories about her father that reality and imagination blur to the point where she's not sure what she remembers and what she thinks she remembers.

She has few precious photos of her dad, but one is of their last Christmas together. She is sitting on the knee of her mother, Lynda, in front of her father and Lynda's boys, Michael and Simon. A month after Kevin was killed, Lynda began a slow and painful spiral and O'Connell would need every bit of fight she could summon to keep going.

Outside the tattooist's home, O'Connell reached her car. It was a high-powered Subaru WRX with a 'boxer' engine and the word 'Shotgun' blazoned across it in plastic decal. She opened the door and looked down at her father's image staring back at her from her flayed skin. Tears started to run down her face.

A day after her father's portrait was inked onto her arm, O'Connell strolled into the Fortitude Boxing Gym in the inner-Brisbane suburb of Newstead as she prepared for a victory over Hungarian whirlwind Edina Kiss, from Budapest.

Her children, son Cooper, then ten, and daughter Taylor, then nine, followed behind carrying their mother's boxing equipment in her training bags. The gym was run by Steve Deller, who has spent almost all his life involved in boxing as a fighter, trainer, manager and promoter. As a young man he also had stints as a roustabout, ringer, rodeo rider and truck driver out on the everlasting plains of Queensland, sometimes mustering wild cattle in the vast expanse between Bedourie and Birdsville. He knows what toughness and self-reliance are all about. His stepson Greg Eadie fought at the Commonwealth Games, and he has coached Olympians Todd Kidd, Jarrod Fletcher, Shane Knox and Paul Miller. Two of his boxers, Fletcher and Dennis Hogan, fought in world championship bouts.

But Deller said when it came to fortitude, O'Connell was in a league of her own. 'Shannon had a pretty shit childhood and she's had to fight for everything all the way. She came up to Queensland to get away from the drug scene in Adelaide that killed her mother, and she changed her life around. She has made a good home for her kids. She struggles hard every day but puts her kids through a private school so they can get a better start in life than she had.'

Because there were few female boxers able to match it with O'Connell, she usually sparred against men, and on the day of our last interview she was dodging the blows of the Queensland men's super-bantamweight champion, Jarrett Owen.

O'Connell's children, fair-haired and beaming, bounced about on the gym's rubber matting while their mother bandaged her hands to stop her fingers breaking under the force of her own punches and then adjusted a leather headguard to minimise the chance of cuts on her face from Owen's blows. She popped in a mouthguard to protect her perfect, pearly white teeth. Then, with her kids watching on, wide-eyed with fascination, she came out punching, as lithe as a panther, with jabs, hooks, crosses, uppercuts.

As her legs carried her forward, a tattoo on her right calf twitched. Under the inked number 78 were the words 'Forever in my heart, forever in my thoughts'.

The number 78 was painted on the side of the motorbike her father rode to his death.

There is not a lot of money in women's boxing, O'Connell told me, but she was using the purse from her fight with the Hungarian to pay her children's school fees.

'I want them to have a better start than I had,' she said. 'After my father died, my family's life fell apart. My mother was consumed with grief. She had come from a bad place; a bad childhood and she had been married – very unhappily – before my dad.

'In my eyes, my dad had been her saviour. They owned a house, and he gave her and us a normal sort of suburban life. When he was taken away from her, my mother was just so lost that it was like she wasn't human anymore. There were suddenly a lot of drugs and a lot of bad people in our house, a lot of violence, especially to my mum over drugs, [such as] heroin and sleeping pills – anything anyone could get their hands on.'

O'Connell blushed a little. 'I would sometimes help my mother inject herself. I was just a little girl trying to survive. There was a lot of abuse to me, too.' She swallows hard. 'All kinds of abuse.'

O'Connell says she dabbled in drugs herself as a teenager but escaped by spending much of her childhood with her 'nan and pop', Mavis and Bill O'Connell.

She took up boxing aged 20 to rehabilitate a back injury she suffered playing netball. Her first coach was the relentless old-school taskmaster Terry Fox, one of Adelaide's best boxers in the 1970s and a man who had raced speedway against O'Connell's father.

Fox was a good coach and O'Connell was a fast learner. She won an Australian amateur championship in her fifth bout and at a tournament in Tonga met Brisbane trainer Chris McCullen, who convinced her to start a new life in Queensland, away from the drug scene that was consuming her mother. O'Connell packed up all she owned – which wasn't much – and headed for the Sunshine State in 2004.

Two years later she gave birth to her son Cooper. That same year her mother died of a heroin overdose in Adelaide. She was 46.

Why boxing? When you've had so much pain in your life, why make it worse? Why get punched in the face when the pay is peanuts and it hurts?

'I've always loved the sport,' O'Connell told me. 'My life has been a fight ever since my father died, and the tough competition you get in boxing has helped me find myself and cope with things like depression.

'The reason I love boxing is because it's tough, and tough is what I know.'

Ebanie Bridges built her boxing career in Western Sydney, training with Arnel Barotillo, a world-title challenger who had fought Manny Pacquiao.

The Blonde Bomber taught maths at Airds High School, south-west of Sydney, and had international success as a bodybuilder. She was 33 when she had her first professional fight and 35 when she won her first world title, the IBF bantamweight title in Leeds in 2022.

'I've loved combat sports since I was a kid and I have a black belt in karate,' she told me.

'Women's boxing was banned in New South Wales for many years, so I took up bodybuilding and competed internationally. But I really love punching people and when I finally got the chance to box I dedicated myself to going as far as I could.'

Ebanie made her amateur boxing debut in 2016 aged 30 and won two New South Wales titles, showing that while she has a head for figures her fists set the toughest tests.

She turned professional in February 2019 on the same night that Tim Tszyu beat Englishman Denton Vassell.

'I like smashing the stereotypes,' she said.

In the December 2022 world title fight in Leeds, Shannon stunned the world champion with her aggression early, but she was down in Round 3 from a big right hand and never a real threat after that. A brutal combination from Ebanie in Round 8 caused referee Howard Foster to stop the fight.

Not long after the win, the American magazine *Sports Illustrated* named Ebanie their 'Women's Breakout Boxer of the Year'.

IN THE BEGINNING

Convict Contests

The first recorded boxing match in Australia started with two hardened convicts spared from the gallows but still fighting for their lives before a mob of liquored-up soldiers and free settlers in old Sydney Town.

Officers of the New South Wales Corps began arranging bareknuckle fights between convicts under rules devised by Jack Broughton, an English champion. The rules were designed to stop men beating each other to death, though the only things banned were kicking, eye-gouging and hitting an opponent when he was floored. Men shaved their heads to stop hair being torn out, and they soaked their faces and fists in brine to toughen the skin. Fights were broken up into rounds – a round being determined when a man was dropped by a blow or fell to his knees to avoid punishment. Opponents could still be thrown to the ground and headbutted or bitten. Sometimes fights lasted for hours.

On 8 January 1814, Australia's first newspaper, *The Sydney Gazette*, provided the first report on a boxing contest in Australia under the headline 'Pugilism'. The contest had taken place the previous day somewhere near what is now the Anzac War Memorial in Hyde Park. The two convicts, John Parton, aka John Berringer, and Charles Sefton, had both escaped the noose in England for minor thefts in those times of desperate poverty.

They fought for two hours and the *Gazette* reported that 'within the few last rounds Sefton's strength had observably declined much more than that of his adversary, to whose superiority he was at length obliged unwillingly to yield'. Sefton lost several teeth and 'was unable to see out of his eyes, so swollen were they from the blows which his younger antagonist had dealt him'.

Women Strike Out

The first record of women boxing in Australia dates from 5 April 1826 when *The Australian* newspaper reported that a 'motley tribe' of ruffians from Sydney's notorious Rocks area had gathered at 6 a.m. on 28 March to see two married women settle a dispute with fisticuffs.

'Mrs Eleanor', originally from Ireland, 'backed by her lord and husband' took up a 'most terrific posture' opposite her foe, 'Mrs Ann' from Chelsea, who advanced to the scratch line 'in a kind of jog trot' to start the fight. 'By a feint Mrs E. planted a tremendous crushing hit upon her opponent's "snuff-box" and the claret followed copiously ... Mrs. A. retrograding a little, returned the compliment with a slap upon Mrs. E's breadbasket.'

In the second round, 'a crushing hit contacted with Mrs A's earrings, which was smartly repaid on the other's peepers'. As the crowd chanted "bravo, bravo", 'the lass from the land of the potatoes' answered a cracking punch to the face, with a whirlwind attack in 'true Donnelly style'.

Rounds 4 to 10 were close. The Irishwoman continued to wrestle with her 'Murphy squeezers' but, after 11 rounds, time was declared and no result recorded.

Anthony Mundine had a reputation for talking himself up in both rugby league and boxing, but he had nothing on Australia's first internationally known bare-knuckle fighter, John Gorrick, also known as Isaac Gorrick, who came to the world's attention for his brash confidence. The son of an English soldier, Gorrick was a Hawkesbury River butcher. Heralded by a huge amount of advance publicity in London that spoke of his devastating right hand, he talked 'very big' about what he was going to do to any Englishman who could muster sufficient courage to face him. Gorrick met all the prominent sporting men of London – known as The Fancy – and told them that he was adopting the fighting name 'Bungaree', after an Aboriginal warrior.

Bungaree was matched with local hero Johnny Broome under the London Prize Ring Rules of 1838, which declared biting, headbutting, and punching to the groin illegal. The new rules said that a man being dropped would constitute the end of a round; he would have 30 seconds to come up to 'scratch': a line drawn across the middle of the ring. At the end of the round, the weary fighters would rest by sitting on the knee of a kneeling cornerman, a practice that was kept up for decades until someone thought stools might be more manly. Boxers would sip rum or whisky between rounds. Those who showed the slightest trepidation were said to have no 'bottle'. The bout was set for 27 May 1842, the day after the Ten Thousand race, and was to be held near the Newmarket Racecourse. Bungaree came into the ring waving a light-blue flag adorned with brilliant cobs of corn surrounding his portrait and the legend 'Advance Australia! Who'd have thought it!'

As Broome's seconds were lacing the Englishman's boots, Bungaree called out, 'Hurry up with those boots. I shall lick him in less time than it has taken you to do that job.' While shaking hands across the scratch line, the Australian remarked contemptuously, 'Well, here you are at last. I'm going to thrash you inside a quarter of an hour.'

Bungaree, stripped bare above the waist, and wearing long white flannel pants, was a picture of Australian pride and physical perfection. But a big right to the solar plexus forced a loud grunt from the Australian. Broome then grabbed Bungaree around the waist, lifted him high and hurled his 150 pounds (68 kilograms) to the ground. Bungaree threw his hands in front of his face, leaving his body exposed to smashing punches.

Nevertheless, as the English papers reported, 'the Australian proved game to the core, and he took his gruel like a hero'. He was stopped after an hour's punishment.

The gold rushes of the 1850s saw boxing boom in regional Australia. Bob McLaren opened a famous gym on Main Road, Ballarat. Just over 100 kilometres to the north, another gold town was named after the English prize-fighter William Abednego Thompson, better known as 'Bendigo' Thompson. Bendigo remains the only city in the world to be named after a boxer.

The longest recorded fist fight anywhere in the world took place on the goldfields on 3 December 1855, on the one-year anniversary of the battle at Eureka Stockade. The bare-knuckle brawl at the Fiery Creek diggings, 50 kilometres to the north-west of Ballarat, lasted an astonishing six hours and 15 minutes. The prize money was £400.

In one corner was Irish-born James Kelly. About to turn 42, he had been fighting in England since he was 16. In the other corner was Jonathan Smith, a 32-year-old from Norwich, England, who had come to Australia as a soldier with the 96th Regiment of Foot in 1840. The fight began at 10.30 in the morning and finished at 4.45 that afternoon. While a lot of 'claret' flowed from the boxers' wounds, spectators availed themselves of bottled stout and sandwiches. The English soldier finally surrendered, shaking hands with his Irish conqueror.

The Great Teacher

Larry Foley, the man who revolutionised prize-fighting in Australia, was not a big man. He stood just 5 feet, 9 inches tall and weighed 147 pounds (175 cm and 67 kg), but he was the most feared boxer in Australia at his peak.

The son of an Irish Catholic schoolmaster, Foley was born on the Turon River near Bathurst in 1849 and baptised at Penrith two years later.

Already a notorious street fighter, he arrived in Sydney at 18 to work for a demolition contractor. He began training with John 'Black' Perry, an African-American who had served with the British army in Ireland, and now ran a gym in Bay Street, Glebe. It wasn't long before Foley's reputation as a fighter spread and he became leader of the Catholic 'Green' gang that was involved in a turf war with the 'Orange' Protestant gang in The Rocks.

Foley leased the United Services Hotel on the corner of William and Riley streets in Woolloomooloo, where he ran boxing classes. In 1877 he joined with the American fighter and bookmaker Jack Thompson and the Englishman Abe Hicken to give boxing demonstrations with Jem Mace, known around the world as The Norfolk Gypsy. Mace was an Englishman who had once claimed the heavyweight championship of the world and is still regarded as the father of modern boxing in Britain. He said Foley was the best fighter in the world at his weight.

In Melbourne, Mace and Jack Thompson also ran classes at the Old England Hotel at 220 Bourke Street.

Foley also bought the White Horse Hotel in Sydney's George Street, and when his boxing classes got too crowded in the basement of the pub, he used old wood and tin from his demolition business to build a gymnasium at the back (the area is now under the Strand Arcade).

* * *

Until Foley's death, on 12 July 1917, three days after suffering a heart attack in a Turkish bath, he was Australia's greatest boxing coach. He popularised boxing to the degree that by the end of the 19th century it was a major sport in Australia. He also made Australia a major force in the sport worldwide. His famous boxing academy, The Iron Pot, was at various times home to champions such as Peter Jackson, Young Griffo, Bob Fitzsimmons, Paddy Slavin, Joe Goddard, Dan Creedon, George Dawson and E W 'Starlight' Rollins, a native of Georgetown, Guyana, who worked on pearling vessels before settling in Brisbane and then making his way to Foley's Sydney headquarters.

Ned Kelly Took a Shot at the World Champ

Ned Kelly, along with Joe Byrne, the lieutenant of his bushranging gang, was said to be among a crowd of 150 people on the New South Wales side of the Murray River, just downstream from Echuca, at dawn on Thursday 20 March 1879. According to reports, the crowd had gathered to watch a bare-knuckle brawl between Larry Foley and Englishman Abe Hicken. The fight lasted a little over an hour. At the end, Hicken presented a 'horrible spectacle': both his eyes were nearly closed, his lips were cut and blistered, his nose knocked out of shape and his whole face pounded almost to jelly.

Foley had major boxing figures Jem Mace and Jack Thompson as his cornermen. Both were of great interest to Ned Kelly. He had used the alias 'J. Thompson' during his horse-stealing career, as a nod to a fighter he admired, and during his raid on the New South Wales town of Jerilderie a month before the Foley–Hicken fight he was always 'blowing' [boasting] and bullying, according to the inhabitants who he took hostage. At one point, Kelly placed nine revolvers on a bar in a pub that he'd made his headquarters and told his prisoners: 'They talk of this Jem Mace as the champion of the world. Why, if they can arrange a meeting so that I am safe from being taken, I will fight him or any other man in the world, and lick him, too.'

In 1873 Kelly had proclaimed himself the heavyweight champion of north-eastern Victoria after winning a 20-round bareknuckle match against another horse thief, Wild Wright, at the Imperial Hotel in Beechworth. Ned missed out on his shot at the world champion and before long, despite his suit of armour, came off second best in a gun battle with police at Glenrowan.

Since he knew the rules of boxing that bore his name better than anyone, the Marquess of Queensberry, touring Australia in 1888, was invited to referee a heavyweight fight between Maitland's Paddy Slavin and 'Irish' Jack Burke, who was actually a London Jew. The fight was set for 9 July 1888 at the Hibernian Hall in Swanston Street, Melbourne.

Ten thousand people battled each other for 2000 seats. The venue was so crowded that the aristocratic godfather of modern boxing had to be lowered into the hall through a skylight. Some of the willing hands who helped lower him also helped lift his gold watch, worth around 100 guineas. An appeal was made for the pickpocket to be a true sportsman and do the right thing, and eventually the watch was returned.

The fight was declared a draw after eight rounds but, the following year, Slavin, a blacksmith who ended up as a sheriff in a far-flung gold town in Canada, knocked out Burke in a return fight.

Peter Jackson: Australia's Black Prince

The first great champion produced in Larry Foley's gym was the West Indian–born Peter Jackson, or 'The Black Prince', Australia's first global champion in any sport. Jackson was a pioneer for black athletes on the world stage.

The great-grandson of a freed slave whose owner's name was 'Jackson', Peter was born near what is now St Croix in the Virgin

Islands. His family was poor, but he was a diligent student who dreamed of playing Shakespeare's *Othello* on the stage. Weighing just under 90 kilograms, and 187 centimetres tall, he had a lithe, muscular physique and a soft, pleasant voice with a slight lisp. A clergyman who knew him once said that Jackson's speech made every sentence something of a 'well-cut jewel'.

Jackson arrived in Sydney in 1879 as a cook on a ship carrying Boston ice to India and Java sugar to Australia. Penniless, he peddled wooden toys around Pyrmont, worked in an orchard and as a woodcutter in the bush near Lane Cove, and crewed on a paddle steamer running between Circular Quay and Manly.

Larry Foley first saw Jackson on a Saturday night at Wynyard Square in 1880. Jackson was fighting off seven thugs from the gang of the notorious Dixon the Dog Hanger, who led a band of street criminals preying on the patrons of bars and brothels.

In his gym at the back of the White Horse Hotel, Foley taught Jackson the skills of modern boxing. Jackson had his first fight in Sydney in 1882, and over the next 17 years fought everywhere from the Wagga Wagga skating rink to the Honolulu Opera House, London's posh National Sporting Club and great auditoriums in San Francisco, Chicago, New York and Vancouver.

In San Francisco, where it has been reported that he may also have introduced the Australian crawl to American swimmers, Jackson beat two of the world's leading heavyweights, George Godfrey and Tom McAuliffe.

The world champion of the time, 'Boston Strong Boy' John L Sullivan, who often boasted he could 'lick any sonuvabitch in the world', refused to fight Jackson, famously telegraphing the Australian's backers with his impossible terms for a title fight: 'White men $10,000 apiece, [black men] double price.'

Unable to secure a shot at Sullivan's world title, Jackson travelled to San Francisco, and on 21 May 1891, he fought

James J Corbett, who was portrayed by Errol Flynn in the Hollywood epic *Gentleman Jim*. Corbett always maintained that Jackson was the best fighter he ever encountered. The boxers were so weary in the 61st round, they could not raise their arms and referee Hiram Cook called off the fight without a result.

The following year, 1892, Jackson was at Covent Garden in London, knocking out Frank 'Paddy' Slavin, his long-time rival. Slavin had reportedly called Jackson 'a yellow n****r' a decade earlier when they were drinking together in Foley's Sydney pub.

On 30 May 1892, in front of a crowd of 1300 that included the Wild West showman Buffalo Bill Cody, Jackson and Slavin fought more than 20 rounds for the heavyweight championship of the British Empire. The two Australians went at it hammer and tongs until Jackson dropped Slavin twice in the tenth round to win 1750 guineas out of a prize pool of 2000. It was the last great fight for both men.

'Gentleman' Jim Corbett beat John L Sullivan for the world title in New Orleans that year but no rematch with Jackson could be arranged, despite the efforts of Thomas Edison to bring them together in front of his newfangled motion picture camera.

For six years Jackson went without a fight, disillusioned, depressed and drinking heavily. He played Uncle Tom on the stage until, broke and nearly 38, he was lured back to the ring, only to be mauled by the young bull Jim Jeffries. Jackson was already dying of tuberculosis when he was knocked out in his next and last fight in Vancouver. He spent months coughing up his lungs in a Canadian hospital until his money ran out and he was shipped home to Australia. Friends took him to Roma in western Queensland, hoping the dry climate would help his condition, but he died there on 21 July 1901 aged just 40. He is buried under a magnificent headstone in Brisbane's Toowong Cemetery.

Young Griffo: Booze, Brothels and Brilliance

Despite the outstanding skills of Peter Jackson, the most dazzling student to emerge from Foley's Iron Pot was Albert Griffiths, who preferred the name Alfred Griffiths and was better known as Young Griffo. Until he was worn out by booze and brothels, Griffo was so fast and clever that the best fighters of his day could hardly land a glove on him.

Most likely born in the mining town of Sofala, near Bathurst, New South Wales, in 1871, Griffo learned to fight as a newspaper boy in Sydney's Rocks. He spoke with a Cockney accent, and was short and stocky with a hairy chest, long arms and the face of a good-natured goblin. He made his professional debut in 1886 and fought in 236 bouts until 1904. He would make pocket money by standing on a handkerchief in pubs, daring anyone to try to knock him off. His fighting style was to flummox and frustrate opponents into submission.

After a display of defensive brilliance and lightning counter-punching that sank New Zealand's 'Torpedo' Billy Murphy after fifteen rounds, Griffo won the world featherweight title, as recognised in Britain and Australia, at the Sydney Amateur Gymnastic Club on 22 July 1891.

'What's the matter? Can't you hit him?' asked the referee, as a shattered Murphy pulled off his gloves in surrender.

'Hit him?' replied Murphy, 'I can't even see the bastard.'

In 1892 Griffo boxed a 22-round draw against Jim Barron in an Australian lightweight title bout before heading to the United States, where he spent the rest of his turbulent life drinking with the likes of John L Sullivan and dazzling crowds with his radar-like defensive skills.

In 1894, Griffo boxed both an eight-round draw against George 'Kid' Lavigne in Chicago and a 20-round draw against world bantamweight champ George Dixon in Boston before losing a hotly disputed ten-round decision to world lightweight champ Jack McAuliffe in New York.

In 1895 in Boston, Griffo was set to box Jimmy Dime but was nowhere to be found come fight time. The promoter finally cornered Griffo in John L Sullivan's saloon.

Griffo was blithering and the promoter ordered him to be thrown in a tub of ice water. Finally, Griffo was revived enough to call for another drink and agree to fight Jimmy Dime only if the sodden John L, snoring on the bar room floor, his walrus moustache twitching, sat ringside as his guest.

Despite being hopelessly drunk, Griffo made Jimmy Dime miss with almost all his punches for eight rounds to earn a draw as John L slurred incomprehensible encouragement from behind a champagne bottle at ringside.

By 1900, Griffo was ravaged by alcoholism and lost in the eighth round at Brooklyn, New York, against Joe Gans, one of history's greatest lightweights. Griffo spent time in a mental asylum for alcoholism but still won more fights than he lost before being forced into retirement. He was virtually penniless when he died a broken man in the basement of a New York boarding house in 1927.

Bob Fitzsimmons: Freckles and Freakish Power

While Young Griffo was the most brilliant of Foley's pupils, the most successful was the Cornish-born, Kiwi-raised Bob Fitzsimmons. Slim, balding and freckled, he had cinemascope shoulders and the legs of a giraffe.

Fitz was born in Helston, Cornwall, the youngest of 12 children, but his Irish father moved his family to New Zealand, settling at Timaru on the South Island in 1872 when Fitz was nine.

Fitz became a blacksmith, building up powerful shoulders and arms out of proportion to the rest of his frame. He was heavily influenced by Jem Mace, who had toured New Zealand

and encouraged him to use his great natural power. Fitz started fighting in New Zealand in 1881.

He had at least six scraps in New Zealand, two of them bareknuckle, before heading across the Tasman to Foley's gym in 1883. He spent seven years there, winning most of his fights but losing two in four rounds when fighting for the Australian middleweight title in 1890 against Montague James Furlong, a frequent rival better known as the alcoholic Jim Hall.

Before long, Fitz was in America. He had immediate success and within a few months was fighting for the world middleweight championship against 'Nonpareil' Jack Dempsey, a boxer whose name would be borrowed by the world heavyweight champ of the 1920s. Though Fitz was a huge underdog, his powerful punching with thin 5-ounce gloves (about half the weight of modern fighting gloves) gave him a chance, and on 14 January 1891, before a crowd of 4000 at the Olympic Club in New Orleans, he dropped Dempsey repeatedly before finishing him off in the 13th round. Fitzsimmons was suddenly a wealthy man, taking $11,000 of the $12,000 prize money.

He gained revenge over Jim Hall in 1893, knocking out his Australian rival in four rounds in New Orleans, and beat a leading American, Joe Choynski. He then stopped the previously unbeaten Kiwi Dan Creedon to retain his world middleweight crown in just two rounds.

In February 1896, Fitzsimmons won a disputed version of the world heavyweight championship against the Irishman Peter Maher. Judge Roy Bean, the infamous Wild West character, helped organise the fight just across the Rio Grande from Langtry, Texas. It lasted just 95 seconds.

Wyatt Earp: Referee With a Six-gun

Wyatt Earp, one-time marshal of Tombstone, Arizona, and the last man standing in the gunfight at the OK Corral, was called in as referee when Bob Fitzsimmons took on the rugged former sailor Tom Sharkey on 2 December 1896 at the Mechanics Pavilion in San Francisco.

Earp entered the ring with his Colt revolver in his holster. After Fitz landed a big body punch in Round 8, Sharkey dropped limp as a rag and claimed he'd been hit when he was down. Wyatt Earp disqualified Fitz and though there were jeers and catcalls, no one protested too much, given Earp's reputation with a six-shooter.

Then came the greatest moment in Fitz's career. On 17 March 1897, in the rambunctious gold town of Carson City, Nevada, Fitz knocked out Jim Corbett, Peter Jackson's old rival, for the world heavyweight title taken from John L Sullivan.

Corbett was more than 7 kilograms heavier than Fitz, and he out-boxed him for much of the fight, dropping him in Round 6. But in the 14th round, Fitz suddenly switched stance from right-handed to southpaw and drove his left hand under Corbett's heart. His famous 'solar plexus' punch left the champ writhing in agony and unable to beat the ten-count from referee George Siler.

The fight card was filmed by Enoch J Rector and at 100 minutes was at that time the longest motion picture ever made.

Fitz lost the title to the undefeated Jim Jeffries, who outweighed him by 18 kilograms and was on a roll, having just annihilated Peter Jackson.

In 1903, Fitzsimmons scored a first-round knockout of Con Coughlin in Philadelphia. His opponent died the next day, but two weeks later Fitz was back in the ring for another win. A month after that he astonished again by winning the world light-heavyweight title (79 kg) with a 20-round decision over George Gardner in San Francisco.

Fitzsimmons kept fighting until 1914, when he was 50.

He died of pneumonia in Chicago three years later, survived by his fourth wife and with little of the fortune he'd made.

AUSSIE WORLD-BEATERS FOR A NEW CENTURY

Huge Deals and Timeless Champions

The promoter Hugh D 'Huge Deal' McIntosh, was the ultimate hustler. He once tried to seduce Rudolph Valentino's wife with a ring souvenired from the tomb of Tutankhamen. Mrs Valentino was a keen student of Egyptology, and McIntosh – pitching a movie deal to the Valentinos – had acquired the precious bauble during the great era of archaeology.

McIntosh had started his working life as a pie-delivery boy and went on to become a miner, chorus boy, doctor's assistant, train driver, bouncer, cow-milking champion, theatrical entrepreneur, politician, newspaper magnate, rabbit breeder, milk-bar giant, and much more besides. He raced cars and pushbikes, supported Olympic athletes and was the major sponsor of the fledgling Sydney rugby league competition and a consummate spruiker.

By his early 30s, he was one of Australia's richest men. He owned one of the grandest homes in Sydney and leased Lord Kitchener's Broome Park, near Canterbury, England, re-laying the cricket pitch there with black soil from Bulli, New South

Wales. A member of the New South Wales Upper House, he boasted of friendships with Winston Churchill, Teddy Roosevelt and William Rockefeller. He owned influential newspapers in Sydney, at one time sacking Kerry Packer's grandfather, Robert Clyde Packer, from his job as editor of *The Sunday Times.*

In 1908, around 16,000 American sailors were due to arrive in Sydney with America's Great White Fleet on a world tour to show off that country's naval might. The prospect prompted McIntosh, then aged 31, to take an audacious gamble and promote a world-title fight between Bill Squires, from the New South Wales town of Narrabri, and Canadian world heavyweight title holder Tommy Burns.

Bill Squires had first come to the notice of Melbourne gambling maverick John Wren three years earlier when he crushed West Indian–born Peter Felix in a round.

Wren started promoting Squires, and a crowd of 10,000 at Melbourne's Exhibition Building saw him drop Tim Murphy eight times in three rounds to win the Australian title on 28 April 1906. On 6 November, on the morning of the Melbourne Cup horserace, 15,000 people braved the rain at Wren's Ascot Vale racecourse to see 'Boshter Bill' knock out Peter Kling.

Squires had been born at Edgeroi Station, near Narrabri in 1879, the son of One Eye Bill Squires, and had worked as a shearer, timber cutter, railway navvy and bush cook. He became a miner at Wallsend near Newcastle and after some bareknuckle fights was coached in the finer points of the gloved business by featherweight champ Paddy King. Not a huge man at about 82 kilograms, he nevertheless had terrifying punching power.

Will Lawless, who wrote for *The Referee* under the byline 'Solar Plexus', once asked Bill how he would describe his fighting style. Bill shrugged his shoulders and replied: 'I just 'its 'em.'

Critics said Bill knew 'no more about the "noble art" than a bandicoot does of biology' and that the first time he met a good scientific boxer, he would be 'knocked dead to the bloomin' world'.

Still, Squires was riding a string of knockouts when he travelled to the small town of Colma, California – at the time a major international boxing venue – to fight the new world heavyweight champion Tommy Burns. A short, stocky Canadian whose birth name was Noah Brusso and whose portrait reminded many of Napoleon, Burns had succeeded Jim Jeffries as world heavyweight champion. Giving his stamp of approval to the new champion, Jeffries would referee the Burns–Squires fight in Colma on the Fourth of July holiday in 1907.

Squires was bigger than Burns and by all reports a much harder puncher. Bookies made him a 10–9 favourite. At the first bell, Squires charged out of his corner throwing haymakers, but his reputation was too good to be true: his threadbare defence was exposed. Burns knocked Squires down three times and the Australian was counted out in the opening round.

'Squires has a glass jaw,' *The San Francisco Examiner* reported, 'and no fighter is stronger than his weakest point.'

Squires had 11 more fights and was knocked out in ten of them. He faced Burns in a rematch at the Neuilly Bowling Palace in Paris on 13 June 1908. Burns was saved by the bell in Round 4, with only the world champion's capacity for taking punishment allowing him to survive a terrific punch to the jaw. He recovered to knock Squires unconscious in the eighth round. It was ten minutes before Bill opened his eyes.

Seeing his opportunity, Huge Deal McIntosh gave Squires a fighting chance at home. He lured Burns to Sydney with a purse of £2000 – the equivalent of about A$2 million today – win, lose or draw. Squires was guaranteed £400, but the bumper crowd would eventually earn him an extra £150 bonus.

McIntosh contracted a timber merchant to hastily erect an open-air stadium – the largest purpose-built boxing arena in the world – on an old Chinese market garden at Rushcutters Bay. McIntosh named it Sydney Stadium. It would have a roof fitted in 1912 and, as the Old Tin Shed, became the home of Australian boxing for six decades, later playing host to other performers such as The Beatles, The Rolling Stones and Frank Sinatra.

Tommy Burns was the guest referee for the first ever fight there, on 21 August 1908, when about 2000 people watched Sid Russell outpoint Peter Felix for the New South Wales heavyweight title. Just three days later, Burns was the main event, defending his world heavyweight title against Squires in brilliant sunshine just after midday on a Monday afternoon. While the American sailors didn't support the fight as McIntosh had hoped, a record Australian crowd of 16,000 – including many members of the government – contributed to a gate of £13,400.

Burns was a 5–1 favourite, but Squires made a lively start and, cheered by the huge crowd, had Burns groggy in Round 7. After ten rounds, both men's faces had been bloodied, but Squires was in front. In Round 11, Burns, despite having a blackened eye and a cut face, began to change the complexion of the contest. He looked a new man. He dropped Squires twice in Round 13, the second time for the 10-count from referee Harry Nathan. Burns had retained his world title again. When Squires finally got up, still dazed, he started throwing punches at imaginary opponents.

History in Black and White

Although Tommy Burns had held the world heavyweight title for two years, there was an enormous shadow hanging over him. Many in the sport believed the best boxer in the world was not Burns, but a black Texan: Jack Johnson, the son of former slaves.

Johnson first came to Australia in 1907. On 19 February that year, at Sydney's Gaiety Theatre, he knocked out Peter Felix in the opening round for what was billed as the 'Coloured Heavyweight Championship of the World'.

The following month, Johnson was at John Wren's Richmond Racecourse in Melbourne, manhandling local football hero Bill

Lang. Born William Lanfranchi, the big local blacksmith had been Richmond's fullback when they won the VFA flag in 1905, and he'd turned professional as a boxer the same year. On 4 March 1907, he faced Johnson before a crowd of 11,000. On this rainy day, Lang was soon out of his depth.

In a clinch in Round 9, the dazed, exhausted Lang asked Johnson what round it was. 'What round, Bill?' Johnson replied, flashing a wicked grin with his gold-capped teeth. 'It's the last.' Moments later, Lang was on his back, out cold, the rain pelting his bloodied face. Johnson returned to America and scored six more wins, one of them over the worn-out old campaigner Bob Fitzsimmons, before heading back to Australia when Huge Deal McIntosh made him the kind of offer he'd been waiting on all his life.

In the interim, Bill Lang put together 11 straight wins over the likes of Peter Felix, Peter Kling, Dick Kernick and Arthur Cripps. In 1908, he was given a chance at world champion Tommy Burns at the specially built stadium on City Road, South Melbourne. Burns would receive £1000 and Lang £600. Lang had already played eight games for Richmond that year. On 2 September, he was ready to make his mark in what was regarded as the most prestigious honour in the world of sport. To help the Australian win the world heavyweight title, Hugh McIntosh would be the referee.

A crowd of 8000 began to fill the stadium from before 8 a.m. The main event started just after noon. The chunky Canadian punched away furiously at close range. So self-assured was Burns that, at the start of Round 2, he came at Lang with both hands down.

Lang instinctively let fly with a half hook, half uppercut from his left hand. It caught Burns under the right side of the chin. The blow lifted the world champion clean off the canvas and dropped him with a huge thud on the seat of his pants. 'A look of blank wonder and astonishment' passed across Burns's face,

The Argus reported. 'Then he gazed at Lang with admiration. The crowd went mad. Men shrieked with joy, cheered and danced, and threw their hats up.' Referee McIntosh started to count quickly, hoping he'd reach ten before Burns got to his feet. But Burns was up at 'six', shaking the fog from his head.

In Round 6, he hurled a right hand all the way from his ankles. Lang crashed to the canvas, rolled over onto his stomach and was counted out.

Fight of the Century

No black man had ever fought for the world heavyweight championship and 'Huge Deal' McIntosh wanted to change that, not because he believed in racial equality – far from it – but with an eye to the massive profit that a legally sanctioned 'race war' could generate. Burns wanted nothing to do with it, but McIntosh made him an offer he couldn't refuse: £6,000 (about $A6 million in today's money).

In his documentary *Unforgivable Blackness*, Ken Burns explained that at a time when black men could be lynched in America for whistling at white women, Jack Johnson flaunted his sexual, intellectual and fighting prowess. When he wasn't battering white men to a pulp, he trampled on society's taboos, living with a succession of white sex workers. He dressed in furs and diamonds, and when most white men still travelled by horse and cart, Johnson roared about in the most expensive automobiles.

'When whites ran everything, Jack Johnson took orders from no one,' Burns said. 'To most whites, and even to some African-Americans, Johnson was a perpetual threat: profligate, arrogant, amoral – a dark menace and a danger to the natural order of things.'

Johnson had beaten the best black fighters: Joe Jeanette, Sam McVea and Sam Langford. Now McIntosh was offering

Johnson the chance to prove he was better than the best white man in the world. The fight was set for Sydney Stadium, appropriately, for Boxing Day 1908.

Writers – including the American novelist Jack London, who, like most of the reporters, was vocal in his support for the white champion – travelled from all corners of the globe to cover the fight.

A year earlier, *The Referee* had reprinted an item from a Californian newspaper in which Johnson claimed he was going to marry a white Sydney woman, Lola Toy. Toy sued *The Referee* for damages. Even though she admitted that she had spent a night at Johnson's hotel, had danced and been photographed with him, she was awarded £500 because of the harm to her reputation that public association with a black man might cause. In 1908, however, crowds of Sydney girls still flocked to see the exotic Texan training for his historic bout. Johnson stuffed heavy gauze bandages down the front of his tights to fatten his reputation.

Hugh D McIntosh had originally signed Johnson to fight Burns for a purse of £1000 but, under constant pressure for a raise from the hulking American, he ended up paying Johnson £1500.

Negotiations were often heated. McIntosh's friend Norman Lindsay, who had drawn the two fighters for the cover of the December 1908 issue of *The Lone Hand* magazine, remembered the safety measure taken by McIntosh during the pay dispute. It was a piece of lead pipe rolled in sheet music on the promoter's desk. McIntosh told Lindsay it was for Johnson if he tried 'any funny stuff'. The title of the tune was 'Sing Me to Sleep, Mother'. Burns prepared for the fight at retail king Mark Foy's plush Hydro Majestic Hotel in the Blue Mountains. Johnson set up camp at the more modest Sir Joseph Banks Hotel in Botany, alongside former New York sex worker Hattie McClay, one of the many Mrs Johnsons in his life. He also trained at a cottage at Manly where he would bodysurf with the locals. He spent time talking about fights with old Larry Foley and he sparred with Bill Lang.

By Boxing Day 1908, Sydney was agog with fight fever. Thousands were milling around the gates by 2 a.m. At 10 a.m., an hour before the fight was due to start, 20,400 fans filled the vast wooden structure. One of them, Charmian London, Jack London's wife, disguised herself in men's clothing to gain admission. Perhaps as many as 50,000 people – mostly men and boys – unable to buy tickets, scaled trees, telegraph poles and roofs to watch from outside the wooden arena.

Accepted wisdom of the time suggested Burns would attack Johnson's body because blacks had thicker skulls than the 'civilised' white man. The white audience was certain that their little champion would emerge triumphant, even though, at 184 centimetres Johnson was 14 centimetres taller than Burns and much more physically imposing. As Jack London wrote, however, once the bell rang Burns had as much chance as 'a dewdrop in hell'. 'The fight?' London wrote. There was no fight. 'No Armenian massacre could compare with the hopeless slaughter.' Burns hit the deck within seconds of the opening bell and for the next 14 rounds suffered a public flogging.

All the while, Johnson flashed his gold-capped teeth in a dazzling smirk that only exacerbated Burns's agony.

'Cahm on leedle Tahmmy,' the big Texan would drawl, before cutting Burns's face some more. 'What's wrong, Tahmmy? You hit like a girl.'

Burns, exhausted and broken, flailed helplessly, cursing his tormenter through shredded lips as Johnson moved away, drawing Burns onto his heavy counterpunches.

'Stand and fight, n****r,' the champion screamed at one stage. 'Fight like a white man.'

The massacre continued until Johnson was finally declared the winner in Round 14 when the Sydney police switched off the movie cameras and told Burns he was done.

While black newspapers in America celebrated Johnson's win as the most significant triumph for African-Americans since the abolition of slavery, *Fairplay* magazine lambasted the new heavyweight champion of the world as a 'huge, primordial ape'. *The Bulletin* magazine, which had changed its masthead slogan from 'Australia for Australians' to 'Australia for the White Man' declared Johnson's taunting of Burns so objectionable that if he had tried it in America he would have been shot dead and the killers acquitted. Journalist Randolph Bedford, writing in the Melbourne *Herald*, described Burns's defeat as beautiful sunlight being snuffed out by ugly darkness. In America, race riots and lynchings greeted news of the black man's success.

McIntosh had made a fortune, with gate receipts totalling £26,000, almost double the previous Australian record he'd set for the Burns–Squires fight four months earlier. He was about to make another £37,000 showing the film of the fight around the world.

Jack Johnson headed home to the United States, but not before spending some time in Brisbane where he paid his respects at the grave of Peter Jackson in Toowong Cemetery.

Hard Yards of the Fight Game

Canadian-born Sam Langford, known throughout the world as the Boston Tar Baby after his adopted hometown, is regarded as one of the greatest heavyweights of all time, though he was never given a shot at the world title.

Langford had 11 bouts in Australia between 1911 and 1913, and while he was here, he beat his arch foe, American Sam McVea, four times in fights for the Australian heavyweight title and the World Coloured Heavyweight Title. He finished his Australian campaign with a 15-round fight against Moree's Colin Bell at Queensland's Rockhampton Stadium.

The bout was declared a draw, though the judges seemed extremely generous to the Australian. After some debate, it was decided that the two weary pugs could settle the issue with a 75-yard (69-metre) race to the dressing-room. That contest also ended in a dead heat.

Australia's First Indigenous Champion

A chubby Queensland stockman with a fondness for lollies and fruitcake became the first Indigenous national boxing champion. Jerry Jerome had a wild, unorthodox fighting style delivered from a southpaw stance: weaving and dancing about, sometimes bounding like a kangaroo, and occasionally even jogging away from opponents in mock terror.

He was of the Yiman people, born at Jimbour Station, 16 kilometres north of Dalby, and he was 34 before he had his first pro fight in 1908. Though rarely in peak physical condition, he had a fast right lead and a powerful looping left swing, and he could punch effectively at long range or close quarters with bursts of devastating combinations.

During his career, Jerome twice knocked out Frenchman Ercole de Balzac, and went up against the English expat Arthur Evernden, as well as the Americans Cyclone Johnny Thompson and Eddie McGoorty, who had both claimed the world middleweight title.

After six wins in his first seven fights, Jerome was matched with Australian middleweight champion Arthur Cripps in 1910 at Brisbane's Olympic Stadium. He lost a decision over 20 rounds. The newspapers said Cripps had maintained the superiority of the white race but that Jerome 'bore out all that has been said of his wonderful quickness in eye and hand, whilst the originality of his methods at times perplexed his veteran opponent. Above all he proved that the white race had not by any means a monopoly of the quality of courage'.

At Brisbane's Olympic Stadium two years later, Jerome defeated 'Black Paddy', an Aboriginal middleweight from Western Australia, over 16 rounds. Then, on 7 September 1912, Australia saw the first Aboriginal national champion in any sport crowned when Jerome, 'fighting like a wild cat', dropped middleweight champ Charlie Godfrey from Bundaberg repeatedly in Round 3 then knocked the wind out of him with a right to the stomach in Round 4.

He went on to beat Arthur Cripps in a rematch and twice stopped the 'Bondi Dairyman' Tim Land.

In 1914, Jerome was being trained by the old West Indian heavyweight Peter Felix – but only after permission was granted by the Queensland Aboriginal Protection Board. A few days short of his 38th birthday, he gave Eddie McGoorty a tremendous fight at the Brisbane Stadium.

In the fourth round McGoorty was caught up in a whirlwind of punches, but in Round 5 Jerome broke a bone in his forearm. His corner threw in the towel at the end of the sixth. Promoter Snowy Baker remarked that if Jerome could keep fit 'he would be the greatest middleweight fighter in the world'.

Jerome retired in 1915, 41 and flabby, having earned £5000 during his career. Although the Queensland Government said that it was keeping a quarter of his earnings in trust, he died in poverty at the Cherbourg Aboriginal Settlement in 1943.

Les Darcy: A Tragic Icon

Ever-smiling teenager Les Darcy, a rock-hard fighting blacksmith from Maitland, New South Wales, took Jerry Jerome's place as Australia's top middleweight.

They just don't make heroes like Darcy anymore. From the age of 14, he was the family breadwinner for an alcoholic father and an ailing mum and her ten children in Maitland, moving them from a hovel to a grand home.

Darcy was a strong, stocky, powerful boxer-puncher who overwhelmed opponents, working on the inside, chopping them down with short body rips and hooks to the head. He had an amazing stamina and ability to absorb punishment.

Darcy had learned to box as a barefoot schoolboy and made his pro debut as a featherweight in 1910, scoring a knockout in 11 rounds over Guv'nor Balsa in the railway hamlet at Thornton, near Maitland. Two years later, aged 17, he lost over 20 rounds to Bob Whitelaw for the Australian welterweight title at Newcastle. In a rematch the following year, Darcy scored a knockout in five.

He lost back-to-back fights against the onion-eared American Fritz Holland at Sydney Stadium in 1914, and then took part in two highly suspicious foul-filled fights against American Jeff Smith, losing the first and winning the second. The second win, on 22 May 1915, crowned Darcy as world middleweight champion as far as most commentators outside America were concerned, but Smith may have thrown the fight in a gambling sting. His purse was withheld and he never fought in Australia again.

On 19 February 1916, at Sydney Stadium, Darcy stopped Manly lifesaver, rugby star and Olympic swimming champion Harold Hardwick in seven rounds for the Australian heavyweight title. During the fight, two of Darcy's teeth were knocked out and an infection slowly developed in his blood.

By the outbreak of World War I he was a political pawn. While he was punching the best fighters from America, politicians were asking why he wasn't knocking out Germans on the Western Front like so many other young Australian men. Still a teenager, Darcy was under constant pressure to enlist even though he had a dozen hungry mouths to feed at home. He tried to join up at a recruiting station in Brisbane, but his mother refused to give her consent and, as he was under 21, he was turned away.

He decided to make money while he could, defying a ban on leaving the country. Once his parents and siblings were taken care of financially, he reasoned, he would enlist and go to war. Telling his friends that he wanted to spend just six months boxing in the United States in order to set up his family, he fled to America.

Politicians in Australia and America labelled Darcy a coward and deserter, and boxing commissions in the United States banned him from fighting. Meanwhile, the infection in his blood was taking hold. By the time the boxing commissions finally relented after he had enlisted in the United States Army Signal Corps, he had become desperately ill.

At the time, the boxer who hated knocking people out and who went easy on sparring partners was regarded as a serious threat to the world heavyweight champion Jess Willard, a giant who stood 30 centimetres taller than Darcy and weighed at least 38 kilograms more. Jack Dempsey, who in 1919 smashed Willard's jawbone through the side of his face and left him a quivering wreck in three terrifying rounds, remarked years later that Darcy could have beaten Willard just as easily.

Darcy was in Memphis, Tennessee, in 1917, when blood poisoning caused him to collapse while training. He died, aged just 21, in the arms of his sweetheart, Winnie O'Sullivan, and was soon deified by Australians. Winnie remembered that he had lovely dove-grey eyes rimmed with black, and that he was always smiling.

Darcy had met fame and adulation with modesty, had faced persecution and hate with his cheery grin and was so sunny in the face of an agonising death that, even decades later, tough men were moved to tears.

Darcy's body was returned to Australia. As many as 300,000 people filed past his coffin in Sydney, while another 100,000 attended his funeral in Maitland.

In 1996, documentary producer Graham McNeice and I travelled to the old mining town of Hill End, west of the Blue Mountains, to uncover the only surviving footage of Darcy's funeral for the film *That's Boxing*. A local resident had the footage in a tin under his bed.

I interviewed one of the mourners at the funeral, Rita Tollis, mother of Mickey Tollis, a star fighter of the 1940s. Rita was in her 80s then, but she remembered the long queue passing by Darcy's casket in Maitland.

Tributes for Darcy did not dim with time. Forty years after his death, Memphis man Luke Kingsley, who got to know him well, recalled that the young boxer 'was as straight as a yard rule. A diamond. I tell you that from the bottom of my heart'.

And Henrietta Cheal, who remembered Darcy as a big loveable boy playing with the kids at Mosman, recalled: 'Ah, he was a lovely fella. And that's the beginning and the end of it.'

Snowy Baker: Hollywood's Great All-rounder

Reginald Leslie Baker, better known as 'Snowy', was one of Australia's finest ever all-round athletes, excelling at 26 different sports and becoming one of the giants of Australia's infant film industry.

He started his sporting life as a running champion at Sydney's Crown Street Public School and ended it as a polo-playing Hollywood hero. He also won Olympic silver in boxing and played halfback for the Wallabies rugby union team against Great Britain.

Born in the Sydney suburb of Darlinghurst in 1884, the husky and handsome Baker went on to study engineering at Sydney University, where he won blues for cricket, rugby, rowing and athletics.

In 1908 at the London Olympics, he squared off in the middleweight final with the Englishman Johnny Douglas, no mean sportsman himself – Douglas was also a pace bowler who went on to captain the English cricket team in 18 Tests and who also played for England in football.

Douglas took the gold medal, but Baker, who already had a gift for invention, told everyone back in Australia that the referee was Douglas's father. He wasn't.

Baker bought Sydney Stadium from Hugh D McIntosh. After Les Darcy sailed for America, depriving Baker of his biggest ticket seller, he waged a vicious campaign against the young champion for failing to enlist.

John Wren eventually bought out Baker's interest in Sydney Stadium and Baker turned his attention to the movies, setting up a film studio at his mansion in the eastern Sydney suburb of Waverley and casting himself as an all-action superhero. Movie fans gasped at his death-defying stunts.

In 1920 Baker left for Hollywood and lived the rest of his life there, becoming manager of the Riviera Polo Club in Santa Monica and befriending the silent film comedian Harold Lloyd. He taught Rudolf Valentino horsemanship for *The Sheik* and coached Douglas Fairbanks on how to crack whips for *Son of Zorro*. At 60, Snowy performed stunts for *National Velvet*, starring Elizabeth Taylor and Mickey Rooney.

Grim Toll of Hard Fights

One of the most curious characters to appear in Australian boxing in the early 20th century was Joe Grim, an Italian-American–born Saverio Giannone.

Known disparagingly as 'the Human Punching Bag', Grim had an extraordinary reputation for being able to take horrific punishment without being knocked out. He had 179 recorded bouts around the world but may have had as many as 500. He had a ritual at the end of each bout, standing at the ropes like a pugilistic Quasimodo and shouting to the crowd, 'Me Joe Grim. I fear no man on earth.'

In 1903 Grim tackled former heavyweight champion Bob Fitzsimmons in Philadelphia over six rounds and lasted the distance, despite going down twice in the second round, once in the third, three times in the fourth, six times in the fifth and eight times in the sixth. A newspaper reporter said he 'took a battering ... that would have killed an ordinary man'.

Two years later, Jack Johnson knocked Grim down 17 times but still couldn't stop him in their six-rounder, telling reporters after the fight, 'I just don't believe that man is made of flesh and blood.'

Grim had 11 fights in Australia in 1908–1909. He won nine of them but was pummelled in Sydney, Melbourne, Ballarat, Zeehan, Perth and Charters Towers. He died in the Philadelphia Hospital for Mental Diseases in 1939.

Australian author Michael Winkler used Grim's tour as the basis for his novel *Grimmish*, which was shortlisted for the 2022 Miles Franklin Literary Award.

THE HUNGRIEST FIGHTERS

Triumph and Tragedy

The cruel dangers of boxing were never more evident than in the fight between mates Harry Gordon and George Mendies at Sydney Stadium on 3 May 1924. Mendies was the son of Portuguese migrants, a brilliant little flyweight (51 kg) who had won the Australian title and fought the world-beating Filipino Pancho Villa in Manila. Having already beaten Mendies once, Gordon didn't want to fight his friend again. However, with a small child and pregnant wife, Mendies needed the money, so Harry agreed to fight him.

Mendies gave away a good deal in weight, height and reach. Yet, for six rounds, he outfought and outboxed his bantamweight (53.5 kg) opponent. Gordon came on strong late in the fight. In Round 15, as Mendies shifted his stance to southpaw and tried a right-hand lead, he left his chin unguarded. Gordon struck with his own right and Mendies went down, his head making a sickening thud against the padded floor of the ring. He was rushed to St Vincent's Hospital for emergency brain surgery but died three days later. The coroner's verdict was accidental death.

Mendies's purse was a meagre £87. After his expenses were paid, there was little left for his pregnant widow and child.

Have Gloves, Will Travel

The roaring twenties produced many world-beating Aussies.

George Cook, from the village of Cobbora near Dubbo, had a 22-year career that began in 1916 and took him all over the world. He scored two wins over the Basque Paulino Uzcudun and a victory over the Black Canadian Larry Gains, and twice fought Primo Carnera during the Italian's march to the world championship.

Albert Lloyd, from the Melbourne suburb of Carlton, scored perhaps his biggest win over the Englishman Phil Scott in London in 1922.

Colin Bell was nearly 38 when, at the Hippodrome in Sydney, he stopped leading English heavyweight Matthew 'Nutty' Curran. The following year, 1922, in a pair of fights at the Olympic Theatre in Mackay, he twice outpointed the New Zealand plumber Tom Heeney in 20-rounders, finally becoming the Australian heavyweight champion as he neared his 40th birthday.

Heeney had nine fights in Australia. He would make his mark on the world scene six years later, fighting world champion Gene Tunney before a crowd of 46,000 at New York's Yankee Stadium in 1928. Former world heavyweight champion Jack Dempsey was in his corner. Writer Damon Runyon labelled the powerful New Zealander 'The Hard Rock from Down Under'. He lasted until the 11th round.

Tommy Uren, from Sydney's Leichhardt, was a powder monkey on the Hurlstone Park–Glebe Island goods line rail construction, and entertained workmates with death-defying bites on detonators. His biggest moment came at Sydney Stadium in a fight against black Englishman Len Johnson on 8 May 1926. The fight was billed as the Middleweight Championship of the

British Empire, although Johnson's previous win over Australia's Harry Collins for the title was not recognised by British officials, as their rules stated that title contestants 'must have two white parents'. Uren troubled the lanky Manchester boxer with his silky skills early in the fight before Johnson ended the debate with a right uppercut to the solar plexus in Round 11.

Temora blacksmith Frank Burns (his real name was Eric Barnes) had four fighting sons, the most successful of them being George Barnes, a huge star of the 1940s and 1950s. Frank had headed to Europe for a series of bouts in the early 1920s and soon after his arrival dived into the Thames to rescue a drowning man. Although he was awarded a Royal Humane Society medal for heroism, he contracted pneumonia, and he was never as strong again.

In Burns's most important fight, at Holland Park in London in 1922, Ted 'Kid' Lewis, the former world welterweight champ, stopped him in 11 rounds for the British Empire middleweight title.

Billy Grime, a fighting milkman from Wombat, New South Wales, smoked throughout his career and drank an egg beaten in a glass of sherry each morning, believing it dried the fat inside his stomach. Grime won the Australian featherweight title from Bill Spargo in Melbourne in 1923 and the lightweight title from him a year later. In 1927 he won the welterweight title from Eddie Butcher at Sydney Stadium, even though he conceded nearly 9 kilograms to the champion.

By the time he took on American Petey Sarron in 1929 at Sydney Stadium, Grime was a veteran of 111 pro fights. He had already fought at Madison Square Garden and other large American venues. Sarron had fought for the United States at the 1924 Olympics and went on to become world featherweight champion.

The 1929 bout was to be the first of five fights between Grime and Sarron, and the only one Grime would win.

When Grime retired in 1933, other stars had begun to dominate the lighter weights in Australia, among them Merv 'Darky' Blandon, Alf Blatch (who would fight all-time great Henry Armstrong at Madison Square Garden), Mickey Miller and Charleville's Bobby Delaney, whose four battles with Bobby Blay at Sydney Stadium were epics of the ring.

Jimmy Kelso's mother died while his father was fighting in the First World War. Orphaned, he learned to fight in a boys home and in the labyrinthine alleys of Sydney's inner-city Surry Hills.

In February 1933, he came in as a last-minute substitute opponent at Leichhardt Stadium to face Al Foreman, the Montreal-born Empire lightweight champion, who was rated Number 3 in the world. Foreman was a 15–1 on favourite, and the crowd was so small for what shaped as a mismatch that Kelso's purse was just £19.

Yet, hungry for success, Kelso ground out a 15-round decision. He went on to beat Bobby Delaney in his next fight for the Australian title.

In April, he was matched with Foreman again for the Empire title. *The Referee* reported that while the 'London Hebrew boxed as a machine, picking his points nicely', Kelso won 'by stealing and picking punches, at in-fighting and bursting to the front during the most important period of the fight – the end'.

Born in Gunnedah, Hughie Dwyer grew up in a Maitland orphanage and learned to box from a correspondence course run by Snowy Baker.

Dwyer outpointed Sid Godfrey for the Australian lightweight title at Sydney Stadium in 1922, then won another 20-round decision over America's Olympic gold medallist Sam Mossberg before a brief visit to America, where he lost to Joe Welling at Madison Square Garden.

Dwyer was to follow his 1927 win over Frank Burns for the Australian middleweight title by beating Al Bourke for the welterweight belt at Leichhardt Stadium. In all, Dwyer spent 14 years as a professional fighter, winning three Australian titles.

His wife, though, didn't share his passion for the sport. Hughie had inherited the trunks of the late Les Darcy, but Mrs Dwyer, thinking the most precious memorabilia in Australian boxing to be a pile of old rags, burned them in the backyard incinerator.

Jack Carroll: Australia's Favourite Fighter

Jeff Horn, Jeff Fenech, George Kambosos, Kostya Tszyu, Anthony Mundine and Danny Green all attracted huge crowds to their fights, but the most popular Australian boxer of all time was an unlikely looking hero who gave battlers a measure of hope and glory during the lean years of the Great Depression.

No great fighter ever looked less like one than the pasty, balding, homely slaughterman whose real name was Arthur Ernest Hardwick, and whose stabbing left hand sliced up opponents like they were sides of beef.

Yet he became the greatest crowd magnet ever seen in Australia, slapping as often as he punched, and cutting opponents to ribbons with the cuffing laces of his gloves. Despite his rough head and powder-puff punch, crowds fell in love with Carroll during the 1930s, perhaps because battlers during the Great Depression could identify with one of their own. He held the Australian welterweight title for a decade and beat some of the world's top middleweights.

Promoter Charlie Lucas, who had managed leading Australian fighters since the days of Jerry Jerome, offered American world champ Barney Ross £12,000 – the largest ever purse for a fight in Australia – to face Carroll at the Sydney Showground in December 1936. Carroll was to receive £3000 and the crowd was expected to reach 70,000. The fight fell through, however, after the Australians failed to send Ross's deposit to his managers in Chicago, fearing they might not see their money again.

It is part of Australian boxing folklore that world light-heavyweight champ 'Slapsie' Maxie Rosenbloom, who had a series of fights in Australia in 1936, returned to America and told Ross: 'That old man out there will not only take your title, he'll cut you to ribbons.'

Writer Lou d'Alpuget, whose daughter would marry former prime minister Bob Hawke, said the fast-moving Carroll had a sandy skull, lolly-pink skin, an apologetic manner and about as much punching power as an angry housewife.

Yet crowds couldn't get enough of him: 30,000 turned up to the Sydney Sports Ground to see him beat American Izzy Jannazzo, another 30,000 were there to see him beat American Jimmy Leto, and 25,000 more sat through pouring rain to see him bamboozle Dutch Olympic gold medallist Bep van Klaveren.

Carroll was born at Kensington, Melbourne, the seventh child of a truck driver. Because his father disliked boxing, he used an alias in the ring. He turned pro in 1923 and won the Australian welterweight title from Al Bourke in Sydney in March 1928.

Carroll's loss to middleweight star Fred Henneberry by a 13th-round stoppage in February 1932 was the last defeat he suffered. He went unbeaten for the next six years.

Back in 1996, I stood under a tree at Dungog in the thick timber country north of Newcastle and listened as Henneberry, still lean and tough, recalled his battles with 'The Red Fox' more than 60 years earlier.

They fought three times. Henneberry won the first by a 13th-round stoppage and lost the next two on points over 15 rounds.

Henneberry reckoned Carroll cut opponents with the laces of his gloves using illegal punches. 'It took me 13 rounds to catch him in the first fight,' Henneberry told me. 'He was very fast. Carroll had a left hand – they called it a straight left. He used to flick with it, backhand style, which is a foul. But he got away with it for a long time.'

Carroll outpointed former American world champion Tod Morgan in 1933 and 1934 and beat top American Wes Ramey and Aussie middleweight destroyer Ron Richards. He also chopped up and stopped Canadian Billy Townsend, who claimed the world junior-welterweight title.

Fighting to Eat

From the 1984 Olympic Games Jeff Fenech sent me a postcard on which he had written his career mantra: 'Tough times don't last, tough people do.' Fred Henneberry proved that. Born in Port Pirie, South Australia, he tramped for three years during the Great Depression before finally finding steady work as a bootmaker's assistant. He became the hellcat of Sydney Stadium, a fierce middleweight who was disqualified eight times in his career, five times in his ten wars with arch foe Ron Richards.

To those who knew Henneberry later in his life, he was a quiet, unfailingly polite old chap, who bowed when introduced to ladies. He had a business selling women's lingerie and although he ran several country hotels he never touched a drop of alcohol.

To those who visited Sydney Stadium in its heyday, however, or who have seen the old newsreels of his fights, he was the toughest, angriest man ever to brawl there. What made such a gentle, kindly man so fierce?

'I was hungry,' he told me at the age of 85. 'Fellows in the 1930s were fighting to eat and usually had three or four others to feed as well. If you didn't put on a show for the crowd, you didn't get paid and you went home hungry.'

As a young boxer just starting out, Henneberry beat Joe Taylor, later the boss of Sydney's illegal casinos. He ended up outliving three other legends he'd whipped: Jack Carroll, Ambrose Palmer and Ron Richards. When he died in the peaceful little town of Dungog, New South Wales in 1997, aged 86, Henneberry was still corresponding with one of his greatest foes, Archie Moore.

Henneberry and Moore had fought at Sydney Stadium in 1940. Moore won with a low blow in Round 7 of what had been a pulsating stoush. Twelve years later, Moore began a ten-year stint as world light-heavyweight champion. He fought for the world heavyweight crown twice and, in 1962, at the age of almost 46, took on a young upstart named Cassius Clay – later known as Muhammad Ali.

Henneberry won the Australian middleweight title from Ambrose Palmer in 1932. Handicapped from the first round when his right eyebrow was cut, Henneberry kept taking the fight to the slick-boxing Victorian. He was finally declared the winner on a foul in Round 9, but it was while he was writhing on the canvas from two low punches.

Henneberry lost his middleweight title to Ron Richards, against whom he engaged in Australia's most notorious boxing feud, a series of ten fights in which 'Fiery Fred' was disqualified five times for headbutts, low blows and rabbit-killers – blows to the back of the head.

Still, Henneberry managed to beat the future middleweight champion of the world, American Ken Overlin in 1938. He fought a draw with top-rated American Georgie Abrams at Madison Square Garden in 1939. *The New York Times* said that 'erratic body fire' cost Henneberry the first, sixth and eighth rounds in penalties – otherwise, he would have won comfortably against a man who pushed the legendary Sugar Ray Robinson to a split decision.

'I fought with what they used to call a lot of devil in me; that means I got up and had a go,' Fred told me, the fire still in his old eyes. 'I asked for no quarter and I gave none. I was a fighter.'

Ambrose Palmer: The Aussie Rules Star Who Made His Mark

Ambrose Palmer became one of the best light-heavyweights Australia has produced, a world championship trainer and an outstanding Australian Rules footballer. His father, Bill Palmer, was a Victorian lightweight champion, and at the age of 15, Ambrose won the Victorian amateur welterweight title. He turned pro two years later and quickly built a reputation as a skilful boxer who had a masterful defence but suffered cuts easily.

Palmer scored a knockout in Round 12 over the Jack Dunleavy-trained Jack Haines in December 1930 to become the Australian middleweight champion. Haines suffered a cerebral haemorrhage during the fight and never fought again.

Two years later, Palmer tackled one of the world's top heavyweights, Young Stribling, a 27-year-old American from Macon, Georgia who, despite his comparative youth, had engaged in almost 300 professional fights compared with Palmer's 30.

Stribling came from a family of vaudeville entertainers and was coached by his parents 'Ma and Pa Stribling'. He dabbled in aviation and raced everywhere on his motorbike. Stribling had gone into the 15th round of a thriller with world heavyweight champion Max Schmeling in *Ring* magazine's Fight of the Year just 12 months earlier.

Stribling was 8 kilograms heavier than Palmer, but promoter Hugh D McIntosh, whose financial empire was crumbling, still thought Palmer would give him a great battle at Sydney Stadium in a promotion built around America's celebration of the Fourth of July 1932.

Palmer was all heart but Stribling had every physical advantage. After ten one-sided rounds, Jack Warner, Palmer's chief second, asked referee Joe Wallis to stop the fight.

'My weight advantage told,' Stribling said. 'I wore him down with lefts and rights in close. But Palmer was a good, game boy until the end. He's a very good fighter and will give anyone in the world a battle at his weight. He gave away too much weight against me. I congratulate him on his pluck.'

Palmer conceded: 'It was a great chance for me to be matched with one of the world's three greatest heavyweights, but Stribling tossed me about like a baby. I knew from the first punch I delivered that his weight and strength would master me. Stribling caught me with a hefty uppercut right on the chin, and I felt as though my head was knocked off my shoulders.'

Stribling had little time to enjoy his win. Back in America the following year he was roaring down a country road in Georgia to the hospital where his wife was convalescing with their new baby, the couple's third child, when he was hit by a car coming the other way. Stribling suffered a crushed pelvis and his left foot was left dangling by a single tendon.

'Well kid,' he said to a friend who came to his rescue, 'I guess this means no more roadwork.'

Stribling was taken to the same hospital where his wife and baby were resting. His left foot was amputated.

At one point he woke, saw his wife, and asked, 'How's the baby?'

He died the next day.

Ten years later, former promoter Hugh McIntosh, once among the most influential men in Australia, died in poverty in London after the collapse of an English milk-bar business he had started. All he could leave his long-suffering wife of 45 years were a few pounds and some moth-eaten clothes.

Palmer recovered from his injuries to beat Americans Dave Shade, Leo Kelly and Olympian Johnny Miler, who had beaten the great Joe Louis as an amateur. He also scored wins over Fred Henneberry and Ron Richards.

After dropping a hotly disputed 15-round decision at the Sydney Sports Ground to America's future world light-heavyweight champion Gus Lesnevich in 1938, Palmer retired.

He returned to play ruck-rover with the Footscray Football Club, now the Western Bulldogs in the Australian Football League. Eighty-three games and 44 goals later, Palmer's football career ended when, sandwiched in a collision with Essendon players, he suffered nine fractures of the skull and six fractures of the jaw.

The injuries were far worse than anything he received in boxing.

He became a fight trainer and from his gymnasium underneath the West Melbourne Stadium guided such champions as Mickey Tollis, Max Carlos, Trevor 'Stretch' Anderson, Rocky Mattioli, Brad Vocale and Johnny Famechon, who took the world featherweight title in 1969.

Ron Richards: The Rise and Fall of an Indigenous Hero

Ron Richards was one of the great success stories of Australian sport and one of its most profound tragedies. He was the first Indigenous sportsman to be a genuine world beater, and he claimed numerous titles, including the British Empire middleweight and the Australian middleweight, light-heavyweight and heavyweight crowns.

He was born Ranold Richards at the Deebing Creek Aboriginal Presbyterian Mission near Ipswich, west of Brisbane, in 1910. His father was a part-time tent show fighter and Ron began working alongside his dad in his other trade as a fencer, developing strength and endurance in his arms and shoulders.

At 15, Richards began boxing at the Smally Higgins tent show at Boonah and had his first recorded pro fights in 1928 at Aratula, near Cunningham's Gap.

With his brother Max, a bantamweight champion, as his best man, Richards married the beautiful Dorothy Iselin in 1935 at St Luke's Church in Charlotte Street, Brisbane.

Sadly, Dorothy died just 18 months later from tuberculosis and was buried in Toowong Cemetery. Richards was not one to waste time, though. He fought again a few weeks later and the following year married Irish immigrant Colleen Boyle in Marrickville, Sydney. At a time when Australia's First Peoples were still not regarded as citizens, Richards owned four city houses and amassed a small fortune valued at £20,000.

He was not above shady dealings either. On 5 December 1936 in Brisbane, Richards stopped a boxer billed as 'visiting American Al Norwood, the light-heavyweight champion of the Pacific Coast'. Norwood's real name was actually Lance May, and he worked at a petrol station in Glebe. While Richard's reputation was tainted for a while by the 'Bowser Boy' gambling scandal, it didn't hurt his popularity or power. Just two weeks later he stopped Fred Henneberry in ten rounds.

Richards was the first of the great champions to be trained by Ern McQuillan at his various gyms around Newtown, Sydney. In 1938 Richards recovered from a loss to Ambrose Palmer to score a 55-second knockout of American Ray Actis, the number-two light-heavyweight in the world. A few months later at the Sydney Sports Ground he dropped and battered New Yorker Gus Lesnevich, who would eventually hold the world light-heavyweight title for seven years and challenge Ezzard Charles for the world heavyweight crown.

Richards beat other top Americans including Atilio Sabatino, the Alabama Kid and Ossie Stewart, and in 1940 outclassed America's Olympic gold medallist Carmen Barth. He twice battled the 'Ol' Mongoose', American Archie Moore, who had a training camp in the Megalong Valley in the Blue Mountains, west of Sydney. To lose weight he'd gained on the voyage from America, Moore ran 10 kilometres in the mountains every day. He claimed to have learned how to control his weight for fights for the next 25 years while training there, saying that in exchange for a red sweater that Moore was wearing, an old

Aboriginal man told him that he could derive all the goodness from meat by chewing it and then spitting it out rather than swallowing. It was a weight-loss secret that Moore used all his life. In their first fight, Richards decked Moore for a nine-count with the first right hand he threw, only to lose in Round 10 on cuts. In their second fight, Moore won a close decision, having been taken the full 12 rounds for the first time in his career.

Richards found difficulties assimilating into a white society that was uncomfortable with him living in their neighbourhood. He started to drink heavily. A year after he retired in 1945 he was broke.

When he was drunk, which was often, Richards was regularly beaten up by thugs around Sydney's Haymarket.

Police in Sydney charged him with vagrancy in 1947 and his Irish Colleen eventually sued for divorce on the grounds of adultery, though she dropped the action.

Classified as a 'half-caste', Richards was sent to the Woorabinda Aboriginal settlement in Central Queensland in 1947 for what the white authorities said was his own protection. In 1950 he was transported to Palm Island, off Townsville, where he spent 17 hard years, many of them as a virtual prisoner.

In 1964 Richards made a visit to Sydney for a few weeks to see his estranged wife for the first time since 1947 and to meet his new granddaughter, Colleen Jr.

'My daughter Bernadette had her about two years ago,' Richards told Hugh Curnow of *The Bulletin* magazine over a few beers at the Warren View Hotel in Enmore, where Richards was spending most of his time.

'I came down to see the little kid. She's a beauty. I love old people and animals and little kids. Don't like fights anymore, just old people, animals and little kids. When they got me up on the platform at the White City stadium the other night and introduced me to the crowd as the former champion middleweight, light-heavyweight and heavyweight boxer of Australia and everyone applauded, it was all right, I suppose, but it's nothing like seeing that little Colleen. She's got real lovely blue eyes and olive skin. My grandfather was an Englishman. He married a half-Maori girl. My father married a half-Aboriginal. Now my granddaughter has got the blue eyes. She's a real beaut, she is.'

Richards was unshaven with a salt-and-pepper-whiskered chin, and he told Curnow that even though Palm Island had a booze ban, 'white blokes smuggle it in for us. They give it to us once a week – on Sundays. They pick us up in a truck and drive us out back of the settlement and open up the beer. Doesn't do any harm, once a week'.

Curnow noted that despite his fondness for a drink Richards still looked fit and strong. He'd been working as a carpenter's labourer on Palm Island for the minimum wage of £19 a week. His gait had been 'peculiar', though, since his legs began playing tricks on him some 15 years earlier. He placed one foot gingerly in front of the other and shifted his weight awkwardly forward, on his heels instead of his toes.

Richards went back to Palm, but in 1966, he heard that his wife Colleen was seriously ill in Sydney, and he returned from North Queensland to help her.

While Colleen survived her health scare, Richards died of a heart attack on 14 January 1967 at his home in Dulwich Hill, aged 56. He was buried at Rookwood Cemetery after a service at St Brigid's Roman Catholic Church in Marrickville.

His pall bearers were his old foe, Fred Henneberry, and other star fighters Jimmy Carruthers, George Barnes, Dimitri Michael, Clive Stewart and Vic Patrick. Forty other famous names in the boxing world formed a guard of honour.

The chief mourners were Ron's widow, Colleen, his 86-year-old mother, Florence, his daughter, Bernadette, his brother, Max, and his sister, May Ford.

Ray Mitchell, Australia's leading boxing authority of the time, wrote: 'When the majority of boxing champions are but names in the record book, the fans will still talk of Ron Richards.' And they do.

Getting Under the Skin of Old Ern McQuillan

Ern McQuillan was a fiery old coot. Even as he was facing the final bell of his long life he was still up for a fight. One of my regular amusements as a young and mischievous reporter on Sydney's *Daily Telegraph* in the early 1980s was to greet Ern's phone calls with the observation that Jeff Fenech would have beaten his fighter Vic Patrick. I never failed to get the desired result – a fiery tirade for several minutes in which Ern would tell me he'd been in the game for 70 years and I'd been in it for five minutes. Ern always landed the finishing blow with an expletive blast for a 'young mug' as he slammed down the receiver.

Ern was a Newtown boy from the old school who believed that a smack in the gob could settle any argument. He trained 60 national champions, more than any other Australian boxing coach, and often boasted of having made more money from boxing than anyone else in this country.

From a succession of gyms in the Newtown area, the last of which became a chocolate warehouse at 69 Wilson Street, McQuillan turned out heroes such as Ron Richards, Vic Patrick, Jack Hassen, Clive Stewart, Bobby Dunlop and Tony Mundine. He ruffled a lot of feathers and won a lot of fights.

Ern was born in Newtown on 16 May 1905 and from the age of seven was a hustler, selling vegetables door to door from his billycart. He took his first boxing lessons from a local trainer named Yank Pearl.

Ern claimed he had 23 pro fights, losing three, and retired after losing to George 'KO' Campbell in a 20-rounder at Leichhardt. Ern's winnings for his previous five bouts amounted to six shillings.

Boxing boomed in the depression and McQuillan's gym was full of hungry fighters. One of them, scrawny bantamweight Pat Craig, became his first Australian champion in 1933. A few years later, Patsy Lucca turned up to train at Ern's gym and, fighting as Vic Patrick, he became Ern's all-time favourite. Jack Hassen arrived soon after Patrick retired and in 1969 another young, raw-boned Aboriginal fighter came to McQuillan's Wilson Street gym to improve his fitness for a shot at rugby league. His name was Tony Mundine, and he was the last of Ern's great champs and the only one to fight for a world title.

Ern McQuillan had a feud with rival trainer Bill McConnell that lasted four decades. Ern always said that he'd trained more top fighters and made more money. Bill countered that he'd produced a world champion in Jimmy Carruthers.

Their argument had started at Newtown Stadium back in the 1930s, when Bill's wife, Millie, clobbered the pugnacious Ern. On 14 October 1957, McConnell and McQuillan staged their most famous stoush, a bare-fist ripper that raged for 15 minutes outside Sydney Stadium.

'I got done like a dinner,' McConnell told the doyen of sportswriters, Mike Gibson. 'We were both pretty pig-headed. Our gyms were just around the corner from each other so I suppose it was inevitable we'd start to blue. We had half a dozen fights. We had one down the back of Newtown Cemetery and McConnell's sister belted me over the head with the heel of her shoe. I got square the next afternoon, though. I cornered him one on one and nearly killed him.'

McConnell was floored by a heart attack in 1968 and died two years later. Shortly before McConnell's death, McQuillan tried to bury the hatchet, helping to organise a boxing show at Sydney Stadium to raise money for his old enemy. 'We raised 800 quid,' McQuillan recalled. 'I took it over to him at his home. You know what McConnell said? "How much did you rip out of this?"'

McConnell dubbed one of his fighters Kid Candle – one blow and he was out – and he recalled a verbal battle with another youngster he was trying to discourage from fighting but who still had stars in his eyes.

'But Bill, what about the time I went the distance with Russell Sands?' the young pug asked.

'You mean the time you went all the way with him in a cab,' Bill shot back.

When Alice McQuillan, Ern's wife of almost 60 years passed away in 1984, Ern dropped his bundle. Often the training duties would be performed by his sons Alan and Ernie Jr, who became one of Australia's best news photographers. Ern still occupied the front office of the building, though, overseeing all the young hopefuls in Reeboks just as he had overseen them in rags 50 years before.

The Quiz King and the Chicago Showboat

Television producer Reg Grundy may have made countless winning TV quiz shows but Vic Patrick told me that, as a fight caller for radio station 2CH, Reg helped bring about Vic's greatest defeat.

It was against the quicksilver Chicago showboat Freddie Dawson at Sydney Stadium in 1947.

Dawson made three visits to Australia between 1947 and 1954 and scored 21 wins in 21 fights Downunder.

In fighting styles, he and Patrick were polar opposites. Southpaw Patrick fought like a shuffling crab, his head tilted to one side, flapping his right hand like he had a broken claw as he probed for openings for the big left. Dawson floated like a butterfly, flicking in and out of range, sticking out his chin as moving bait, taunting, fainting, mocking as he tried to lure his opponents into stinging combinations.

Patrick was cut early in the fight. In Round 2 he was clearly hurt by a Dawson right hand. But in the fifth, Patrick began to find his range with his right leads and stung Dawson with his famous left to the body, left to the head. In Round 8, he rocked Dawson with solid combinations, forcing him to come down off his toes and hang on for survival.

Patrick pressed the advantage throughout Rounds 9 and 10, and then, in the 11th, landed what everyone in the stadium thought was the payoff punch – a smashing left to Dawson's body. The American crumpled and fell through the ropes onto the ring apron.

Vic would later say that Dawson landed on Grundy's microphone. 'Reg pushed him back into the ring and if it wasn't for that I'd have probably beaten Freddie by KO,' he said.

'After I dropped him, I didn't think he'd get up but Freddie was a great boxer, a strong man and very fit.'

Grundy remembered the fight very differently, and the film of the fight bears out his version.

Dawson went through the bottom rope and landed on his backside. He was in bad shape as referee Joe Wallis counted six over him. Dawson struggled to his feet and Patrick swarmed in. But the American was cunning beyond his 23 years, and with 54 pro fights already on his résumé he knew how to survive.

Vic's memory was spot on when he told me: 'Dawson held on for the rest of the 11th round and came at me in the 12th like the Spirit of Progress [train]. The next thing I was seeing stars and hearing little birdies tweeting.'

Patrick lay on the canvas for three minutes, unconscious until Ern McQuillan carried his beloved fighter from the ring in his arms as though he were a small child.

Vic Patrick had taken on all comers for nearly a decade until worn out by constantly fighting bigger men. He had his last bout in 1948. For many years after that he was Australia's top referee. He also owned pubs in Surry Hills, Gymea and Lakemba.

'For me, boxing was a great sport that helped me support my family and gave me strength and confidence,' he told me. 'Boxing builds up a person's character. After all, even if you're just a preliminary boy it takes a lot to lace on a glove.'

In Vic's last-ever interview, he told me that the biggest influences on his career were Ern McQuillan and his offsider, Art Kennedy, who first taught Vic to throw punches properly. His hero was Ron Richards, and his biggest adversary Tommy Burns.

Tod Morgan was the toughest opponent he faced, and Ron McLaughlin and Les Sloane the hardest hitters. Hockey Bennell, he said, was the most skilful, Freddie Dawson the fastest, and the lanky Kiwi Bos Murphy, who towered over him on his way to a decision victory at Petone, the most awkward.

The great old champ passed away in 2006.

Sixty years after suffering a beating from Patrick in their epic battle, Tommy Burns joined a cavalcade of fight stars to farewell his old rival inside the South Chapel at Rookwood in western Sydney.

Tommy was 84 at the time, a small frail man with wispy white hair, very different in appearance and bearing to the Australian movie star of the 1940s who at the same time was the biggest drawcard ever at Sydney Stadium.

Over the years I worked with two of Tommy's sons, Tony and Peter Murphy, who were both outstanding journalists, and Tommy, whose real name was Geoff Murphy, signed Vic's order of service for me as 'Spud Murphy', his nickname as a kid.

He wrote a little note above it, too, in a shaky hand.

'Hasta la vista, Vic. See you again in heaven, mate ... but I'm in no hurry.'

Tommy died in 2011.

Tommy Burns: The Handsome Hero

Tommy Burns's parents moved around a lot when he was a kid, running bakeries that invariably went bust.

'I started out punching dough for humans,' he once said. 'I ended up punching humans for dough.'

He was born Geoffrey Mostyn Murphy in Mullumbimby, northern New South Wales, in 1922, and was a celebrity from day one.

At 5 kilograms, he was said to be the biggest child ever born in the town, and for a long time after his birth, locals would knock on his parents' front door, asking if they could see the giant baby.

His first recorded pro fight was at Proston near Wondai in Queensland in 1936 when he was just 14.

He earned 4 shillings, which was four times his weekly wage in the bakery. Though he never really liked hitting people, he was encouraged to pursue boxing by his older brother Dudley, 'a mad fight fan'.

Desperately poor and working as a farm hand, he fought a few times in Lismore and then made a name for himself at Brisbane Stadium in the early 1940s.

By then, 'Spud Murphy' was boxing under the alias Tommy Burns, borrowed from the old heavyweight champ. 'Spud' used an alias because he didn't want his mother to know he was fighting. Even when he became one of the most famous sportsmen in Australia, his mother still refused to watch him fight, preferring to pace around the block counting her rosary beads and praying that no one in the fight got hurt.

By the time Murphy/Burns was 17 he was unbeaten in 24 pro fights, and Bert Potts, the cigar-chomping manager of Brisbane Stadium, wanted to push him into main-event bouts. Burns believed he was too young and instead went to a cattle station outside Barcaldine in central Queensland, where he spent a year and a half as a 57-kilogram jackaroo and horse breaker.

Back in Brisbane, he was guaranteed £50 to fight smart-boxing Lisle Law for the Queensland lightweight title on 18 April 1941. Burns struggled to make the weight so badly that in the weeks leading up to the bout he ate only a few grapes a day and drank black tea with lemon. But for £50 he was willing to cut off a leg if he had to.

After finally making the weight at 3 p.m. on the day of the fight following an hour of brisk exercise, Burns was famished. His trainer Alby Graham told him to eat a rare steak to regain some strength, but as a devout Catholic, Burns would not eat meat on a Friday.

Alby suggested they go and see a local Catholic monsignor to receive compensation so he could eat the red meat but, sticking to his guns, Burns retorted: 'Alby, if the bloody Pope himself says I can eat steak on a Friday I still won't eat it.'

When Burns climbed into the ring he knew there was no way he could fight 12 hard rounds.

He managed to make it to the 10th but was on the verge of being knocked cold when Alby Graham skied the towel.

It was a painful defeat, but it was Burns's only loss in his first ten years as a professional boxer and the fight drew the biggest attendance ever for a bout in Queensland until that time – 5675 – who paid a record £835.

Burns made £176 for the bout, more than he could make in a year of manual work.

With World War II raging, Burns hoped to become a fighter pilot but instead his lack of formal education saw him assigned to the Austral Motors factory in New Farm, Brisbane, that was turning out armoured vehicles.

Newly married to Betty, Burns moved to the Sydney gym of Jack Dunleavy, and fighting in the heavier welterweight (67 kg) division, the ruthless slugger with movie-star looks became a massive drawcard at Sydney Stadium.

In 21 fights at the Old Tin Shed, 15 were sold out, and his popularity was repeated in Brisbane and Melbourne.

Burns's run of victories set up the massive 1946 showdown with Vic Patrick, the most eagerly anticipated Australian stoush since the original Tommy Burns against Jack Johnson.

Despite his shattering defeat, the new father was back in the ring three months later.

The following year, he lost on a disqualification against Welshman Ronnie James.

Again Burns fired back, stopping Hockey Bennell for the Australian welterweight title left vacant by Vic Patrick's retirement, and on 3 March 1947 he was matched with black American O'Neill Bell in what many of the old-timers reckoned was the most savage fight ever staged at Sydney Stadium.

'Both of us took a journey into hell,' Burns said.

Bell had come to Australia after beating former world welterweight champion Fritzie Zivic a few months earlier. Among the many great fighters he had battled were the 'Raging Bull' Jake LaMotta and Sugar Ray Robinson.

For the first ten rounds, Bell handed out as much misery as he received. At the end of each round, Burns, his face horribly misshapen, begged referee Joe Wallis for one more. Finally, in the tenth, Burns overcame his gangly opponent with a series of short, jolting punches. When Bell finally went down from a huge right cross, he sprawled on the ropes in his own corner. Referee Wallis counted to six but was oblivious to the fact that the bell had sounded immediately after he had counted 'one', the sound having been drowned out by the roar of the crowd.

Bell came out for the 11th round, but it ended only seven seconds after it began, Burns smashing Bell down with a two-handed attack.

His pulsating fight with Bell finally over, Burns raised his busted hand in victory, but his handsome head was swollen like a soccer ball.

'Good grief. My face was such a mess,' Burns later recalled. 'It was so swollen and both my eyebrows were busted open.

'My trainer, Alby, couldn't drive a car so I had to drive myself all the way from Rushcutters Bay to my home at Narrabeen on Sydney's Northern Beaches.

'I had one hand on the steering wheel and the other holding one of my eyes open, all the while trying to work the manual gearstick.

'Every time I wanted to see anything on the road I had to use my fingers to force my swollen eyes open. The eyebrows were all stitched up.

'The writers of the time said it was a great fight – perhaps the greatest ever seen. But I wouldn't know. I only saw it through one eye.'

Burns spent three days in bed after the fight.

Not long after his epic victory over O'Neill Bell, Tommy Burns appeared in the Charles Chauvel epic film *Sons of Matthew*, set on the rugged Lamington Plateau in the Gold Coast hinterland. Based on the lives of the pioneering O'Reilly family, the movie featured Burns as a hero who knocks out the bad guys and strips off for a skinny dip in a scene designed to make female audiences swoon.

Burns was set to fight world welterweight champ Sugar Ray Robinson in Chicago in July 1948 but lost a decision to black American Benny Evans in Sydney in March that year, a decision that was a shock to the crowd and an even bigger shock to Burns. He later said it was the lowest point of his career and suspected that his Australian promoters had influenced the decision of referee Joe Wallis so as to stain his record, ruin the Robinson fight and prevent the loss of their biggest drawcard overseas.

In 1948, Burns retained his Australian welterweight title against Mickey Tollis but lost the title to Queenslander Kevin

Delaney after suffering an injury to his jaw before the bout. He retired from boxing for two years, but appeared on stage in Brisbane in the play *Golden Boy*, playing a character like himself, who didn't like fighting but did it for the money.

Burns's marriage was failing and he took off to America to think about the future. Ezra Norton, the head of Truth Newspapers, paid him £20 a week to work as a sports correspondent while in the US.

While there, he met former world heavyweight champs Jack Dempsey, Joe Louis, Gene Tunney and the original Tommy Burns.

'When I met Burns in America I recall his wife standing beside him stroking his back. They were past 60 years. She said, "Isn't he beautiful?" and I suddenly realised what affection was. I'd never known affection as a kid ... When there's nine in the family things can get tough. But ours was never a close-knit family. We all split up. I was close to Mum but I hardly knew my father.'

Burns returned to Australia in 1950 and realised that his marriage was over. He needed money in a hurry and gambling kingpin Joe Taylor gave him a job as a nightclub singer doing a Frank Sinatra tribute show.

'I'd kept myself fit and I saw that Mickey Tollis, who I'd fought twice before, was the welterweight champion of Australia. So with Joe Taylor as my manager I challenged him.'

'We fought in October 1951, but it was obvious early that Mickey was over the hill, and even though I hadn't fought in two and a half years I had no trouble.'

Burns next faced Don 'Bronco' Johnson, a big dag from North Queensland who would have been right at home in a Dad and Dave comedy. Bronco showered in his socks, wore long side-levers and a 10-gallon cowboy hat, and sometimes strolled through city streets with a baby crocodile under his arm.

The son of a bullock driver from Queensland's Atherton tableland, inland from Cairns, as a young man Bronco wore a long beard and ran his own rodeo show. He was also said to have killed a crocodile in the wild with a knife.

When he first arrived at Ern McQuillan's Sydney gym after an impressive amateur career in Queensland, Bronco was dressed like Hopalong Cassidy.

His fighting style looked like it was based on bar-room brawling from a cowboy movie, and McQuillan thought he was someone's idea of a practical joke. But even though Bronco's windmilling punches created enough breeze to knock the hats off spectators, McQuillan could see his raw power and potential. 'If he hit you in Pitt Street,' McQuillan said, 'you'd wake up in North Sydney half an hour later.'

Bronco lived in a caravan beside the beach at Cronulla with his wife, Sheila, and their baby, where they cooked their dinner on an open fire.

When the fight with Burns was set, Bronco was unbeaten in 11 pro fights and was confident he'd make it 12.

Half a century later, he recalled that he thought he'd be fighting 'a pretty boy mug lair'.

In the conservative post-war years, Burns was a flamboyant figure in parachute-silk shirts, shark-skin slacks and two-tone shoes.

'He was a prominent film star and a good-lookin' fella,' Bronco told me. 'I thought, I'll stir the possum in this fella; I'll knock him around a bit. But after a couple of rounds I changed my mind. He was no lair. He was a tough bird.'

Burns's mates had told him Bronco was very raw – that he didn't know a left jab from a free kick. But it turned out to be the most intense five rounds Burns ever fought.

In Round 5, Bronco was still on his feet but helpless.

At the end of the fight Burns said: 'Thank God for that,' because he wouldn't have been able to come out for the next round either.

According to Burns, on the way back to the dressing-rooms, Bronco said to him: 'Aw, big dough mate. We'll do it again.'

'Bloody hell, not with me you won't,' Burns replied.

He later admitted: 'I couldn't breathe after the fight because he'd broken my ribs with one of those punches that came up from the floor.

'When I finally came to get my prize money ... from [promoter] Harry Miller, he told me he'd love me to fight Bronco again. I said, "Harry, you fight him. I'm not getting in the ring with him again."'

Lanky Len Dittmar, a balding fitness fanatic with the best left jab in the business, outboxed Burns over 15 rounds in Sydney in 1952 and then Burns travelled to Mt Isa to beat Harry Hayes from Griffith in the New South Wales Riverina. The promoter shot through without paying Hayes a penny and without giving Burns the £700 he still owed him.

Burns then beat Lithuanian migrant Pran Mikus but retired after two losses to George Barnes. The first paid him £2300, the biggest purse of his career. His final defeat against Barnes came in 1954 over 15 rounds during a rainstorm at the Brisbane Exhibition Grounds. Burns fought in bare feet because of the rain, thinking it would give him more grip on a slippery canvas. Instead, his heels and soles were cut to ribbons.

In his later years Burns would make some spare cash, often for the many charities he supported, by showing fight films in clubs and halls around Australia. But he always told his audiences: 'The man who says he likes fighting, well his IQ must be a cent in the dollar. I fought in a business I detested. I enjoyed the glamour and the excitement, but I detested the physical combat. I find it difficult to believe that anyone would take up boxing unless it was to earn good hard cash and there was no other opportunity for them.'

Burns had a huge female fan base but resented it. Women only paid half the admission price for ringside tickets at Sydney

Stadium, and the thousands of seats they occupied could have gone to bigger-spending men, who often found the stadium sold out, still with their money in their pockets.

'I would always bow to the four corners of the ring before a fight,' Burns recalled. 'People thought I was bowing to all the ladies – the truth is I was counting them and figuring out how much more I could have earned if there were men in those seats.'

He told *The Bulletin* magazine that he'd always had trouble with women. 'I've been in five domestic matches. I got knocked out every time. Five different nationalities.

'Maybe I have something that attracts women. I don't know. When I was in America, I met Joan Crawford. Joan was very nice to me. She took me by the hand and showed me around ... that's all I'm going to tell you.'

THE FABULOUS FIFTIES

George Barnes: The Soldier
Who Just Kept Coming

George Barnes was a 168-centimetre dynamo whose father, Frank Burns (real name Eric Barnes), had been the Australian middleweight champion in the 1920s.

Born in Temora, New South Wales, George took up the sport aged 15 at the North Sydney Police Boys Club. Like his father, he worked as a blacksmith's striker, and in 1948, after serving with the Australian Imperial Force in New Guinea, Barnes turned professional.

In April 1954, a few months after beating Tommy Burns, George was matched with American Freddie Dawson over 15 rounds before a crowd of 15,000 at the Sydney Sports Ground.

A brilliantly timed right hand from Barnes decked Dawson in the opening round, but Dawson was in command for the rest of the fight. Still, Barnes became the first Australian to last the distance with the slick American, and his manager and father-in-law Jim Barker won £5000 after betting that his boy would be there at the final bell.

In a 14-year career, in which he always favoured relentless attack over defence, Barnes failed to go the distance just once – in his last fight, when Gary Cowburn stopped him in six rounds at Sydney Stadium in 1962. When referee Vic Patrick halted the fight, Barnes burst into tears from sheer embarrassment.

Trained in Sydney by Arthur Fennell, Barnes's biggest wins were a pair of 12-round decisions in 1952 over American Wallace 'Bud' Smith, who became world lightweight champion in Boston three years later.

Smith came to Australia with a formidable record, having fought for the United States at the 1948 London Olympic Games. In 1952 in Melbourne, he gave Frank Flannery a boxing lesson; it was thought he would do the same to Barnes at West Melbourne Stadium on 6 June. Yet Smith, a 3–1 on favourite, was sensationally outfought, outboxed and outpointed.

After Barnes stopped veteran Englishman Eric Boon, a rematch with Smith was arranged two months later at Sydney Stadium. The American was installed as a 5–4 favourite, but again Barnes proved too good. In 1955, Smith upset the odds, outpointing fellow American Jimmy Carter for the world title in Boston.

Barnes blamed the lingering effects of a bout of malaria he'd suffered in New Guinea during World War II for three early losses (1950–1952) against Frank Flannery, a Melbourne sensation.

Flannery loved to incite crowds to hate him for his rough-house tactics. He was a swaggering villain, Jimmy Cagney in gloves. 'I got clouted with a bottle occasionally from people in the crowd, and once some old tart hit me over the head with an umbrella,' he told me. 'But if they wanted to boo me they still had to buy a ticket and it cost as much to jeer as it did to cheer.'

Flannery was born in Footscray in 1927 and grew into an angry little man, never standing more than 5 feet, 3 inches tall (160 cm).

At 15 he began training at Jack McLeod's gym in Footscray, scoffing at the other fighters and telling McLeod which of the 'mugs' he could flatten. He started out as a cheeky little gym mascot and had his first fight weighing 6 stone 2 pounds (39 kg).

Hank Stanley, a Melbourne fight promoter, became Flannery's lifelong friend and was ringside to see most of his mate's great battles.

'The night Frank fought Jack Hassen, both men got knocked down so many times there were more ups and downs than Christine Keeler's pants,' Stanley recalled.

'Then there was all the drama around Frank's fight with Alfie Clay. 'Before the Clay fight Frank had a gastric stomach and Frank's brother Bobby came up with this old remedy of port, wine and brandy.

'He took a two-litre bottle into the corner for the fight and gave Frank a good sip between every round. They were 15-rounders in those days and after ten or eleven rounds, Frank was as high as a kite on the port, wine and brandy.

'Bobby said to him: "Frank, your title's slipping away." So Frank got this real determined look on his face, drank down the rest of the brew and went out to win the last three rounds and salvage a draw.'

Jack Hassen and his Broken Heart

As a young sportswriter in Sydney in the early 1980s, I yarned with Jack Hassen at his home in La Perouse and got to know him well.

In his old age you could sometimes catch Jack at the fight clubs in Sydney, the poor offspring of the Sydney Stadium where he'd made his fame and a fortune he could not keep. More likely you would catch him down by the wharves, where he spent 35 years working after his boxing career fell to pieces. By then he was a little old man with receding grey hair, thick glasses and a gentle manner.

After the retirement of Vic Patrick, and with Tommy Burns in America, Jack became the highest-paid boxer in Australia. But he paid a heavy price for his involvement in the sport.

Born in Cloncurry, western Queensland, in 1925, Jack was orphaned at the age of two and raised by the parents of another hard-hitting Indigenous fighter, George Bracken, on Palm Island.

When he was 12, Hassen was sent by the government to work in Cairns as a chemist's messenger. Jack told me that the chemist gave him his first new shirt. He then became a labourer and stockman, working for 'a Hindu chap we called the Galloping Ghan'. He was working at Kenmac Station near Hughenden when he started fighting in Jimmy Sharman's travelling boxing troupe. Before long, he was fighting pro bouts in Townsville, then Brisbane and, finally, Sydney, where he was trained by Ern McQuillan.

Jack had a big punch but little defence or footwork and McQuillan knew he'd be a crowd favourite.

Starting at Sydney Stadium in 1948, Hassen put together wins over George Kapeen, Roy Treasure, Tommy Stenhouse, Pierre Montane and Andre Famechon, before dropping a decision to tricky Los Angeles lightweight Rudy Cruz.

Hassen was then matched with the clever Melbourne fighter Archie Kemp, a 25-year-old truck driver. They fought at Sydney Stadium on 19 September 1949 for the Australian lightweight title. Kemp was in fantastic shape, sparring with his mate Jack Rennie, later the trainer of Lionel Rose.

Following the example of Rudy Cruz, Kemp ducked, dived and dodged Hassen's heavy punches while piling up the points through the first six rounds. But he didn't duck enough. In the 11th round Hassen got his man in a corner and battered him. Hassen looked appealingly towards referee Joe Wallis, who motioned him to continue. Hassen hit him again and Kemp staggered and fell, blood oozing from his mouth.

Kemp was rushed to St Vincent's Hospital for an emergency brain operation immediately after the fight, but was buried in Melbourne three days later, leaving a wife and two-year-old son.

Hassen wasn't worth a stamp as a fighter after that. Of his last seven fights, he scored only one victory, against Ken Bailey, and was knocked out five times – by Frank Flannery, Mickey Tollis (twice), Freddie Dawson and Joe 'Old Bones' Brown, an American who became world champion.

For more than half a century, until his death in 2002, Hassen was haunted by Archie Kemp's ghostly face. Even in the grip of Alzheimer's late in his life, one of the few things he could mutter to me when he was interviewed for the last time was: 'Poor Archie, poor Archie. I'll never forget it.'

Years earlier Jack had told me: 'Some blokes are strong but I'm not. What happened in that fight shook me to pieces. His wife sent me a telegram, saying it wasn't my fault. But I've never been able to get it out of my mind.

'Still, if it wasn't for boxing I'd still be up on the mission, or still be out West with a couple of dogs taking the sheep up to Barcaldine.'

Jimmy Sharman and the Travelling Boxing Shows

Travelling boxing troupes were an annual treat for Australians in less sanitised times, black eyes accompanying the fairy floss and toffee apples at fairs and agricultural shows. And with Jimmy Sharman's show the most famous, they were still going strong into the 1950s, still introducing many of Australia's budding champions to prizefighting.

In 1847, 'Big Ike' Reid started a touring boxing show following his win over George Hough at Sydney's Middle Harbour. Big Ike was a Port Phillip convict who had obtained his freedom for good conduct as a servant on the expeditions of Sir Thomas Mitchell.

Later, in the 1870s, Jem Mace's boxing shows did much to popularise the sport. In the early years of the 20th century, Bill Doherty toured the Western Australian goldfields. Ernie Bell, brother of heavyweight fighter Colin Bell, and a Maori named George Ruenalf, ran shows on the east coast. So did Sam Norman, who occasionally employed a young Les Darcy. Snowy Flynn's shows featured such fighters as Bill Squires, Peter Felix, Hock Keys, Jackie Green and Llew Edwards.

For many young men across the country, the highlight of their sporting life would be when they laced on a glove to fight one of the touring professionals inside the boxing tent – even if they were battered to defeat. Often, the tent fighters themselves – including the likes of Dave Sands's brother, Percy (who fought under the name Ritchie Sands) – suffered long-lasting injuries as a result of the concussions they endured over many years.

Yet the shows flourished, including those of Roy Bell and Selby Moore in Queensland, and a troupe run by roly-poly heavyweight Les McNabb in New South Wales.

The most successful travelling show was Sharman's. At different times, the Sharmans employed Tommy Uren, Frank Burns, Jack Hassen, George Bracken, Billy Grime, Dave Sands, Jackie Green, Frank Burns, George Cook, Bindi Jack, Mickey Miller, Archie Bryant, George Flemming and Greg McNamara. Rud Kee, who billed himself as Champion of China, was a fixture in the show for more than half a century from 1916, first as a fighter then as a ticket seller. Academy Award–winning actor Victor McLaglen, who had once sparred Jack Johnson, also boxed in Sharman's troupe. Another Hollywood star, Errol Flynn, said that the £2 he made fighting one of Sharman's boys in Townsville was the hardest two quid he ever earned. Others to fight for Sharman included Geoff Clark, the former ATSIC chairperson, Pastor Doug Nicholls, who became Governor of South Australia, and Max Stuart, the convicted murderer and Arrernte elder.

Gunditjmara and Bundjalung elder Archie Roach, a lauded singer, songwriter and Aboriginal activist, who was also Lionel Rose's cousin, had a stint in the tent shows, as did his dad. Archie Snr fought as Snowball Roach (because of his white hair) while Archie was known as Kid Snowball.

Sharman's champions would be lined up on a platform as one of the fighters banged a drum and Sharman or an offsider bellowed to the crowd, 'Who'll take a glove?' and 'A pound or two for a round or two.'

Sharman was born at Narellan, south-west of Sydney, in 1887, one of the 13 children of a poor dairy farmer. He claimed that his grandfather was an Irish bare-knuckle champion. Sharman said he scored 83 knockout wins in his first 84 fights in the Riverina and that in 1911 he broke the jaw of Jack Carter at the Olympic Skating Ring in Wagga Wagga, winning a £500 wager and putting his opponent in hospital for 19 weeks.

Sharman ran his show from 1915 to the 1950s, when he passed on the reins to his son, Jimmy Jr. The younger Sharman was a former rugby league player, having debuted as a fullback for the Western Suburbs Magpies in 1934. He'd become the side's regular fullback after the retirement of Test captain Frank McMillan and played 59 games for the club in a six-year career.

Jimmy Jr's son, also called Jim, was exposed to the world of fairs, circuses and travelling vaudeville from a young age, but became a world-renowned entertainer in another field. Born in 1945, this Jim Sharman became an internationally famous theatre director by his late 20s. He directed the rock musical *Hair* in Sydney, Melbourne, Tokyo, and Boston and then *Jesus Christ Superstar* in Australia and London. He is best known for directing and co-writing the screenplay for the cult stage musical and film *The Rocky Horror Picture Show* in 1975.

Jimmy Sharman Snr's tent show staged its last fight at Shepparton in October 1971. The travelling boxing troupes of Roy Bell and Fred Brophy, however, still tour Queensland and the Northern Territory. In most other states, tent boxing has been banned under health and safety rules.

Rude Farewell for the Alabama Kid

Ernie Johns learned to fight in the tent show run by his father, Harry Johns, and won the Australian bantamweight title fighting as 'Young Regan' at Leichhardt Stadium in 1953. During his career, he met other champions such as Trevor King, Keith Francis and Bobby Sinn.

The top fighter in Harry's troupe was the American southpaw Clarence Colin Reeves, who was known as The Alabama Kid. He was from Georgia, and not Alabama. Another leading fighter of the 1950s, Bryan Membrey, who became a renowned artist, remembered how 'The Kid', standing on the platform in front of the tent ready to take on all comers, looked 'sensational dressed in the American stars and stripes with a red coloured gown in contrast to his dark cocoa skin'. A crowd of 16,000 watched Ron Richards outpoint The Alabama Kid at the Sydney Sports Ground in 1938, but in a return bout four years later, The Kid won by a knockout in eight.

Following his loss to Doug Brown in Moss Vale, New South Wales, on 2 April 1948, The Alabama Kid was arrested by immigration authorities. Despite having an Australian wife and two Australian-born children, he was imprisoned in Long Bay Jail then deported back to the United States as a 'prohibited migrant'.

He had come to Australia for one fight in 1938. Instead, over the following ten years, he fought 75 professional bouts in Australian rings, and hundreds more in tent-show fights.

Dave Sands: Death of a Young Hero

Dave Sands beat some of the best middleweights in the world and was widely admired for what the eminent historian Richard

Broome called his 'quiet manliness and dedication'. A heavy-handed Indigenous counterpuncher in the mould of Ron Richards, he twice beat the American Carl 'Bobo' Olson, who went on to become world middleweight champ.

Sands was the best of the 22 Australian champions trained by Tom Maguire in Newcastle between 1919 and 1955. Despite his standing as one of the best fighters in the world, he was only too willing to help his family with the domestic chores, such as sewing, and he relaxed listening to Bing Crosby and boogie-woogie music.

Born on 24 February 1926 at the Burnt Bridge Aboriginal mission, near Kempsey, New South Wales, to George Ritchie, a rodeo-rider and timber-cutter, and his wife, Mabel, Sands was the fifth of eight children.

His brothers Clem, Percy, George, Alf and Russell also boxed, and in 1939, Percy was the first of the brothers to train with Maguire in Newcastle, adopting the ring-name of Ritchie Sands, as a nod to 'Snowy' Sands, a local railway guard and boxing fan who had helped Percy dodge the train fare from Kempsey.

Eventually, all the Ritchie brothers adopted the name Sands and wore green satin shorts with a white star.

At 15, Dave joined Percy living at Maguire's gym, dossing down among the equipment. He had his first fight soon after at the Greater Newcastle Stadium, knocking out Leo Corrigan in the first round on a show promoted by the old champ Hughie Dwyer.

Maguire, or 'Mr Mac' as his fighters called him, exploited the brothers, and Dave fought 22 times as a teenager in 1943, often overmatched against bigger opponents.

By the age of 20, Dave had fought 55 times. He captured the Australian middleweight title against Jack Kirkham in 1946 and that same year scored a fourth-round knockout over Jack Johnson in Melbourne to win the Australian light-heavyweight title.

In 1947 he knocked out the American O'Neil Bell in two rounds at Sydney Stadium.

Maguire worked Sands hard and in 1947–1948 he went 18 fights without a loss, beating top foes including the Alabama Kid, Kiwi Don Mullett, Doug Brown and Len Dittmar.

After Sands smashed Frenchman Tony Toniolo in less than two minutes in February 1949, the English promoter Jack Solomons brought him to London.

Suffering the after-effects of a vaccination, Sands was outpointed by Tommy Yarosz at the Harringay Arena in his first fight, but won six in a row in Britain, battering the highly rated Frenchman Robert Villemain, who, just five months later, outpointed 'The Raging Bull' Jake LaMotta.

Sands then won the British Empire middleweight title with a first-round knockout of Dick Turpin.

There was talk of Sands fighting Turpin's more dangerous brother Randolph and negotiations began for a world title fight with Sugar Ray Robinson, who had won the world welterweight and middleweight titles, and who many experts still regard as history's greatest champion.

At Sydney Stadium in March 1950, Sands won a 12-round decision over Hawaiian-born Carl 'Bobo' Olson, dropping him in the first round. He then blasted out Henry Brimm, who had once fought a draw with Robinson, and he won the Australian heavyweight championship from Alf Gallagher.

At the Earls Court Arena in London in 1951 Sands defeated American Mel Brown on the undercard to Randolph Turpin's stunning points win over Robinson in a huge upset for the world middleweight title. Sands had been in the box seat for the fight but negotiations took too long as he and 'Mr Mac' fell out. Turpin, the new world champ, said the only time he wanted to feel Sands's right was when he shook hands with him.

As Sands waited for his world title shot he beat Olson and Henry Brimm in rematches in America.

Back in London, Sands was leading after six rounds against the undefeated West Indian Yolande Pompey when he was stopped on a cut eye in seven.

He came back to Australia to regroup and won four fights in a row.

In May 1952 at the West Melbourne Stadium he stopped Al Bourke in five rounds in a fight for the Australian and Empire middleweight titles.

Then, on 9 July 1952, Sands did a favour for promoter Arthur French and defended his Australian heavyweight title for just £160 against Jim Woods in Wagga Wagga.

On 11 August, Sands should have been spending his seventh wedding anniversary at home with his pregnant wife, Bessie. Instead he was driving a truck laden with 13 friends and relatives on a bush road at Dungog where he and his brothers ran a timber business. Sands was off to do some timber cutting as he awaited news of a showdown with Sugar Ray. When the truck skidded in loose dirt and overturned, everyone on board was sent flying – except the driver.

Dave was crushed against the steering wheel and died that night in Dungog hospital, aged just 26.

His wife, Bessie, and their son and two daughters survived him; a third daughter was born in November.

Twenty-five years later, Bessie recalled that 'Dave was a gentle soul, a gentleman. We only had seven years together'.

Sands had earned about £30,000, but mismanagement and generosity to his kin meant there was little left.

A public appeal raised £2500, sufficient to bury him in Newcastle's Sandgate cemetery and to pay off his home near the beach at Stockton.

The following year, Sugar Ray Robinson went into a temporary retirement and Bobo Olson outpointed Randolph Turpin for the vacant world middleweight crown at New York's Madison Square Garden.

'This title should have belonged to Dave Sands,' Olson said. 'It would have been his had he lived.'

Dave's brother Russell Sands won the Australian featherweight title and Alfie claimed the Australian middleweight crown.

Alfie's son Russell Sands often trained at Ray Wheatley's gym at St Marys in western Sydney. He beat Frank Ropis for the Australian welterweight title in 1984, before losing it to Brisbane tearaway Brian Janssen the following year. Russell liked motorbikes but they didn't like him. In 1986, he had a steel rod inserted in his leg after being run over by a car.

The following year, aged just 23, he was burnt to death in a car crash.

Elley Bennett: The Little Man with the Huge Punch

For a time, Elley Bennett was the number-one ranked bantamweight in the world and he hit opponents so hard he lifted many of his victims clean off the canvas.

One of his old rivals Trevor King boxed heavyweights in the gym and said Bennett hit harder than any of them. He also had the biggest smile, a wide, white aperture that was always there no matter how much punishment snaked through his porous defence. He was notorious for soaking up pain and crashing home his coma-inducing right hand in the dying seconds of a fight to win. Not surprisingly, severe headaches from too many hard hits forced him to retire.

Born in Pialba, Queensland, the son of a bullock driver, he was raised at the Barambah Aboriginal mission (later called Cherbourg) near Kingaroy.

Elley started work as a farm labourer at 13, digging peanuts and cutting sugar cane, and he learned boxing by punching a bag of sawdust hanging from a mango tree.

Soon he was fighting in tent shows around Maryborough. A Brisbane pro fighter named Stan McBride saw Elley score a quick knockout in Maryborough at Christmas time 1945 and convinced him to try his big punch in Brisbane.

Snowy Hill, a former Queensland champion turned trainer, put the gloves on with Bennett for a sparring session and was hit in the body so hard that he had breathing difficulties for months.

Under Hill's guidance, Bennett turned pro at Brisbane Stadium in 1946 and fought nearly every month, blasting out Stumpy Butwell for the Queensland bantamweight title in 1947.

Bennett hated training, did none for his Brisbane battle with George Kennedy and arrived at the stadium after having downed six meat pies and three malted milkshakes for a bet. He decked Kennedy in the first, but Kennedy recovered and stopped Bennett in the 13th.

In 1948 in Melbourne – minus the pies and malted milks – he knocked out Mickey Francis for the Australian bantamweight title.

He also bowled over Frenchman Emile Famechon twice and, before a crowd of 13,000 at Sydney Stadium, blitzed American Cecil Schoonmaker in six rounds.

Bennett could be out-boxed, though, and America's former world champ Harold Dade dodged his blows to beat him over 12 rounds in 1949.

He returned to top Melbourne's Bobby Scrivano and score a pair of stoppage wins over another top American, Vic Eisen, but dropped a decision to Mexican southpaw Ernesto Aguillar.

In a bout for the Australian featherweight title on 9 April 1951, Bennett was hopelessly behind on points against Ray 'Mustard' Coleman, a fearless campaigner who also took great punishment in 100 fights. Fifteen seconds into the 15th and final round, Bennett lifted Coleman off his feet with a left hook-right cross and he was out cold.

The 'Bible of Boxing', America's *Ring* magazine, rated Bennett as pound for pound the hardest puncher in the world, but negotiations for a world bantamweight title fight with American Manuel Ortiz and then Vic Toweel of South Africa went nowhere.

Bennett boiled down from featherweight to bantamweight and lost his national title to the 1948 Olympian Jimmy Carruthers.

The following year the rising star Trevor King proved too tricky over 12 rounds but Bennett managed to retire a winner in 1954, stopping Bluey Wilkins in eight rounds in his last appearance at Brisbane Stadium. He complained of frequent headaches.

He was a founding member in 1969 of the National Aboriginal Sports Foundation, but he had a long battle with alcohol and was a regular before Brisbane Magistrates Court for vagrancy and drunkenness.

By 1973 he was living on an invalid pension in a rented flat in Brisbane. He blamed his financial woes on gambling.

Trevor King remembered meeting his old foe in 1978 when Bennett was in a Brisbane lockup on his 60th charge of drunkenness.

'I'll never forget it,' King told my friend, journalist Peter Muszkat. 'There was this pathetic little man, his mind all jumbled and dribbling at the mouth. When they let me in to see him he put his arms around me and cried like a little baby.'

Bennett died of pneumonia in 1981 in Bundaberg, aged just 55.

Jimmy Carruthers and the First-Round Explosion

Jimmy Carruthers was a slick, stylish boxer known for his smooth skills rather than his knockout power, but he delivered one of the most explosive performances yet seen in a world title bout.

The fair-haired, fresh-faced 'Pride of Paddington' stunned the raging favourite Vic Toweel in the first round before 28,000 fans at Johannesburg's Rand Stadium on 15 November 1952.

Southpaw Carruthers threw 147 punches in the 139 seconds the fight lasted.

The South African world champ threw just one punch. It missed.

Carruthers became Australia's first officially recognised world boxing champ as the title claims of fighters such as Les Darcy and Young Griffo had been disputed overseas.

He was born on 5 July 1929 and grew up in Sydney's Paddington, then a rough working-class suburb.

His parents had migrated to Australia in 1924, from Workington, in the north of England.

Jimmy joined the Woolloomooloo Police Boys Club at the age of eight. He had his first amateur fight at 15 and won the Australian championship in 1947. At the 1948 London Olympics he won two bouts but sustained an eye injury and had to withdraw from the quarter-final with the eventual gold medallist Tibor Csík of Hungary.

Carruthers turned professional in 1950 under the guidance of manager Dr Jim McGirr and trainer Bill McConnell.

He stopped Teddy Fitzgerald at Leichhardt in his pro debut, and then beat accomplished pugs Keith Francis, Bluey Wilkins and Bobby Scrivano before being matched with power-punching Elley Bennett in 1951 in just his ninth pro fight.

The pair went toe to toe for 15 rounds before a crowd of 12,000 at Sydney Stadium. Carruthers proved too slick and quick and took the Australian bantamweight title.

Wins over Taffy Hancock and the spicy Ray 'Mustard' Coleman followed.

Years later, Carruthers took the points in a vicious bare-knuckle fight with 'Mustard' at The Domain, a park in central Sydney.

In May 1952 Carruthers outpointed American Johnny O'Brien, then boarded the ship *Dominion Monarch* with wife Myra and trainer Bill McConnell, bound for South Africa and his showdown with Toweel.

At just 5 feet, 3 inches (160 cm), Toweel was the shining star from one of the world's great boxing families. He was also a 1948 Olympian and had taken the world bantamweight title in only his 12th pro fight by out-hustling Manuel Ortiz, a veteran American who had made more title defences than Toweel had fights.

As the new champ, Toweel dropped Englishman Danny O'Sullivan 14 times, then outpointed Spaniard Luis Romero and Scot Peter Keenan.

Going into the Carruthers fight, Toweel was unbeaten in 27 pro fights. The Australian, 10 cm taller, was undefeated in 14.

Thirty years after the bout, Carruthers told me that Toweel had turned up to their first meeting in what looked like a £300 suit with a brand-new car.

'He looked like a millionaire, and I looked very shoddy with rolled-up sleeves. I wanted what he had. But the fight was postponed after I suffered blood poisoning and before we got into the ring I'd been in South Africa for five months. The longer I waited the hungrier I became.'

A devout Catholic, Toweel prayed for two hours in his uncle's private chapel before the fight and the women in his family offered prayers beneath pictures of the saints, illuminated by candles he had lit.

But instead of divine protection on fight night, Toweel was hit by a cyclone.

In Australia, thousands of fight fans sat around their crackling radios in disbelief at what they were hearing.

Carruthers leapt into the attack from the opening bell with a savage straight left that stunned the world champ.

Fists flying like a buzzsaw, Carruthers then drove the champion through the ropes with savage shots from both hands and Toweel was down and out for the first time in his life.

* * *

In 1996, I interviewed Vic Toweel, who was then living in Campbelltown in western Sydney. He had donated one of his kidneys to his grandson Vic Jr.

Toweel told me he had gone into the Carruthers fight severely dehydrated after struggling to make the 53.5 kilogram bantamweight limit.

'I was caught by surprise and after the first blow, I couldn't remember anything.'

The win was a huge upset, but Carruthers proved it was no fluke four months later when he stopped Toweel in 10 rounds in a return bout, this time before an even bigger Rand Stadium crowd of 35,000.

Carruthers now had the whip hand as the biggest name in Australian boxing. Turning his back on Stadiums Ltd he decided to promote his own shows.

In a fight backed by the Federation of Police Boys Clubs, which had helped him get to the Olympics, Carruthers's world title defence against American Henry 'Pappy' Gault at the Sydney Sports Ground in 1953 drew a then Australian record crowd of 32,500, who shelled out more than £42,000 through the gate. Carruthers earned a record purse for an Australian boxer of £8625.

One of the three judges who gave him a unanimous decision was newspaper magnate and former amateur heavyweight champion Frank Packer.

Carruthers suffered a bad cut over his right eye. After the fight, which was the first official world title bout held in Australia since the historic Burns–Johnson encounter in 1908, it was found that he was also carrying a 30-foot-long tapeworm.

He next won a 12-round non-title fight in 1954 against Brisbane's 'Bulimba Bull Ant' Bobby Sinn, who was riding a streak of ten big wins.

Then Carruthers was off to Thailand for a title defence in Bangkok in May 1954 against Chamroen Songkitrat.

The bout was staged in an open-air arena during a tropical storm. Both boxers had to fight in bare feet because of the slipperiness of the ring and then dodge glass on the canvas from the exploding lightbulbs.

With 19 wins in 19 fights, Carruthers retired as world champion.

He took over the licence of the Bells Hotel at Woolloomooloo but, seven years later, aged 32, he followed a well-worn and unhappy boxing trail by returning to the ring.

He wanted money to invest in a motel, but comebacks rarely go well.

Heavier and rusty after years of inactivity, he lost for the first time, outpointed and badly cut by Italian Aldo Pravisani at Sydney Stadium in 1961.

Referee Vic Patrick said that Carruthers's win over Bobby Sinn was a masterclass he'd never forget, 'but against Aldo Pravisani I didn't recognise him'.

Licking his lips in the crowd of 13,000 was the 1958 Commonwealth Games gold medallist Wally Taylor from the cane fields of Mackay. Taylor's brother Ollie had won a bronze medal at the 1960 Olympics.

'Watching the fight that night I believed I could beat Carruthers,' Wally told me.

'I was 21, young and strong, and Carruthers was 32. I was a confident fella and I didn't believe a guy who'd spent so long out of boxing could beat me.'

Taylor won another 12-round decision and then Carruthers copped a hiding in five rounds against American Don Johnson in Melbourne.

Carruthers then beat the overmatched Louis Magnifico in Sydney and a worn-out Johnny Jarrett in Adelaide before his career ended with a disqualification loss to the modestly performed Jimmy Cassidy in Wellington, New Zealand.

He enjoyed a new career as a boxing referee and for years ran a popular health food bar in the Sydney CBD.

He was just 61 when he succumbed to cancer.

Vic Toweel always remembered his nemesis with respect and affection. 'Jimmy Carruthers was really a gentleman, a really nice chappie,' Toweel told me. 'He didn't brag or swank or show off. A very nice man.'

Pastor Trevor King Fighting the Good Fight

Trevor King climbed out of a wheelchair and blew away his iron lung to become a world-class featherweight who won 63 of 64 pro fights and whipped the only man to better him in a return.

As a boy, doctors had told him he'd never walk without a cane but in 1953 at Sydney Stadium in 40°C heat, the 22-year-old handed out a boxing lesson to Elley Bennett.

For ever after, Trevor waged war, rescuing hostages from the demon drink, saving damaged, broken men from drug addiction. He lost count of the hundreds of tearaways, runaways and rejects, bruised by life's harsh blows, who turned their lives around at his Westside Mission among the Arabian horses and dogs on 35 hectares at the end of a dirt road at Windsor.

Trevor taught his young charges life skills, the value of mateship, and the lessons of boxing: physical endurance and mental strength.

He was born in Cessnock during the Great Depression to an alcoholic father who drank even more after Trevor's mum died young from cancer. At 11 he was a skinny bespectacled runt with legs like toothpicks after being bedridden for a year with polio and rheumatic fever.

To help him recover he was put in the care of a masseur and former fighter named Taff Thomas, who gave the kid boxing exercises to do while his frail frame was supported by a specially built steel tripod. The rehabilitation worked wonders and in just four years King was strong enough at age 15 to begin boxing as a professional.

He was unbeaten in 41 fights when he dropped a 12-round decision to Austrian-born Sigi Tennenbaum at Sydney Stadium in February 1952, but he erased the only stain on his career three months later with a 15-round decision in a bout for the New South Wales featherweight title.

King signed to fight Ghana's Roy Ankrah for the Empire title in Singapore but first agreed to a return fight with Elley Bennett. Three weeks before that bout was to take place King was knocked off his motorbike by a car in the Sydney suburb of Auburn.

Gangrene set in, but refusing amputation, he rehabilitated himself with exercises. He won a comeback fight in 1960, stopping Kiwi Mike Corliss, and set his sights on Australian lightweight champ George Bracken.

King's boxing career was finished once and for all by a car accident that left him with head injuries. His record was 61 wins in 62 fights.

He joined the Salvation Army, then the Methodists, and spent his life fighting the good fight.

Tony Madigan and his Battles with Muhammad Ali

Tony Madigan once told me that while his aggressive style of fighting threw most opponents off their game, he couldn't overcome Muhammad Ali's speed.

Still, Ali always remembered the handsome Aussie as one of his toughest foes.

They first fought in Chicago in 1959, when 17-year-old Ali was known as Cassius Clay. Madigan was already a rugged veteran of the Helsinki and Melbourne Olympics and a gold medallist at the Cardiff Commonwealth Games.

Clay won their first fight on points and a year later repeated the feat at the Rome Olympics on his way to the 81-kilogram gold medal. Madigan came away with bronze, as did Brisbane bantamweight Ollie Taylor, whose daughter Kristine became an award-winning producer for the ABC and made a marvellous episode of *Australian Story* about Jeff Horn.

Madigan, who died in London in 2017 aged 87, was one of Australia's great heroes during a golden sporting age.

His early years were spent in Bathurst and Maitland, New South Wales, but when his father, an oral surgeon, died from cancer in 1938, Madigan's mother moved to Sydney to work as a dentist.

Madigan attended Ashfield De La Salle and Waverley College in Sydney and took boxing lessons from the great old champ Hughie Dwyer. He also played rugby union as a breakaway for Randwick and Sydney's Eastern Suburbs.

As a teenager Madigan sparred with the leading Australian pro fighters of his day, such as Jack Hassen at Ern McQuillan's gym.

He boxed at the Helsinki Olympics in 1952 and reached the middleweight quarter-finals. A young American, Floyd Patterson, won gold and went on to become a two-time world heavyweight champ.

Madigan stayed in Europe after the Games. To eat, he felled trees in Sweden before hitchhiking back to London, where he took a job as a broker for an Australian importing and exporting company. In 1953, he lost to Private Henry Cooper in the British light-heavyweight final at the Wembley Pool, but he represented England five times that year, and in 1954 won the British title at the Royal Albert Hall.

He also took a silver medal at the Vancouver Commonwealth Games.

Madigan moved to Germany in 1955, selling encyclopaedias for a Rhineland publishing company. He was driving to the ski fields with a 23-year-old Sydney friend, Helen Stokes-Smith, the daughter of retired Sydney Stadium fight doctor Kenneth Stokes-Smith. Madigan swerved to avoid a truck parked on the icy road, the car slid out of control and Helen was killed.

Madigan was badly injured, but he fought at the Melbourne Olympics a year later and made the quarter-finals in the light-heavyweight division.

He qualified for the 1958 Empire Games in Cardiff after arriving late for the trials. He had been driving from Brisbane to Sydney when his car overturned at Glen Innes. After walking away from the wreckage, he'd hitchhiked the rest of the journey.

Madigan won gold in Cardiff, taking out the final against Ossie Higgins, an Ipswich Town soccer professional fighting for Wales, and was presented with his gold medal by Prince Philip. On the way back to Australia, he won the Diamond Belt International tournament in Mexico, effectively making him the top amateur boxer in the world.

So impressive was his performance and such was his charisma that Eddie Eagan, an Olympic gold medallist and former commissioner of boxing in New York, took the now 28-year-old veteran back to Long Island and introduced him to Cus D'Amato, Floyd Patterson's trainer and later the man who also moulded world champions Jose Torres and Mike Tyson.

D'Amato told Madigan that he would already beat all but the top five light-heavyweights in the world and that if he turned pro he would be world champion within two years.

Legendary heavyweights Jack Dempsey and Gene Tunney watched Madigan train at New York's Stillman's Gym and encouraged him to make money from his looks and powerful punch.

In New York, Madigan worked for the Australian arm of cigarette company Rothmans and appeared in magazine ads and TV commercials for cigarettes and beer.

But he remained an amateur boxer for all his career.

He won the New York Golden Gloves in February 1959, and along the way battered Sigmund Wortherly, 'The Black Assassin', who claimed that he was also a hitman who murdered at least 30 people in New York.

The following month, Madigan lost for the first time to the young Cassius Clay in Chicago.

Of his Rome Olympics battle with Clay, Madigan told me: 'It was a close fight that could have gone either way. I was the aggressor and he was boxing on the retreat and the judges favoured his style.

'Even in those days, Clay was always talking, talking non-stop, but he was a gracious winner. A few days later he said to me, "The crowd thought you won but I got the gold medal."

'Ali went on to become a truly great fighter and at his peak there is no way I would have wanted to fight him a third time.'

Madigan married a German psychotherapist, Sybilla, in November 1960 and was the Australian team's flag bearer at the opening ceremony of the Perth Commonwealth Games in 1962, where he won light-heavyweight gold again, beating Ghana's Jojo Miles in the final.

In the lead-up to the 1964 Tokyo Olympics, Madigan fought a series of tough battles with Brisbane's Fred Casey, the pair going 2–2 and Casey earning his Olympic place.

Madigan retired to London and the South of France after a lucrative career in property. He was the most successful of all of Australia's amateur boxers, fighting at three Olympics and winning bronze in Rome. He also won gold medals at the 1958 and 1962 Commonwealth Games and silver in 1954.

Tony Madigan missed out on winning an Olympic medal in front of his Australian crowd in Melbourne in 1956.

When Madigan was outpointed in his quarter-final by Russian Murao Uskas, 22-year-old Mildura welterweight Kevin

Hogarth was left as Australia's lone representative in the boxing tournament.

Hogarth fought his way to the semi-finals at West Melbourne Stadium, using his superb jab to beat Hungarian Andras Dori, but he then lost to Irishman Fred Tiedt.

Hogarth didn't realise that losing semi-finalists would still be presented with a bronze medal after the gold medal bout two nights later.

As the three other medallists stood on the victory dais and Hogarth's name was called out, the first Aussie to win a boxing medal since Snowy Baker 48 years earlier was nowhere to be found.

Hogarth was at a harness racing meeting instead.

Bracken Lifted Lionel Rose to the Top of the World

In 1958 the Save the Children Fund charity brought four Indigenous youngsters from a bush settlement in Gippsland to Melbourne as a treat to show them the big city.

Ten-year-old Lionel Rose was one of them. He was overawed by the tall buildings, the lifts and escalators, the trams and all the people. He had never seen a light switch before.

Lionel acquired a taste for the city and a couple of weeks later he and his grandmother, Adelaide Rose, who was almost 70, hitchhiked 100 kilometres to Melbourne to see Lionel's boxing hero George Bracken beat Max Carlos at the West Melbourne Stadium.

Lionel was wearing a suit jacket, shorts and tie that the charity had given him.

When Bracken's hand was raised in victory, Lionel was hoisted into the ring to celebrate this magical moment in both their lives.

'George Bracken was my idol,' Lionel told me decades later. 'If not for Georgie Bracken, I probably would never have started boxing seriously. He was devastating.'

Shock-punching Bracken was born at the Aboriginal mission on Palm Island off Townsville in 1934 to an Indigenous mother and an Indian father, who had taken the surname Braikenridge from a Scottish regiment.

When he was five, Bracken's family moved from Palm Island to Ingham, where his father found work as a carpenter. Bracken's interest in boxing was sparked by an elder brother, Dave, a brilliant amateur fighter who died from a snakebite, and from young Jack Hassen, who was raised by the Brackens after being orphaned.

Like Hassen, George also learned his craft touring with Jimmy Sharman's boxing tent, which he joined in Townsville.

Good-looking, articulate and ambitious, Bracken once told me that he 'never for one moment liked boxing', but he saw it as one of the few opportunities at the time for a young Aboriginal man to make good money.

'If I had been a white man at 17 or 18 with the same opportunities as everybody else, I would never have put gloves on professionally,' he told me.

But he was not a white man. And for a black youth, one of ten children who had worked on cattle stations from the age of 11, boxing represented a golden chance in life.

Bracken and the other stockmen would thrill to the news of Hassen's feats at Sydney Stadium and they would spar for hours, using towels tightly wrapped around their fists instead of gloves. At 17, while on a holiday from Grenville Station, Bracken went to the annual show at Townsville 300 kilometres away. He tried the buckjumping and bullock riding. Then he met old Jimmy Sharman, who was looking for someone in the crowd to fight an air force champ from the nearby base.

'Not me,' Bracken said, but his mates pushed him into it.

'I was scared, real scared,' he said. 'Then in the first round I threw a right hand, hit him on the chin and they took him out. His friend then jumped in and challenged me.

'I really wanted to get out. I thought he'd clobber me something bad. But Sharman talked me into staying.

'I hit that opponent on the chin, too, with my right, and they took him away as well. I got 30 shillings for the two fights and Sharman talked me into joining his troop.'

Near the end of 1952, Sharman's troupe had travelled south all the way to Geelong, where 18-year-old Bracken met the old featherweight champ Kid Young (Leo White), who encouraged him to stay at his house and become a true professional.

Trained by Young and Max Pescud, Bracken made his professional debut in 1953. Two fights later he stopped promising Bryan Membrey.

In 1957, Bracken scored a second-round knockout over Ron Krogh to capture the vacant Australian lightweight title at Brisbane.

He lost two decisions to Max Carlos before beating him on points in 1958, with little Lionel Rose leading the cheer squad.

Then Bracken scored what he considered one of his most satisfying triumphs.

The South African Johnny van Rensburg had used a racial slur against Bracken at the weigh-in for their fight at Melbourne's Festival Hall in 1959.

'The bell rang for the first round and I went straight after him,' Bracken said.

Bracken nailed the South African with a left hook and then dropped him with a right hand. Referee Terry Reilly counted Van Rensburg out. But in all the noise of the crowd's cheers no one had heard the bell. It saved Van Rensburg, though not for long. Bracken flattened him for good in Round 5.

Later Bracken was a singer, music composer, a police liaison officer, and a television identity who spoke out strongly against the imprisonment of Aborigines in settlements and missions.

He never really liked hitting people and he especially hated fighting other Aboriginal boxers.

'I knew we were all in there to make a quid for ourselves,' he told me, 'and I knew how hard it was, and what we all had to go through to get somewhere.'

THE SWINGING SIXTIES

Gattellari's Battle with the Boos

Handsome, charismatic and cheeky, Rocky Gattellari rose to the top of the world by being tough, fast and clever.

As an Italian migrant boy in primary school in Sydney's outer-western suburbs he had to fight hard for acceptance. 'On my first day at school I learned that if you fought the boys who were picking on you and you beat the shit out of them they respected you,' Rocky once told me. 'So I suppose those bullies did me a favour – they taught me how to fight.'

Born on 6 September 1942, Gattellari was the fifth of seven sons of a Calabrian shepherd family who, wary of the local mafia, had migrated to Australia in 1954.

Life was tough for a dirt-poor Italian family in a new land. Gattellari grew up among the market gardens at Bonnyrigg in Sydney's south-west, fighting gangs of bodgies and bikers to show them he was one 'dago' who wouldn't give in. He used his fists nearly every day and became a brilliant amateur fighter, beating Jackie Bruce and the amateur establishment for a place in the Australian team for the Rome Olympics.

The Italians treated Gattellari as a traitor and he copped a controversial decision early in the tournament against the eventual gold medallist Gyula Török of Hungary.

With movie star looks and the confidence to match, he was always going to create headlines when he turned pro on 18 September 1961, knocking out Queensland drover Freddy Ah Sam in the third round at Sydney Stadium.

Soon he was matched with Jackie Bruce again, this time for the Australian flyweight title. Gattellari won in Round 6 and in his next fight drew 11,000 people to Sydney Stadium when he stopped American Sal Algieri in the first round.

Gattellari loved the limelight, and adored the opportunity it gave him to mock the critics who decried him as a flashy immigrant too big for his little boots.

He posted wins over Brisbane's Jackie Treschman, Scottish Olympian Danny Lee, the American Ray Perez, and in a fight for the Australian bantamweight title, Queenslander Noel Kunde.

He became a huge drawcard because of the speed of his fists and his cocky swagger, but crowds were rarely on his side.

'The Italians would cheer but the majority were the Australians and the boos sounded like an aircraft taking off,' he told me. 'I'd be waving to the crowd and people would be shouting 'wog' and 'dago'. They came to see me get beaten, but I did my best all the time to shut them up.'

Unbeaten in 16 fights, Gattellari was given a great chance to beat Italy's veteran world flyweight champ Salvatore Burruni, and more than 30,000 came out to see the fight at the Sydney Showground on 2 December 1965.

'The Rock' abandoned his usual all-out attack to box cautiously. By Round 12, Burruni was well ahead on points, but Gattellari cut Burruni and the wound spurred on the little champ.

Burruni roared into Gattellari in Round 13 and dropped him three times for a knockout victory.

It was the Rock's first professional defeat.

According to *The Canberra Times*, most of the members of parliament in the House of Representatives that night temporarily lost interest in the verbal fight over the Trade Practices Bill at about 9.30 p.m.

'A count of heads showed three Opposition members, five Liberals, one Country Party member and three ministers present,' it reported. 'Moments after the knockout, Mr Cameron (Labor, SA) entered the House and told the Deputy Leader of the Opposition, Mr Whitlam, who gasped 'Oh, no' and passed on the news to the Attorney-General, Mr Snedden, who in turn informed the temporary Chairman of Committees, Mr Drury.'

Gattellari won five more fights and on 11 December 1967 squared off with Lionel Rose for the Australian bantamweight title. It was billed as the biggest fight at Sydney Stadium since Vic Patrick and Tommy Burns. Appropriately, Patrick was appointed referee.

Fans queued for more than a kilometre from the old Sydney Stadium at Rushcutters Bay back up Bayswater Road to Kings Cross.

Again, Rocky fought his heart out against a naturally bigger man.

Rose told his trainer Jack Rennie in the interval between rounds 12 and 13 that he was going to knockout Rocky in the next.

Which is what he did. Rocky was badly hurt and recovered in hospital.

He retired after a fight in Naples in 1968, but 11 years later he came back to be humiliated in three rounds by Paul Ferreri at Sydney's Hordern Pavilion.

In later years Rocky ran restaurants and became a successful finance broker.

The Imposter Exposed

Billy Booth was one of Australia's best amateur fighters, beating Lionel Rose and Japan's Olympic gold medallist Takao Sakurai before fighting at the 1964 Tokyo Games.

After he retired from boxing, Billy spent more than 30 years holidaying at the same spot on the New South Wales north coast.

On the first day of his holidays one year, Bill was intrigued to read the profile of a local fight trainer on the back page of the town's newspaper, and how the trainer's greatest moment in boxing came when he beat Billy Booth as an amateur.

Bill had never heard of the impostor and just as his wife put a breakfast of bacon and eggs in front of him, Bill blurted out his disgust at the fraud: 'What the hell is this crap?' he said.

'Well, if you don't like your breakfast,' snapped Mrs Booth, 'you don't have to eat it.'

The highlight of Australia's involvement at the Tokyo Olympics boxing tournament was provided by heavyweight Athol McQueen, a raw-boned dairy farmer from Kyogle in northern New South Wales.

Big Athol, then 23, beat Japanese heavyweight Tadayuki Maruyama in his first fight and then faced a Philadelphia meatworker named Smokin' Joe Frazier.

Athol became the first fighter to deck Frazier but the powerful American got back to his feet and, unloading his infamous left hook, powered on through the tournament to win the gold medal and become one of the most feared heavyweights of all time.

Ray of Sunshine for the Fighters

Ray Connelly became Australia's most famous boxing announcer thanks to his colourful introduction of fighters using potent polysyllables previously only licensed to the Oxford, Macquarie and Webster dictionaries. He alliterated awesomely down glovedom's glory road as boxing's loquacious and lauded Lord of the Ring.

Ray once introduced Azumah Nelson to the crowd as 'the immortalised Nimrod of tempestuous temerity' and once hyped Jeff Harding to the fans as 'passionately orbiting towards catastrophic magnitude'.

Harding told Ray after winning his fight that he didn't know what half the words meant. 'But keep saying them, Lord,' Harding said, 'You make me feel good.'

TV Ringside and Its Knockout Stable

After a century and a half of fierce fights across the country, Australian boxing faced a new challenge on the night of Sunday, 16 September 1956. The black-and-white image of the urbane former disc jockey Bruce Gyngell came flickering into lounge rooms across the country. 'Good evening,' he said, 'and welcome to television.'

This new medium created new possibilities for stay-at-home entertainment. Sydney Stadium manager Harry Miller knew almost immediately that the crowds that flocked to the fights there every Monday night would soon dwindle. It would be a similar story for John Wren's Festival Halls in Melbourne and Brisbane, and for other fight venues around Australia. Rather than kill boxing, however, television soon came to complement the fight game and take it to a new audience.

Channel 7's *TV Ringside* first hit Australian screens in July 1966, with Ron Casey and the wisecracking 1920s middleweight Merv Williams as commentators, and colourful characters such as Terry Reilly and Des Crabbe as referees. The show became a Monday night staple.

While the Nine and Ten networks copied the format, *TV Ringside* remained the market leader. Until June 1975, it broadcast 319 programs featuring 1450 televised fights, showcasing some of the enduring heroes of Australian sport as well as crowd pleasers such as John Wright, Jack Kriss, Carmen Rotolo, Hillary Connolly, Kahu Mahanga and Bob Liddle, later a prominent Indigenous leader, who was awarded an OAM in 2013 for 'service to the community through roles with Aboriginal organisations, particularly in the oil exploration and production industry'.

As *TV Ringside* made the audience for pro boxing boom, Tasmanian amateur Wayne Devlin won eight consecutive Australian titles between 1970 and 1977, while Brian Tink, Benny Pike, Mal Challinor, Dennis Talbot and Phil McElwaine were all amateur standouts of the era.

In the 1980s I called a number of big fights for Sky Channel, usually in partnership with the former Manly rugby league prop Peter Peters, but also with the Melbourne broadcaster Ron Casey and the Sydney broadcaster of the same name.

Sydney's Ron Casey, who made his name as a radio shock jock, was also the publisher of the *Australian Ring Digest* during the 1950s, and in the 1970s hosted *TV Fight of the Week* on Channel 9.

Ron and his mate, the great welterweight Tommy Burns, provided the commentary when former world heavyweight champs Smokin' Joe Frazier and Jimmy Ellis did battle at St Kilda's Junction Oval in 1975. Frazier won in the ninth round and travelled to the Philippines to face Muhammad Ali in his next bout, dubbed 'The Thrilla in Manila'.

Ron could throw a punch, too. On 16 July 1991, he was a guest on the Nine Network's *Midday Show* hosted by Ray Martin, when he became involved in a heated debate with singer, actor and Vietnam veteran Normie Rowe. Casey jumped up to confront Rowe, who pushed Casey back into his chair. Casey responded with a big right cross to Rowe's chin.

Jack Rennie: Finding a Diamond and a Rose

The popularity of televised fight shows in Australia in the late 1960s was boosted no end by the fact that this country had produced two of the finest fighters in the world – Lionel Rose and Johnny Famechon.

When I was a small boy my local barber, like many businesses of the time, had a picture of 'Fammo' over the mirror in his shop, the way Catholics might have a picture of the Pope.

Famechon climbed to the top of the world featherweight standings while Lionel Rose was climbing to the top of the bantamweight division under the guidance of trainer Jack Rennie.

Jack Rennie was born on 13 July 1930 in Melbourne. From a young age, newspaper photos of Dave Sands and Vic Patrick covered the wall of his bedroom and he became a handy welterweight who fought from 1946–1950, winning 17 of 28 pro fights, though it was always said that he was too nice to ever knock anyone out.

Jack was only 19 when he retired as a fighter.

In 1949 he played Australian rules football with the Essendon seconds and then Williamstown in the VFA until a broken wrist put him out of football, and increasing weight meant that a boxing comeback was beyond him.

'I started coaching a football team at Moonee Ponds and on rainy days I'd take them to the gym for some boxing training to keep them fit. Some of the players turned out to be pretty handy fighters and in 1958 I found I had a team of footballers and a team of fighters.'

At the same time, 100 kilometres to the south-east, ten-year-old Lionel Rose was living in a dirt-floor humpy, one of a handful of similar huts erected at Jacksons Track in a Gippsland eucalypt forest. Each ramshackle dwelling contained as many as a dozen children.

Lionel was enrolled at Labertouche Primary near the small town of Drouin, but his childhood was spent wagging school, smoking cigarettes and learning boxing moves from his father. Roy Rose was a young timber cutter supplying wood for a factory in Drouin, but he suffered from a congenital heart defect that meant he was only able to work infrequently. In better times, he had made some extra money in the travelling boxing troupes.

'Through my father I was a Gunditjmara,' Lionel recalled. They were a fighting tribe and, though he died when I was 14, Dad told me a lot about them. He was a good man, a tent fighter. He used to tell me a lot of stories about the mission where he grew up.'

Roy also told Lionel about the great Aboriginal fighters of the past: Jerry Jerome, Ron Richards, Jack Hassen and Dave Sands.

Every day, from the age of six, Lionel would practise his punches – the fast left jab, the shock left hook, the thumping straight right. Lionel would fill a flourbag with sand and gravel from Jacksons Track, hang it from a tree and punch it until his knuckles bled.

'Oh, yes, he was a lively chap,' Lionel's mother, Gina, told the American magazine *Sports Illustrated* in 1968. 'He used to play away the days. He'd come home and tell me everything that happened in school that day, and then the teacher would stop by and ask me where he had been. My husband paid fines twice because Lionel stayed away from school, and the third time he couldn't afford it and my husband was in jail for 48 hours.'

The local police liked Roy Rose, though. They didn't even lock the door. They told him he could go home if he cleaned the place up, but he stayed in jail for two days to teach Lionel a lesson.

When Lionel was ten, the Save the Children charity, looking to publicise the plight of Aboriginal Australians, brought him and three other Indigenous youngsters to Melbourne for a short holiday.

Graham Walsh, a press photographer for Melbourne's *Sun* newspaper and a former boxer, was assigned to cover the story. Walsh brought the boy to his Blackburn home to meet his wife. In later years, Walsh would often recall how Lionel was fascinated by the light switches and taps, turning them on in the shower and sink again and again, amazed at water that was not only running, but hot.

Walsh gave Lionel a pair of his old boxing gloves: the first pair of real gloves that Rose could call his own. When asked what he most wanted to see in the big smoke, the little boy told Walsh that his one wish was to see the fights at the newly rebuilt West Melbourne Stadium, known today as Festival Hall. Walsh took him to meet the Italian welterweight Bruno Visintin, who was training in Melbourne. He then arranged for Lionel to be ringside two weeks later, where, on 3 October 1958, he saw Visintin lose a decision to Johnny van Rensburg.

Lionel, dressed in shorts, suit jacket, long socks and tie bought by the charity, sat goggled-eyed at Melbourne's premier boxing stadium waiting to see his first proper boxing match.

The announcer, Fred Tupper, called Lionel into the ring and introduced him to the crowd. It was something that Rose would grow accustomed to in later years, but that night Lionel was so nervous that, when a microphone was put in front of his face and he was asked what he wanted to be when he grew up, he couldn't speak. Instead, he whispered into the announcer's ear and the message was then relayed to the crowd: 'Lionel's ambition is to become a fighter like the late, great Dave Sands.' Lionel would later recall that the statement 'nearly brought the house down'.

It was two weeks later, on 17 October, that Lionel and his grandmother Adelaide Rose hitchhiked from Jacksons Track to Melbourne to see George Bracken fight at the stadium. As they waited by the roadside with their thumbs extended, the old lady and the little boy endured racial slurs, but it was not enough to stop them.

They made it to Melbourne and Lionel was invited to join Bracken in the dressing-room before his bout against Max Carlos. Bracken recalled: 'I had a good chat to him that night. He was so excited. I showed him a few moves and he was thrilled. I fell in love with him. I really did and he became my mascot from then on. He hardly missed another of my fights.'

Lionel wanted to emulate Bracken in the same way that Bracken had wanted to emulate Jack Hassen.

Lionel watched, mesmerised, as Bracken, hero to Indigenous Australians everywhere, outboxed Carlos over 12 rounds to win on points, avenging a pair of defeats in the preceding two years. Seeing this handsome, articulate, wealthy young black man scoring a momentous victory, Lionel's resolve to be a champion fighter was cemented. When Bracken's hand was raised in victory, Lionel was hoisted into the ring. As the applause eventually abated, Bracken left the ring with his arm around his young fan. Lionel whispered to Walsh: 'I'll always remember this night.'

A few weeks later, the Aboriginal Welfare Board moved the Jacksons Track community to a settlement near the Drouin Racecourse. The old humpies were bulldozed. Lionel's new two-room house was made of weatherboard, with a tin roof and wooden floor.

A few kilometres away, in the town of Warragul, a local boxing coach and railroad repairman named Frank Oakes was busy training an eager bunch of youngsters at the community hall. He would later remember: 'One night at the Warragul Gym I saw a little dark face pressed up against the window. It was Lionel. I went outside and brought him in and asked him to do a little bit of work on the heavy bag to keep warm. Later on I found he'd walked about five miles [8 kilometres] from his home at Drouin to get there.'

Lionel soon struck up a friendship with Jenny Oakes, the trainer's daughter. It was the 1950s, and other children wouldn't play with Jenny because she'd let an Aboriginal boy into her house. Yet Lionel would become the love of her life and they would stay together for half a century.

After six months of training in Warragul, Lionel was ready to fight. He went to Sale for an amateur night. He was just 12 and weighed 35 kilograms. There were no boxers his weight, so he was matched with a state champion, Jim Beaumont, two years older and 7 kilograms heavier. 'He belted hell out of me,' Lionel recalled. He nursed his wounds for the 90-minute ride back to Warragul, his face puffy and sore, embarrassed that every other boy in his team had won.

Lionel hung up the gloves for two years. By 1962, however, he was the eldest of nine children in a tiny home, his father's invalid pension the only money coming in. He decided to box again, hoping to eventually make enough money from the sport to support his family. In one of the proudest moments of his career, he won an amateur bout at the Warragul Technical School in front of his father. He was then offered a fight as a curtain-raiser to the professional fights at Festival Hall. With huge excitement, Roy Rose told everyone about how his son would shine in boxing's famous theatre. Tragically, only a couple of nights before the bout, Roy passed away, aged just 34.

Lionel decided to go ahead with the fight, knowing that it would have been his father's wish. He went straight from the funeral to Festival Hall. On the way to Melbourne, he told Frank Oakes: 'I guess it's all up to me now – I've got to feed the kids.' Lionel not only won his bout but was judged the best boxer of the night.

By 1963, Rose was a thin-legged, big-chested youth with outsized biceps. He was just 15 when, with Frank Oakes guiding him, he won the Australian senior amateur flyweight title at Hobart Town Hall. In the tournament to select Australia's 1964 Olympic team for Tokyo, he was narrowly outpointed over three rounds by the Sydney southpaw Billy Booth. Rose had lied about his age to compete; even if he had won, he would not have been allowed to fight at the Games as he was still under 16.

Oakes realised that Rose needed more advanced coaching and sparring so, on weekends, he sent him to his old friend Jack Rennie, who realised immediately that Lionel was a rare find. 'He was a natural. His footwork, hand speed, the way he moved. It was all instinctive,' Rennie recalled. 'You couldn't teach that; I couldn't teach that. I knew he would make it; his reflexes were so fast. He was a prize to come to my gym.'

In a 50-year career as a fight trainer until his passing in 2013 Jack was an inspiration to other Aussie boxing coaches including my mentor, the great Johnny Lewis, and he turned out other star boxers including Paul Ferreri, Harry Hayes, Graeme Brooke, Jimmy Thunder, Tony Miller, and Mick Croucher. Lionel Rose was the most successful.

In Jack's tiny backyard gym at Marco Polo Street, Essendon – a gym not much bigger than a garden shed – Rose sparred against Bob Allotey, Rennie's flyweight from Ghana and, gradually, began staying for more than just the weekends. Before long, Rose moved in permanently with Rennie, his wife, Shirley, and their two boys, Mark and John. Lionel lived in their spare bedroom until he married Jenny Oakes in 1970.

Jack had spent four years at night school to become a production manager in a local printing firm, and every night after work he spent his time honing the teenager's natural speed, reflexes, toughness and courage, using his rudimentary equipment in that tiny gym.

Rose was only 15, but already he drank and smoked heavily. 'I had to be a father to him,' Rennie said. 'I had to stand on his toes when he got out of line. He'd been a chain smoker since he was ten years old – 30 cigarettes a day. I gave him a pipe to puff on instead because I thought that was better than the ciggies. Shirley and I bought him books, too, and enrolled him in correspondence courses because he'd only had six years at school and even then wagged most of the days. Together we made a great team.'

Rose – known as 'Slim' to his friends – began his professional career in 1964, outpointing Mario Magris for £20 over eight rounds in Warragul. He won 16 of his first 18 fights, and on the undercard of Rocky Gattellari's world title fight with Salvatore Burruni in Sydney in 1965, he outpointed Toowoomba-born Arthur Clarke.

In 1966, Lionel outpointed Noel Kunde over 15 rounds for the Australian bantamweight title.

Rose then defended his national championship against Gattellari.

There was huge national interest in the fight. 'It was the first bout relayed interstate on television,' commentator Ron Casey recalled. 'We used the coaxial cable for the first time for a boxing bout and it drew a huge audience in Melbourne.' Gate receipts totalled more than $50,000, an Australian indoor record. Rennie, however, would always complain that he and Rose only got $500 in television rights for the event. 'The fans were there from early in the afternoon, hours before the first prelim bout,' Rennie remembered.

Rose's advantages in size and speed were immediately obvious, but The Rock stayed with him through 12 hard rounds, soaking up enormous punishment. In Round 13, Lionel took a desperate left hook from Rocky and fired back with his own left hook. Rocky stumbled. Lionel leapt in with five sizzling hooks. With tremendous speed, two straight lefts followed, then a hook off a jab, a straight left and another hook off a jab. A big right exploded off Rocky's chin; he went down with his head folded under him, his upper body underneath the bottom rope on the apron of the ring.

No one could have blamed Rocky if he had stayed down. Yet, somehow, he got back to his feet. Referee Vic Patrick asked him if he wanted to continue. Incredibly, The Rock nodded. Rose drove Gattellari into the ropes with punches to the head and body. Rocky spun away to the centre of the ring, but Lionel followed, his gloves firing nonstop. Finally, a huge right over the top sent

Rocky crashing to the canvas, out cold. Patrick counted to five and then, realising that Rocky was badly hurt, quickly called for the doctor and ambulancemen. The Rock was unconscious for half an hour, but, after a clearly distressed Lionel visited him at St Vincent's Hospital, he made a full recovery.

Two months later, Rennie received the offer he and his young fighter had dreamed about. 'We were watching telly at home when the phone rang,' Jack recalled. 'I told Lionel, "There's a Jap on the phone ... he's talking about a world-title fight with Fighting Harada." Lionel was listening in on the conversation and he kept saying to me, "Take it, Jack, take it." He was jumping around all excited, but I asked the bloke if he would call back tomorrow night ... I was a bit worried that Lionel wasn't quite ready. He was only 19, but he wanted it, there was no way I could have knocked it back.'

Rose and the Rennies set up a training camp by a Gippsland beach at Kilcunda where Rose would eventually spar dozens of rounds with the brilliant young Kiwi Denny Enright. Despite a record that had now grown to an impressive 27 wins out of 29 fights, Rose was still a teenager. The sporting press gave him no chance. He would be the first Aboriginal man to challenge for a world boxing title, only getting the fight because he came cheap: $7500 compared with $70,000 for Harada. One of the conditions insisted on by the Japanese was that the scoring referee and two other judges all be Japanese.

Rose was a shy boy who had never been out of Australia. If the occasion didn't overwhelm him, the wise heads believed, the stocky Masahiko 'Fighting' Harada, a human whirlwind, certainly would. 'There weren't too many people who gave me a chance against Harada. Ten people were there to see us off at Essendon,' Rose recalled. Japan and a fearsome champion were daunting prospects for a country boy making his first overseas trip, but Rennie believed that Harada's aggressive style would suit his fighter.

Rose couldn't stomach the Japanese food, so Shirley Rennie brought a frying pan and steaks with her and cooked all his meals in the hotel. In the bewildering metropolis of Tokyo, Rose gave interviews while puffing on his pipe, telling reporters, tongue firmly in cheek, that back home he boxed kangaroos and lived on a diet of gum leaves. The Japanese press couldn't work him out.

When the bell rang for Round 1 in the title fight, neither could Harada. In the Budokan Hall, near Emperor Hirohito's Imperial Palace, with no more than a dozen Australians in a crowd of 14,000 to cheer him on, Rose went to work.

'I knew Harada was a charger,' Lionel told me. 'So I was prepared to meet him head-on. Jack trained me beautifully for that fight and I was able to counterpunch him all night as he rushed in. Before the fight, Jack told me that because all the judges were Japanese, I had to hit Harada twice every time he hit me. I knew I was as fit as I could possibly be so I just went flat out from the start.'

The Australian gave a magnificent display of courageous fighting, his superior height and reach, and strong, fast left hand combining with short, sharp shots to the body.

After marking up Harada's face and opening a small nick on the champion's right eyebrow with his constant left jab, Rose scored a flash knockdown in the ninth with a right to the jaw. He rocked Harada again in the 14th when Harada was on the ropes. Even though the Japanese crowd urged their man to rally in the 15th, Rose remained unflappable. For three minutes, the pair slugged away toe-to-toe.

At the end of the 15th, both fighters raised their arms, then fell into each other's embrace: two proud warriors who had used up every bit of ammunition. Rose felt that he had dominated the action, but there was still a nervous wait as the Japanese judges tallied their scorecards.

'Don't forget,' Jack Rennie told me, 'it wasn't really all that long after World War II and we didn't know what to expect.'

Finally, referee Ko Toyama tallied the scorecards, then theatrically pointed towards the Australian corner and shouted 'Rose-san'. Rose accidentally knocked Rennie over as he leapt to his feet in celebration; the new world champion had won a unanimous decision.

'I can't remember sleeping that night, or for a couple of nights afterwards,' Rose recalled 30 years later. 'Everybody called me "Champ". I was champion of the world! I was on cloud nine for weeks; some people say I am still on it.'

With memories of Kokoda, Changi and the Burma Railway still raw in the minds of World War II–generation Australians, Rose had beaten Japan's national hero on home soil for the championship of the world. There was elation throughout Australia's population of 12 million that night, but among the nation's 130,000 Aboriginal people, Lionel Rose was now Superman. In the slums of Redfern, men danced in the street. In the dry bed of the Todd River, outside Alice Springs, they fired rifles into the air. On the outback stations they hollered so loudly that their voices carried almost to the Aboriginal community beside the Drouin Racecourse. 'For them,' *Sports Illustrated* said, Rose's moment of victory 'was a millennium, a glimpse of Valhalla from a valley of squalor, a vicarious justification of the hope that their own futures might rise beyond futility.'

Rose and his team caught the first Qantas fight from Tokyo, arriving in Sydney a day after the win. In Rose's luggage, alongside his white satin fighting trunks and black leather boxing boots, were his spoils of war – a commemorative samurai sword and three glittering trophies more than a metre high. In Sydney, the team then boarded an Ansett flight to Melbourne and the homecoming of a century on 29 February 1968.

Schoolchildren from throughout Melbourne were given time off to honour him. Half the city's population lined the route into Swanston Street, the enormous crowd bringing inner-city Melbourne to a standstill.

King Lionel: 'Elvis Presley Called Me "Mr Rose"'

On 29 February 1968, Rose stood on the balcony of the Melbourne Town Hall looking out at a quarter of a million people. The crowd roared. He shaped up to Melbourne's Lord Mayor, Reginald Talbot, and shook hands with various state and federal ministers and Victorian Premier Sir Henry Bolte.

The world-title win was just the start. In his first bout after beating Harada, Rose outpointed Italian Tommaso Galli in a non-title bout. It was a warm-up for a $40,000 payday for a return to Japan in July 1968 against Tokyo Olympics gold medallist Takao Sakurai.

The Japanese southpaw proved slick and elusive in the first round and, in the second, drove home a straight left that put Rose on his backside. It took Rose six rounds to catch the fleet-footed challenger, but from then on he maintained the pressure, winning a majority decision.

The following month, Rose made his debut at the Inglewood Forum, outside Los Angeles, winning a close decision in a non-title fight with Mexican Joe Medel. In December, he returned to the same venue to face another Mexican: power-puncher Chucho Castillo. Rose's purse was $75,000 and Castillo's $20,000.

In the lead-up to that fight, Rose won over a special fan. He was nearing the end of a hard training session when he got the message that Elvis Presley wanted to meet him. Rose drove straight to the MGM lot, where Elvis was shooting the movie *The Trouble with Girls*. They spent two hours together, talking about music and boxing. The King gave Rose an autographed United States dollar bill as a gift for his mother. 'Elvis was a gentleman,' Lionel recalled. 'He called me "Mr Rose".'

Two days later, it was time to fight Castillo. Rose built an early lead but suffered a bruise under his left eye in the fourth round. Though blood trickled from a cut, he seemed untroubled. Rose used his counterpunching style to tremendous effect against Castillo, who was the aggressor for most of the fight. In the tenth, Castillo landed a solid right to the jaw and a left to the body, and Rose went down. He was up after a short count. Castillo came out fast in the eleventh but by that time Rose had recovered. Referee Dick Young scored the fight for Castillo, but judges Lee Grossman and John Thomas both had Rose narrowly winning the fight, and he retained his belt.

The Mexican fans went berserk. 'They were hurling bottles full of urine at us,' said Rennie, who suffered cuts on his leg and arm. Dick Young had scalp lacerations and the flying glass cut several policemen. Although double the usual number of police were on duty, they were unable to maintain order as fires were set in the seats. Fourteen fans were hospitalised. Film stars, including June Allyson and Jonathan Winters, ran for their lives. Outside on the street, Kirk Douglas had his new car blown up. Other cars were overturned. The Australians took cover under the ring until the storm passed.

When he was finally safe back in Australia again, Rose was on top of the world. By contrast, the ATV-0 television network run by airline and media mogul Reg Ansett was in trouble. Older sets and aerials could not pick up the new station's television signal. Needing a major drawcard to get Australia's third network into people's homes, Ansett paid $140,000 (including $70,000 for Rose) to televise a live fight between Rose and Liverpudlian Alan Rudkin, the champion of Britain and the Commonwealth. The fight was set for Saturday night, 8 March 1969, outdoors at Melbourne's Kooyong Lawn Tennis Club.

Rose again had much difficulty making the bantamweight limit of 53.5 kilograms but, despite the strain, took control of the fight early with jolting lefts to the face. Halfway through the fourth, Rose slashed a wide gash on Rudkin's left eyebrow with a long right hand. The 14,300 spectators thought the end was near, but the gallant little Briton kept coming right up until the bell to end Round 15.

While Rose took the decision, Reg Ansett was the big winner. The fight was the most-watched television program in Australian history up to that time, with an estimated three million viewers. Seventy-two per cent of Australian households tuned into the event, a record that would stand until the year 2000, when another Aboriginal sports star, Cathy Freeman, inspired by Rose, would win gold at the Sydney Olympics.

Writing in *The Age*, boxing expert and former amateur champion Mike Ryan said that Rose risked serious problems by dehydrating himself to fight as a bantamweight. Indeed, Rose would likely have relinquished his title, if not for American promoter George Parnassus offering him a record bantamweight purse of $110,000 to fight the undefeated slugger 'Rockabye' Ruben Olivares of Mexico.

On 22 August 1969, Rose was back at the Inglewood Forum to face Olivares, who was undefeated with 51 wins, 50 inside the distance. Even the one man who had gone the distance with him had been knocked out in a return. Rose quickly discovered why. In Round 2, a short chopping right to the side of his head sent Rose crashing to his knees. When he got up at the count of four, blood cascaded from his lower lip. A six-punch salvo knocked out his mouthguard.

In Round 3, a right uppercut sent his mouthguard flying across the ring again. A left uppercut early in Round 5 repeated the dose. Olivares also delivered a dreadful body battering. A ten-punch assault, capped by a crunching hook, sent Rose to his knees for the second time. Rose regained his feet at six. He did his best to keep the Mexican tidal wave from pulling him under, but Olivares ended the fight with a right to the chin that put Rose face down.

Rose's run of success was over. Nonetheless, he kept boxing for seven more years. With the help of Melbourne record producer Johnny Young, he also made hits of another kind: the country and western ballads 'I Thank You', 'Please Remember Me' and 'Pick Me Up On Your Way Down'.

Lionel Rose could still be a brilliant boxer on occasion. He beat Don Johnson and Freddie Wicks, and upset future world lightweight champion Ishimatsu 'Guts' Suzuki in Melbourne in 1970 by a ten-round decision. Despite losing to Jeff White for the Australian lightweight title, Rose cashed in on his popularity in Japan when he and Rennie secured another world-title try against WBC junior-lightweight (59 kg) champion Yoshiaki Numata on 30 May 1971 at Hiroshima. Numata beat Rose by a 15-round decision. Lionel suffered subsequent defeats against Blakeney Matthews and Billy Moeller in Australia and then, in 1976, a brutal stoppage against Mexico's Rafael 'Bazooka' Limón. That year, in his final fight, Rose was knocked out in two rounds in Noumea by Maurice Apeang, a Tahitian who fought for France at the 1972 Olympics.

A Loveable Rogue

Lionel had his left hand clutching a scotch and Coke, a smoke wedged between his lips and the long thin fingers of his right hand latched on to my forearm like an eagle's talon squeezing the life out of a slippery lizard.

By 1996 he was a small, bespectacled invalid pensioner who'd endured three heart attacks, but even three decades after he became the world bantamweight boxing champion, I could still feel the steel strength of his hands.

'Come on big fella,' he said drawing close as if to tell me some cherished secret from his storied career. 'How's about a lazy hundred for an old battler?'

Lionel was never backward in coming forward as a fighter and he was relentless on the snip. In fact, some say his greatest win was not at Tokyo's Budokan Hall where he conquered Fighting Harada for the world crown in 1968, but rather many years later at a government function when it's said that he managed to extract $100 from the then prime minister, Paul Keating.

Lionel was in fine form at the launch of a documentary I wrote for producer Graham McNeice called *That's Boxing* in 1996, when the greats of the Australian fight game stretching back to the 1930s all assembled at the Maritime Museum in Sydney.

Lionel must have hit all the old pugs for a lazy hundred with varying degrees of success and my enduring memory of that night is of his eyes lighting up when he heard his old foe Rocky Gattellari was now a finance broker who could arrange loans. Lionel threw his arm around the Rock and with a huge smile said, 'We'll have to talk later.'

Lionel was impossible to dislike. Despite his triumphs and humiliations, he remained the same loveable rogue for all of his 62 years, a little battler from the bush with the smile of a Cheshire cat.

His was not a blameless life. After his fall from the pinnacle of public acclaim he was fined for possession of amphetamines and cannabis, spent a few days in prison for driving while disqualified and was once caught breaking into a school with intent to steal.

His pub crawls were monumental. After his boxing career peaked when he was just 20, he lost all his money, a block of units at Essendon, a house he paid for with cash, country properties and a share in a beachside holiday home. Even his remarkable, long-suffering wife, Jenny, the daughter of his first trainer and his sweetheart since primary school, couldn't tolerate him anymore and left him.

But, just like the rest of Australia, the kindly kindergarten teacher let Lionel back into her heart, and she cared for him for the rest of his life.

Despite suffering heart attacks, Lionel kept smoking – 'carefully', he said – though he smoked two packs a day (when he could afford them) after ditching the pipe. He bet on horses – usually slow ones – and drank whisky instead of beer.

In 1991, his life was dramatised in the miniseries *Rose Against the Odds*. By 1996, he told me that he had spent all his money on 'wine, women and song'. He estimated that he had about '2000 close relatives' who shared the money he made from boxing.

A decade later, before Anthony Mundine's biggest victory over Danny Green at Sydney's Aussie Stadium in 2006, Mundine and his father were joined in their dressing-room by Lionel, their hero. Lionel was wearing thick glasses and there was a stutter in his step. Though not yet 60, he looked much older. His joy at the success of another Indigenous fighter, however, had him smiling as broadly as that day on the balcony of Melbourne Town Hall almost 40 years before, when he had waved to an adoring crowd of 250,000 people.

Although he suffered a stroke in 2007 that left him with speech and movement difficulties, Lionel's charisma and good humour were still captivating when he appeared in Eddie Martin's 2008 documentary *Lionel*, which celebrated his extraordinary career.

There was a national outpouring of grief following Lionel's death aged 62 in Warragul on 8 May 2011, not long after the unveiling of his statue in the town. It was testament to an 'everyman' who reflected in all of us our successes and failures, our strengths and foibles. On the day that Australia's first Indigenous world champion passed away, Australian boxing was still celebrating the crowning of its latest, Daniel Geale, who had just beat Sebastian Sylvester in Neubrandenburg, Germany, for the world middleweight title.

Lionel had brilliant boxing skills and there was enormous courage in the little weight-drained body that carried him to 42 wins in 53 pro fights.

He was also humble and fallible, and his success in sport made us feel good as a country and as a people.

It was not only Rose's boxing skills that were to prove an inspiration. Arguably, the public recognition of an Aboriginal boy's acceptance into a white family – the Rennie household in the 1960s – did as much for reconciliation in Australia as the political rhetoric over land rights at the time and the 1967 referendum to include Aboriginal people in the census.

Jack Rennie's son, John, recalled that Rose 'was immensely courageous, funny, and most of all someone who overcame the prejudices of that time'. Lionel 'never forgot who he was and where he came from and always made me feel like his brother,' John said. 'Lionel had a hard road in later years, but his spirit and heart never changed and the friendship between him and my father never waned.' John's brother Mark Rennie recalled: 'Lionel was my big brother in all ways. I loved him and he loved me. I know: he told me so many times. I will miss him.'

Lionel was given a state funeral at Festival Hall, where his dreams had been launched and where he fought 23 times. Victorian Premier Ted Baillieu remembered that, as a boy, he had been glued to the radio in his brother's bedroom for the Harada fight. 'As the crackling voice of Ron Casey proclaimed Lionel Rose was champion of the world, we jumped around and hollered our support,' Baillieu said. 'It's hard to imagine now what an event that was. Melbourne went nuts.'

When he arrived home from Tokyo after beating Harada to see unprecedented public jubilation, Lionel insisted his mother Gina ride alongside him in one of the American convertibles on hand for his public parade.

As a black Australian, Gina had known hard times all her life.

As the media hung off his every word, Lionel, just 19 years old, was careful to promote a unified country. He did not express the bitterness he must surely have felt over those hard years sleeping on a dirt floor at Jacksons Track, eating possum and watching his father die a worn-out man aged just 34.

During all the euphoria, as 250,000 people cheered him, a reporter asked the little teenager whether his world title win would help his people and their struggles. Lionel said it would certainly bring recognition but, in a nod towards reconciliation, he added: 'I'm not too clued up with all this. I think of myself as an Australian. I think everyone else is an Australian here with me. I don't go in for all this black and white thing. To me, we're all Australians.'

Johnny Famechon: An Artist on Canvas

As Australian boxing reached its zenith with Lionel Rose's victory over Harada, Johnny Famechon was about to give this country two world champions at the same time.

On 21 January 1969, on a freezing London winter's day, 'Fammo' was inside the opulent Royal Albert Hall putting the heat on the extroverted WBC featherweight (57 kg) champion José Legrá, known as the Cuban Eel and the mini Muhammad Ali.

Flash, cocky and extremely quick, Legrá combined his flying fists with the grace of a ballet dancer. Undefeated in his previous 54 fights, he was the raging favourite to beat the sharpshooter from Melbourne. He was also 6 centimetres taller than the Australian, and much more physically imposing.

Famechon had never been beaten inside the distance, but Legrá did his best to tarnish that record, with a huge surge in the last four rounds as he tried everything, including a couple of exaggerated uppercuts, or 'bolo' punches. Fammo ducked and weaved, dodging his blows.

The 15th round was a sensation as Famechon fought Legrá toe-to-toe. The two boxed desperately, but Famechon prevailed. There was a huge ovation when the referee and sole judge, George Smith, gave Famechon the nod on points: 74–73.

'They told me the world was my oyster if I won,' Famechon explained to me years later at his home in the Melbourne bayside suburb of Frankston. 'Seeing as how I enjoy oysters, I went for it with everything I had.'

Born Jean-Pierre Famechon in Paris in 1945, the future world champion had come to Australia as a small boy, following his father, Andre Famechon, a tough brawler who battled some of Australia's best.

Andre's brother, Emile, the French flyweight champion, also became a main event fighter in Australia, and another of Fammo's uncles, featherweight Ray Famechon, fought the sublimely skilled Willie Pep for the world featherweight title in 1950.

Fammo was 11 when he was separated from his mother and brother. He was told that they were going back to their native France for a holiday while he stayed at a boarding school in Sunbury, Melbourne. As Antoinette Famechon left her husband and set sail from Melbourne, however, she knew that neither she, nor her nine-year-old son Christian, would return.

By his teens, Jean-Pierre, an apprentice electrician who was now known in Melbourne as Johnny Famechon, was starting to earn comparisons with Pep for his brilliant boxing. Disregarding the opinion of his father, who felt that his son didn't hit hard enough to be a boxer, Fammo signed on with Ambrose Palmer as his trainer-manager. He had long been impressed by the skills of another Palmer fighter, Max Carlos, and carried out Palmer's famous 'method' of boxing to the letter, perfecting a darting, weaving, hit-and-not-get-hit style.

Famechon never fought as an amateur, deciding that if he was going to get punched he might as well get paid for it. He was just 16 when he turned pro, with a three-round draw against flyweight Sammy Lang earning him £3. Famechon won the Australian title in 1964 with a 15-round decision over Rome Olympics bronze medallist Ollie Taylor.

A stoppage win over Billy Males followed, and Fammo outpointed the American Don Johnson. Then, at Melbourne's Festival Hall in 1967, he scored an 11th round stoppage of Scotland's John O'Brien for the Commonwealth featherweight title.

After winning the world championship from Legrá, Famechon made his first defence against a boxer well known to Australians:

Masahiko 'Fighting' Harada. Set for 28 July 1969 at Sydney Stadium, the undercard was to feature other top Australians Tony Mundine, Paul Moore and Paul Ferreri. The referee and sole judge would be the former champ Willie Pep, all the way from Connecticut.

For the entire 15 rounds, Harada kept walking forwards, throwing heavy punches, just as he had done against Lionel Rose. Harada went down in Round 5, but Famechon was decked three times. In Round 11 an ankle injury affected his mobility. At the final bell, Pep tallied his scorecard and signalled a draw.

Immediately, the crowd started hooting. A check of Pep's scorecard revealed that Famechon had actually won by a point – 70 to 69 – six rounds to five, with four even.

Famechon returned to London for two non-title fights, then flew to Tokyo to defend his title against Harada in a rematch on 6 January 1970.

Famechon had won only 19 of his 64 fights by knockout and did not have a reputation as a heavy puncher. He had a point to prove, however. In the 14th round, Fammo clipped Harada with a right hand. Ambrose Palmer screamed from the corner: 'Go, Johnny, go!' and Fammo knocked Harada clean out of the ring. He knocked him out of boxing, too; Harada never fought again.

On 9 May 1970, Fammo defended his title against Mexican southpaw Vicente Saldivar in Rome, but Saldivar won a unanimous decision over 15 rounds. Just 25 years old, Famechon never fought again. He later became a top referee and, despite a daily diet of six Gitanes cigarettes, an avid long-distance runner.

Famechon may have been the slickest boxer Australia ever produced, but in retirement, overcoming horrific adversity, he rose to even greater heights.

Once he could dodge punches the way Superman dodged bullets, but nothing had prepared him for the first knockout loss of his career, when he walked into the path of a car doing 100 kilometres per hour down the Hume Highway at Warwick Farm in Sydney's west. He was sent cartwheeling through the air and onto his head. That was August 1991.

At the time of the accident, Famechon had no identification on him, and in Liverpool Hospital, where the emergency team fought to save his life, John Famechon became John Doe. What was left of his broken body looked so fit that doctors estimated he was in his late 20s. He was actually 46. But his head was so badly damaged that he was unrecognisable.

'John was in a coma for three weeks,' his wife, Glenys, told me years later, 'and during that time he suffered a stroke that completely paralysed the left side of his body. He had been at a sporting function at Warwick Farm and was heading back to his hotel when the car hit him. He spent a month in Liverpool Hospital and then months in hospitals in Melbourne.'

Glenys had met Famechon, a father of two, on a blind date a year before the accident, following the break-up of his marriage. Now the great champion sat slumped in his wheelchair as though he'd been poured into it; his once rock-hard body limp as an old rag, his head tilted to the right and his chin lolling on his chest. The wasted muscles in his frail neck could no longer hold the weight of his damaged brain.

Famechon was unable to walk, barely able to talk, unable to dress himself. The trauma to his brain made it hard for Johnny to fathom the doctor's words: 'This will be your life now ... you must accept it.'

Glenys was now faced with the choice of caring for a new boyfriend in a near-vegetative state, or simply walking away.

And yet, before Floyd Mayweather Jr, before Sugar Ray Leonard, there was Famechon using the 20 feet by 20 feet canvas of the boxing ring to create masterpieces as the best featherweight in the world. Nimble feet and an even more agile brain. Exquisite timing and a sixth sense for avoiding danger.

'Just look at the old films of him in the sixties,' said Jeff Fenech, who held the same world title 20 years later. 'The skills, the speed, the class. Johnny Famechon was an artist.'

There was a portrait of the artist as a young man in Famechon's Frankston house in December 1993 when he was first visited by Ragnar Purje, a martial arts wizard with a passion for education. Ragnar looked at the portrait and remembered all those great performances at Melbourne's Festival Hall and Sydney Stadium, in Paris, London and Tokyo.

Ragnar and Famechon had met through a mutual friend who believed that Ragnar's studies of the brain and cognitive function might help reignite the old spark in his ailing friend.

Famechon could barely communicate above a slurred whisper but for three hours Ragnar sat with him, captivated by the potential encased in that damaged head.

For three hours he held Famechon's left hand, which had atrophied into a useless closed fist. For three hours Ragnar opened and closed that fist, moving the fingers about, getting the brain used to simple muscular tasks.

'I've been involved in karate for more than 40 years,' Ragnar told me, 'and from my martial arts background and studies in physical education and sports science I believe the only way you can get through to the brain is through movement. The only way children learn and stimulate their brains is through moving about. That was certainly the case with Johnny.'

Ragnar excited Famechon's mind by talking to him about his boxing career and beating the greatest of his day. He would draw Johnny's attention to the portrait of him as world champion. 'What does that photo mean to you?' he'd ask.

'How good-looking I am,' Famechon would mumble in a barely audible whisper.

It was the start of verbal sparring between the two that lasted almost 30 years.

'Humour was John's way of coping with what had happened,' Ragnar said. 'His brain still had that sharp wit and I looked at ways of making it heal the rest of him.

'At the end of our first session I asked John if he wanted me to come back. His head was still buried in his chest and I could hardly hear what he was saying but he mumbled, "Okay – but I'll take it easy on you."'

Famechon probably would have stayed in his wheelchair if not for Ragnar driving the 120 kilometres from Geelong to Frankston every Saturday to give the stricken champ a workout he found more gruelling than 15 rounds.

Ragnar, who had three Master of Education awards and was teaching on the Gold Coast when I met him, would start by opening and closing Famechon's fist, moving his fingers. Before long he was helping Famechon lift his arm. Then he got him to do it all by himself.

Within three months, Famechon was taking his first steps out of the chair. Small steps with a walking stick. But steps just the same.

'When that happened we just cried, the three of us, and had a big group hug,' Glenys said. 'John had come out of a very bad place.'

For the next six years Ragnar was at Fammo's side, making the exercises harder and more complex, getting Fammo to ride a stationary bike while dodging light punches, multiple tasks that fired up the old champ's brain like the furnace of a vast, complex but damaged machine.

'We would finish every session exhausted,' Famechon said, 'and I wished he would go away. But he kept coming back.'

Ragnar said much of the credit for Fammo's comeback to life must go to Glenys, who stuck by Fammo's side through thick and thin, in sickness and in health.

After the accident Johnny still planned to marry Glenys but said he wouldn't do it until he could walk down the aisle by himself.

He kept her waiting for a few years but finally walked down the aisle unassisted in a Frankston wedding chapel in March 1997.

The 137 guests included Fammo's former sparring partner Lionel Rose and Ragnar Purje, the man who had helped Fammo walk and talk and live again.

'Fammo screamed with talent in his boxing career,' Ragnar told me, 'but it was after his accident that he really showed the qualities of a champion.

'He showed the world what you can achieve with pride and determination. And a will to win.'

Johnny Famechon AM passed away aged 77 on 4 August 2022. Like Lionel Rose, he was awarded a state funeral.

Bobby Dunlop: The Ironman of Australian Boxing

Superfit Bobby Dunlop was the hot favourite to beat former world light-heavyweight champion Jose Torres when they entered the ring at Sydney Stadium on 1 April 1968.

Torres was something of a poet and a dreamer who would later write critically acclaimed biographies of Muhammad Ali and Mike Tyson.

The Puerto Rican had won a silver medal at the Melbourne Olympics in 1956 and, nine years later, trained by Cus D'Amato, had taken the world light-heavyweight title from tricky Willie Pastrano, the slick boxer whose style influenced the moves of his training partner, the young Muhammad Ali.

But when he arrived in Sydney, Torres was coming off his second defeat at the hands of Nigerian Dick Tiger, who had taken his world crown. Rumours abounded that the big-punching Torres was more interested in drinking with his buddy, the novelist Norman Mailer, than he was in putting up much resistance against this tough kid from Australia.

Dunlop was an imposing physical specimen at 185 centimetres, 79 kilograms, lean and superbly conditioned.

He was born in Ivanhoe, Victoria, the son of a policeman, and started boxing with Melbourne trainer Billy Murphy.

Dunlop made his professional debut at age 17 in 1963 and at 19 challenged unsuccessfully for the Australian light-heavyweight title, when he was disqualified for backhanding against Clive Stewart at Newcastle.

Dunlop moved to Sydney to train with Ern McQuillan and scored big wins against tough opposition, including Roy Thurgar and the heavyweight Foster Bibron.

At 21, Dunlop was ranked in the world's top ten light-heavyweights, partly on the recommendation of America's former world heavyweight champ Rocky Marciano, who had seen him fight at South Sydney Leagues Club.

In February 1968, Dunlop scored a seventh-round stoppage over Young McCormack to capture the Commonwealth title. The next day he was at work, laying a concrete footpath for Ashfield Council.

Dunlop was now 22 and the betting market suggested that José Torres, 10 years older, was past it when they squared off on 1 April. Torres hadn't fought in 11 months and, by the look of the spare tyre around his midsection, many experts predicted he would quickly go belly up under the stadium lights.

But Torres still possessed knockout power, and while he was training at Billy McConnell's Chippendale gym he knocked out former Aussie champ Billy Stanley while sparring.

Torres came out against Dunlop with his hands held high in front of his face in the distinctive peek-a-boo style that Cus D'Amato taught all his fighters, including Mike Tyson.

Dunlop landed some good jabs in the first round and shook Torres in the second, but it only stoked the fire in the belly of the paunchy, punching poet.

Dunlop was susceptible to overhand rights, and that was Torres's best punch.

By Round 6 Dunlop was badly cut over the right eye and was helpless against the ropes. Torres motioned to referee Vic Patrick that he should save the Australian from worse.

Renowned columnist Jeff Wells wrote: 'It was an act of compassion by Torres which so moved Patrick that he offered to shout Torres a schooner of beer – which is something no journalist who has gargled away half his wages at Patrick's Invicta Hotel [in Surry Hills] could remember happening before.'

Dunlop got his career back on track when he outpointed Italian Giulio Rinaldi, who had been in the ring with all-time great Archie Moore among other world-rated light-heavyweights.

Then, moving into the heavyweight division in 1969, Dunlop captured the Australian title when he stopped Tokyo Olympian Fred Casey in Brisbane.

He then defeated Canadian Al Sparks over 15 in a Commonwealth light-heavyweight title bout in Melbourne but lost in Round 9 to world-rated heavyweight Henry Clark in Auckland.

Clark had defeated heavyweight contenders Leotis Martin and Eddie Machen and lost against the fearsome former world champ Sonny Liston.

Dunlop gave Clark the fight of his life for eight rounds before the power and extra weight of the American proved too much.

After retiring from the ring at just 24, Dunlop became a merchant seaman based at Maroubra in Sydney's east.

He also took up smoking, and the once super-fit Commonwealth champ passed away from a heart attack in Kempsey aged just 54.

THE SIZZLING SEVENTIES

Tony Mundine: Speed + Power = Excitement

Lionel Rose inspired Indigenous men and women around Australia, including the lightning-fast Tony Mundine.

For pure excitement, there were fewer more sensational boxers and I considered it a wonderful privilege to have worked beside his trainer of the time, the livewire Charlie Gergen, in Mundine's corner for his fight against the rugged Canadian-based Scot Murray Sutherland at Brisbane's Festival Hall in 1982.

In the dressing-room before that fight, Tony told me all about the brilliant sporting prowess of his seven-year-old son Anthony, who everyone called 'Choc', because he loved chocolate so much.

Tony had 96 professional fights between 1969 and 1984, and more than a quarter of them were in Brisbane, which became a second home to him.

'Yeah, I had a lot of big fights at Festival Hall and at the Milton Tennis Stadium, open air,' he said. 'I fought some good fighters in Brisbane – Jackson McQuade, Lonnie Harris, Carlos Marks, Jesse Burnett, Steve Aczel. I fought Bunny Sterling, from England, for the Commonwealth middleweight title at Milton in 1972.

I knocked him out in the last round to win the title. They were 15-round fights in those days, you don't have them anymore.'

Tony did it tough growing up in northern New South Wales in the 1950s and 1960s.

'I knew hard times, but that's life, and I kicked on. I still have a lot of relatives up in Baryulgil, near Grafton. We come from the Bundjalung people. Most of our people in Baryulgil worked in the asbestos mines and cancer was everywhere. My dad was 6 feet, 3 inches (190 cm) and solid. When he died at 51 he was like a bloody matchstick. The cancer killed a lot of his brothers too and some of my sisters. Where I grew up we had no electricity. After my youngest brother Leon was born, my mother's spine was damaged and she lost the use of one of her legs. She had to raise nine kids in a shack dad built at Baryulgil. We had no running water, either, and when she had to wash clothes she used to drag herself on one leg to the creek and sit there from daylight to dusk.'

Tony worked in the asbestos mine in the mid 1960s for about 18 months and also worked as a stockman for two or three years.

'But I also had a few fights in Grafton in the travelling boxing tent show of Jimmy Sharman. Every October the boxing tents came to Grafton. We'd get £5 to fight three or four rounds. That was a lot of money back then, especially for a poor teenage boy. I had maybe half a dozen fights in the tents and I did pretty good.

'Then in 1968 something big happened in the lives of all Aboriginal people. Lionel Rose won the world bantamweight title against Fighting Harada in Japan. It lifted me a lot and it was a real boost for Aboriginal people right around Australia to see this young Aboriginal boy on top of the world. It inspired me that I could reach the top, too.'

Tony left Baryulgil for Sydney, at first hoping to make it big in rugby league. He had played in the centres for a team in Grafton and at 17 was offered a place with the Redfern All Blacks in the South Sydney Junior Rugby League.

'I played a little bit in Sydney. But I was working out at a gym and I ended up training with Ern McQuillan, who trained many Australian boxing champions. Boxing came naturally to me. There are Aboriginal kids around Australia who all have natural sporting talent but I was lucky that I was able to develop that talent. I had my first professional fight in 1969.'

Unlike his son in later years, Tony had neither the luxury of a huge support base nor the financial backing to promote his own fights and he was often overmatched against dangerous opponents.

He turned pro in 1969 with McQuillan as his trainer. In his fifth fight, he had to climb off the canvas to beat Ray Wheatley at the Manly-Warringah Leagues Club, and he suffered a shock loss to New Zealand slugger Kahu Mahanga in a *TV Ringside* classic.

But he came back to fight on the last-ever card at Sydney Stadium on 9 June 1970, before Huge Deal McIntosh's vast arena was demolished to make way for the Eastern Suburbs railway line.

Tony knocked out Filipino Ravalo with a left rip to the body in Round 2, the last punch thrown at the Stadium. Jimmy Carruthers counted out the stricken fighter before raising Mundine's hand.

The fight card for the final program also saw boxing brothers Paul and Alan Moore, and the slick Garry Dean appear.

A crowd of 10,000 left the building to the strains of *Auld Lang Syne* after former champions Carruthers, Vic Patrick, George Barnes, Jack Hassen, Hughie Dwyer and Rocky Gattellari climbed into the ring to wave farewell.

In 1972 Mundine was the Australian middleweight champ and he was too fast for heavyweight champ Foster Bibron. Mundine was 74 kilograms and Bibron 95.5 kilograms.

Mundine was also too fast for heavyweight Maile Haumono, the father of rugby league strongman and boxer Solomon Haumono.

Tony beat former world champion Denny Moyer of America, Frenchman Max Cohen and all-time great Emile Griffith in Paris, which he rates as the best win of his long career.

Despite another shock knockout defeat against American Bennie Briscoe in Paris in 1974, Mundine challenged Carlos Monzón for the world middleweight title in Argentina later that year.

Monzón, who would later be convicted of murder, hadn't lost for ten years and was South America's strutting symbol of overt machismo. The President of Argentina, Juan Domingo Perón, had recently died and the country was in chaos, with machine gun-toting soldiers on every corner.

The atmosphere in Luna Park Stadium that night was nightmarish, with the crowd of 25,000 smashing against high wire fences screaming, 'Kill Mundine, kill Mundine.' More fearful of the crowd than his formidable opponent, Mundine started superbly, but was knocked out in the seventh round. In the dressing-room, he wept for 15 minutes into his blood-soaked towel.

'Carlos was the best fighter I ever faced, the hardest puncher too,' Mundine told me. 'He was very tall and he had great range and timing. He had a terrific eye and the ability to pick off your punches.

'I went seven rounds with him and I thought at one stage I had him gone but back in those days I had trouble making the middleweight limit (72 kg). Now they have a super-middleweight division (76 kg) which would have suited me, but back then I had to lose about 11 or 12 pounds (5–6 kg) every fight. I lost a lot of strength just making the weight limit.'

In 1975 at Sydney's Blacktown RSL, Mundine took the Australian and Commonwealth light-heavyweight titles in 12 rounds from tough Steve Aczel, who later joked that Mundine had caught him with about 200 lucky punches.

Under new trainer Charlie Gergen, Mundine rekindled his love affair with Europe, going close to outpointing Olympic gold medallist Mate Parlov in a WBC cruiserweight (86 kg) eliminator in Italy in 1979, and outpointing Ugandan world-title challenger Mustafa Wassaja in France three years later.

Mundine's rematch win over Aczel in 1980 at Brisbane's Festival Hall was the first professional fight I saw, and I got to know him well on his regular appearances in Queensland, including his loss to the Native American Yacqui López in a fight promoted by the then 19-year-old Peter Foster, later notorious as an international conman.

Mundine finally retired after being outpointed by New Zealander Alex Sua at Carlaw Park in Auckland in 1984. He said that he was going to spend his retirement watching his son Anthony play rugby league and basketball. It was to be in boxing, however, that Mundine junior would make his mark.

Even after his 70th birthday in 2021, Tony still looked fit enough to fight professionally.

'I never smoked, drank or took drugs and I tell everyone to eat clean and take care of your body and your mind,' he told me. 'I've got three kids, 12 grandkids. I've still got a brain and I still keep fit by training every day. I'm proud of who I am; proud of what I did.'

Until he saw his son Anthony become a champion in rugby league and boxing, Tony's biggest source of pride was the home he bought his parents at Earlwood, in Sydney's inner-west, with the money he made from boxing. 'Even if I didn't earn anything else, that home I bought my parents made all the years in boxing worthwhile.'

Thirty-five years after I was in his corner when he dropped a decision against Murray Sutherland, a future world champ, Tony could only gasp in astonishment at the achievements of son Anthony, by then a three-time world champion, preparing for his rematch with Danny Green at Adelaide Oval in 2017, a rematch that Mundine lost on points.

'Back when he was a little boy, Choc was scoring tries all the time in junior rugby league,' Tony told me. 'He was scoring nine or ten tries a game. I used to give him a dollar for every try he scored. That was a fair bit of money 35 years ago. He was sending me broke.

'Anthony was a great basketballer and footballer as a kid and whatever else he wanted to do. He had great natural ability but back then I didn't think that he would go on to win three world boxing titles. To be fair, he was fighting at a time when there were a lot more organisations and weight divisions. When I was fighting you only had one world champion in each weight class. Now you have four.'

Who would have won if father and son had fought each other in their primes?

'My son is a great boxer but I was a bigger puncher,' Tony explained. 'I could punch with either hand. When I hit someone clean it was goodnight. I used to knock people clean out.'

Henry Nissen: From the Holocaust to Humanitarian

Little Henry Nissen was a hero to fight fans for his whole-hearted performances as the Commonwealth flyweight champion.

He was a good boxer but a great humanitarian, who became a tireless social worker, helping the homeless and underprivileged.

Though just 155 centimetres and 51 kilograms, Henry was a giant among his peers.

His harrowing and inspiring journey began in the Officers' Headquarters in a displaced persons camp outside the former Bergen-Belsen concentration camp in Germany.

Henry was born there ten minutes before his brother, Leon, on 15 January 1948. His parents were Holocaust survivors. His mother Sonia was a Ukrainian Jew and his father Sam

Nissenbaum, a Polish Jew. The couple had met in the Soviet Union, where they were hiding from Nazis.

The combined Bergen-Belsen camp, where at least 70,000 victims of the Nazis perished, had been converted to a refugee camp after the war. All 20 of Sam's Polish Jewish family had been murdered and Anne Frank, whose diary became a literary classic, had died there only weeks before liberation.

The Nissenbaums eventually migrated to Australia, where they settled in Melbourne's North Carlton near the gym of former Australian middleweight champ Peter Read, and at 14 the twins started training to avoid the blows of the bigger boys in the schoolyard.

Read had fought for Australia at the 1956 Melbourne Olympics, where he'd lost to silver medallist José Torres.

In 1970 Leon became Australian amateur flyweight champion by beating Joey Donovan, an Indigenous star who had fought at the Mexico City Olympics two years earlier.

At the Edinburgh Commonwealth Games that year, Leon lost to silver medallist Leo Rwabwogo of Uganda and hung up his gloves.

Henry, though, decided to turn pro.

In just his third pro fight, he won the Australian flyweight title by outpointing Harry Hayes, a cousin of Lionel Rose, over 15 rounds at St Kilda's Earls Court. He also beat other top Aussies Willie Leslie and Brian Roberts.

In 1971 he stopped Scotland's Johnny McCluskey for the Commonwealth crown at a time when Australia had four other Commonwealth champs – Paul Ferreri, Bobby Dunne, Charkey Ramon and Tony Mundine.

Henry lost his title to Big Jim West three years later, and after losing a rematch he retired with a pro record of 16 wins in 18 fights.

In recent years he has worked six-day, 80-hour weeks in support of Melbourne's homeless, believing that the whole human race is just one big family.

Hector Thompson and the Hands of Stone

Hector Thompson was a mighty body puncher who famously gave all-time great world champ Roberto Durán one of the toughest nights of his career and left the Panamanian legend known as 'The Hands of Stone' in hospital.

He also suffered the ultimate boxing tragedy of a fatal victory, not once but twice.

Born in Kempsey, New South Wales, and raised in a boys home, he turned professional in 1970 under the guidance of Newcastle trainer Ron Short.

He had 16 fights in his first year, one of them a tenth round stoppage of Croatian-born Melbourne fighter Roko Spanja, who died from the injuries.

Thompson lost a decision to Ray McGrady but then outpointed Bobby Cotterill and *TV Ringside* favourite Hillary Connolly before taking the Australian lightweight title from Leo Young in Melbourne.

Thompson was to become a big crowd favourite at Brisbane's Festival Hall for his wily trainer and promoter, the rock-faced hard man Reg Layton.

In 1972 Thompson outpointed Jeff White over 15 rounds to win the Australian light-welterweight title and then outpointed Kiwi Manny Santos for the Australasian title.

A 15-round decision over Ghana's Joe Tetteh followed for the Commonwealth crown.

Thompson then challenged Roberto Durán in Panama in 1973 for the world lightweight title.

Forty-four years later I cornered Durán at the Horn-Pacquiao fight and asked him about that battle.

'Hector Thompson was a very good boxer, a great boxer,' Durán told me, 'but I stopped him in eight rounds. It was an exciting fight. When he arrived in Panama, Hector tried to scare me. He told me he used to eat raw meat and that he was going to kill me. I said, "I eat beans and rice and I will knock you out."'

Thompson had made a name for his ability to absorb punishment and then grind down opponents in the later rounds. But Durán hit harder than anyone Thompson had ever faced.

Still, he made a great fight of it before succumbing to a fusillade in the eighth. Ismael Laguna, another great Panamanian lightweight, recalled the fight as one of Durán's toughest, and remembered how Durán had been so dazed by Thompson's punches that several times he forgot where his corner was.

Back in Australia, Thompson scored two big wins over Argentina's Carlos Maria Gimenez and American Jimmy Heair.

He stopped former world light-welterweight champ Alfonso 'Peppermint' Frazer but suffered a knockout in three rounds to Mexican Javier Ayala when the Australian sustained a torn cartilage in his knee.

Thompson hit back hard, beating Japan's world title contender Lion Furuyama and Samoan Ali Afakasi by tenth-round knockout, to retain his Commonwealth crown in Brisbane.

At the end of 1975, Thompson challenged Antonio Cervantes, of Venezuela, for the World Boxing Association (WBA) light-welterweight title, again in Panama.

The lanky South American had already made nine title defences but Thompson began the fight well, and after six rounds was so full of confidence that he told Reg Layton that he could feel Cervantes weakening.

But in the seventh round, Cervantes, who was ahead on points, cut Thompson's eye and Layton stopped the fight before the start of Round 8.

On April Fool's Day 1976, Thompson stopped American Chuck Wilburn in ten rounds at Blacktown in Sydney. Wilburn tragically died of his injuries.

The next year, Lawrence 'Baby Cassius' Austin took Thompson's Commonwealth crown.

His career finished in 1980 with back-to-back knockout losses to Frank Ropis and Steve Dennis.

Charkey Ramon and the Opera House Brawl

Charkey Ramon was a tough farm boy born Dave Ballard. He was given his fighting name by the eccentric trainer Bernie Hall, the first boxer to go the distance in Australia with the American lightweight Freddie Dawson.

Bernie believed that the black Americans were the best fighters (Charkey as in charcoal) and the Mexicans weren't far behind. Bernie liked the Mexican name Ramon.

Dave Ballard and his brother John, a lightweight Bernie nicknamed Bricky Squire, were first taught the basics of boxing by their father Squire Ballard, who owned several thousand acres at Gulgong near Mudgee, New South Wales.

Dave was the New South Wales amateur light-middleweight champion and a veteran of tent show boxing. He turned pro in 1970 and fought ten times in his first five months.

He suffered his only loss the following year when the much bigger Samoan Fred Etuati outpointed him in Sydney over eight rounds.

But in 1972 Ramon scored a third-round knockout over Paul Lovi to win the Australian light-middleweight (70 kg) title and then captured the Commonwealth title with an eight-round stoppage of Englishman Pat Dwyer in Melbourne.

He outpointed Frenchman Jacques Kechichian in Noumea in a two-man war and scored an 11-round stoppage of Canadian Donato Paduano in a Commonwealth title defence.

In the last fight of his career Ramon stopped tough Mexican Manuel Fierro in seven rounds in Brisbane, solidifying his spot as the top contender for world champ Koichi Wajima of Japan.

A surfing mishap wrecked Ramon's shoulder and he never boxed again.

His last fight inside the ring was on 2 April 1982 at the Sydney Opera House. I had been in Sydney only a few weeks when I found myself ringside, covering my first fight night in the big city.

Alex Temelkov and another Bernie Hall fighter, Ken Salisbury, were boxing for Ramon's old Australian title. Temelkov repeatedly fouled Salisbury and the pugnacious Hall, his silver mane swishing, leapt onto the ring apron, grabbed Temelkov in a headlock and prompted a 14-man brawl inside the ring.

Charkey, wearing the referee's bow tie, was king hit from several angles but gave a lot better than he got, the old body punches as solid as ever.

The Morwell Rock who Conquered the World

Born in central Italy in 1953 to a father who idolised heavyweight great Rocky Marciano, Rocco Mattioli came to Australia with his family at age six.

He left the Morwell Sacred Heart Convent School in Gippsland at 15 with a reputation for street fighting, though he said it was only because he was always being called a 'wog'.

He became an apprentice boilermaker and later a favourite on *TV Ringside*, almost always guaranteeing a knockout.

A tremendous puncher with an aggressive, brawling style, Rocco was first coached by Ambrose Palmer. He turned pro in 1970, beating Tony Salta, Glenn Grinsted and Alby Roberts. He had just one loss in his first 20 fights before being outhustled over ten rounds by slick Paul Moore at Brunswick in Melbourne.

'I remember Mattioli being a very strong, hard puncher but he was suspect against skilful, technical boxers in those days,' Paul Moore told me. 'He went on to win a world title and I feel honoured to have fought him.'

Mattioli won a close rematch against Moore and in 1973 stopped Jeff White in 12 for the Australian welterweight title in Melbourne.

He outpointed America's former world junior-welterweight champ Eddie Perkins in 1974 but the following year suffered his first stoppage loss, on cuts, to Samoan Ali Afakasi, in a fight for the Australasian welterweight title.

But Mattioli was resilient. He came back to score a fifth-round stoppage of America's former world welterweight champ Billy Backus at Melbourne's Festival Hall.

Leading American welterweight Harold Weston outpointed Mattioli in Melbourne in Rocky's last bout before he decided to base himself back in his native Italy.

There he drew with Italy's popular former junior-welterweight champ Bruno Acari and won seven straight before a crushing knockout of Germany's Eckhard Dagge in Berlin gave him the WBC junior-middleweight (70 kg) crown in 1977.

Back in Melbourne the following year, The Rock pounded Elisha Obed of the Bahamas at the Kooyong tennis courts and then stopped José Manuel Durán of Spain in Abruzzo, Italy.

In 1979 he finally crumbled against West Indian–born British southpaw Maurice Hope, losing his world title in the ninth round in San Remo, Italy, after breaking his wrist early in the fight.

Hope stopped him again in 11 rounds at Wembley in London in 1980.

Rocky retired two years later.

Paul Moore and his brother Alan both won the Australian welterweight title after starting their boxing careers on their father Selby's travelling boxing show.

Paul recalled: 'Everyone who went to the country shows in the sixties would remember the fighters lined up and people willing to have a crack at them. My first job was at 15, banging the drum to stir up the crowd, and it was always the case that most people would say, "I want to fight the little bloke banging the drum."'

Paul went on to have 53 professional bouts, starting at Festival Hall, Brisbane, in 1968, and ending at the Palais des

Sports in Paris in 1973 on the undercard to Tony Mundine's win over Emile Griffith.

Wally Carr and his Flying Grandson

Rugby league's flying winger Josh Addo-Carr said the passing of his grandfather Wally Carr did not destroy him but only made him stronger.

Wally, who won Australian titles in three weight divisions, had lost a short battle with stomach cancer in early April 2019 at the age of 64.

The Canterbury-Bankstown winger told *The Sydney Morning Herald* that he'd spent the weeks before Carr's death flying between Sydney and Melbourne, desperate to spend as much time with his grandfather before his health took a final turn.

A Wiradjuri man who was born and raised in Wellington, New South Wales, Carr won twelve titles across six different divisions and fought everywhere from featherweight to heavyweight.

Wally never knew his father, who took his own life before Wally was born. As a boy, he was taken from his mother, and he told Phil Mercer of the BBC that growing up, he moved around often and lived with six different families in six different towns.

At 16, he made his way from the cotton fields around Warren in western New South Wales to Sydney, where he lived with his aunt.

He watched his first professional boxing match on television in the days of *TV Ringside*.

'She had the TV on one night,' he recalled, 'and the fights were on, and all these blackfellas were fighting. I said, "Aunty, how much do the blackfellas get a fight?" She said $50, $100 a fight. I said, "Oh, fair dinkum?" I said, "Well, that's me – I am going to learn to fight," because I was only getting $32 a week wages.'

His first visit to the gym was a painful experience. 'I had blood pouring out of me but I wouldn't go down, naturally, and the trainer said, "You're not real good at fighting, brother, but you've got plenty of ticker."'

'Wait a While' Wally made his debut as a featherweight in 1971.

He went on to fight professionally for 15 years and had 100 professional bouts.

In 1976 he shocked the boxing world by scoring a sixth-round knockout over world rated Kiwi Monty Betham to capture the Australasian light-middleweight crown at the Wellington Town Hall in New Zealand. Betham's son Monty Jr represented New Zealand in rugby league and won eight of nine pro fights.

In 1977 Wally beat the super-talented Johnny Layton for the Australian 70 kilogram title at the Marrickville RSL.

The following year he stopped big-punching Fijian-born Al Korovou in Round 13 to capture the Australian middleweight crown.

Moving up to light-heavyweight, Carr captured another national title in 1984 when he outpointed Tommy West over 12 rounds at Marrickville.

In a non-title battle with world super-middleweight champion Chong-Pal Park in South Korea, Wally made the local hero fight for every point before winning a decision.

Wally announced his retirement in 1986 after a fifth-round stoppage loss to world-rated Doug Sam in Canberra.

Boxing had taken him around Australia and to Korea, New Zealand, New Caledonia, Zambia, Papua New Guinea, Fiji and Indonesia. But without it, his life began to unravel. Gripped by drug and alcohol addiction, he became destitute.

He told the BBC: 'I slept in a park for three years, slept in empty houses, very heavy on marijuana, very heavy on cocaine, and one of my daughters came over to visit me and found me on a footpath.

'I'd just had a heart attack. I just said enough is enough and I stopped everything that day.'

One Flash Boxer

One of the slickest boxers I've ever saw was Jeff 'Flash' Malcolm, who was the star of the Newtown Police Youth Club when Jeff Fenech started training there.

Malcolm was a brilliant southpaw who spent more than 30 years perfecting the art of hitting without being hit, compiling 100 professional victories along the way.

He was just 15 when he had his first pro fight, and he went on to fight the cream of Australia's talent in a career that spanned four decades.

Hector Thompson took a split decision over Malcolm at Orange in 1978 but the following year the Flash outpointed Barry Michael and then Lachie 'Baby Cassius' Austin for the Commonwealth junior-welterweight (63.5 kg) crown.

Perhaps Malcolm's greatest win was a one-sided decision over the American rising star Bobby Joe Young in Ohio in 1983. Young had beaten the great Thomas Hearns twice in the amateurs and became the only man to score a professional win over the legendary Aaron Pryor.

American Manning Galloway outpointed Malcolm in a WBO welterweight title bout on the Gold Coast in 2001, but the Flash fought on for another 11 years until he finally posted his century of wins at age 46.

A Heavy-hitting Author

Shane Weaver was once an Australian boxing champion and, according to his autobiography, a human punching bag, drug dealer, heroin junkie, standover man and alcoholic deadbeat.

He once worked as a psychiatric nurse, hoping that life with the psychotics and faeces eaters would silence the screaming spiders in his own nightmares.

He ran away to Perth with his wife and kids to escape murderous drug dealers after ripping them off, and for years was barely surviving, working long exhausting hours washing dishes in a Perth restaurant.

He had eight children from two marriages but was impotent for many years and needed injections in his penis to sire the last three.

Some of his finest moments were fuelled by blind rage at a time when he said he was a 'cyclone of hate'.

A self-described bog-ugly, bed-wetting teenager, Shane Weaver was once ambivalent about his sexuality and used to frequent the most notorious pubs in western Sydney's Blacktown wearing eye shadow and lipstick, ready to beat anyone to a pulp who looked at him sideways.

Weaver, who boxed under the name Shane Patrick, turned pro in 1971. He won the Australian title four years later at the Blacktown RSL, with a 15-round decision against Darwin southpaw Ricky Patterson after the retirement of Charkey Ramon.

Weaver honed his skills sparring with a young Ray Wheatley who, in the words of Weaver, was 'a light-heavyweight who moved like a lightweight'.

Rather than dull his mind, the savage fights he had with Ricky Patterson, Terry Fox, Joe Keresi and Alex Burns only added to the lurid tapestry of his life, which he laid bare, like a festering sore, in his autobiography *Blacktown*.

In the book, Weaver wrote of his dysfunctional family, detailing his mother's suicide attempts and the whippings from his stepfather, a traumatised, crippled Korean War veteran.

Weaver's remarkable memoir hit bookshelves in Australia in 2003 with all the impact of the non-stop assault that made him a champion boxer. By then, he was the creative director of OgilvyOne Worldwide and living in a luxury apartment overlooking the ocean in Hong Kong.

I later met Shane in a restaurant in Sydney. A man full of surprises, the once merciless boxing champion from a hard-scrabble existence in Sydney's west was wearing a kaftan.

Dean of American sports columnists Red Smith once said there was nothing to writing; all you did was sit down at a typewriter and open a vein. 'But for me writing this book was more like a cross between an exorcism and an enema,' Weaver told me. 'I had to get it all out but I found the whole experience both painful and therapeutic.

'I feel much more liberated than before I wrote the book. The spiders still scream occasionally and probably will until I die. But they are less strident than before.'

Shane was 50 when he wrote the book and he told me that the pain and suffering of his early years fuelled the intense rage that made him both a champion fighter and social misfit.

He said his success in advertising was a by-product of his own more deeply personal victories, vanquishing the demon drink, healing the wounds with the five children from his first marriage, and becoming the kind of husband and father he always wanted to be.

It was an astonishing journey for a man who wrote away to an ad agency for a job when he was down and out, telling them that, as an alcoholic former boxer experienced at working with lunatics, he knew what made people tick.

And it was an amazing trip for the former junkie who ended up in Cairns Base Hospital after slashing his wrists with a butcher's knife when his real dad rejected him.

In his book, Weaver wrote that a beer-bellied truckie with razor stubble, green teeth and tobacco breath was kind enough to give him a ride all the way from Cairns back to Sydney, feeding him hamburgers and Cokes down the Pacific Highway.

In return, the truckie only wanted a few kisses and some oral sex.

As Weaver wrote at the end of this jaw-dropping book: 'The truth is not always pretty but it is never as ugly as a lie.'

Shane died in 2004 aged just 51.

Arthur Tunstall aged 94 and Still Settling Old Scores

The colourful and controversial Arthur Tunstall had a passion for amateur boxing for most of his 94 years. But he found the real love of his life at a swimming pool when he was only 19.

Tunstall was never a boxer himself and counted his greatest victory as winning the hand of Peggy Craven, whom he wed in 1946. They were married for 67 years until her death in 2013.

Tunstall spent more than 60 years involved in Australian boxing and was an Olympic official from 1960 until 2000. He called everyone 'pal' whether friend or foe.

Feisty and dogged, he was in one scrap after another all his life. He occasionally scuffled with reporters and, right in front of me, was once bashed over the head with a laptop computer by a disgruntled Samoan boxer at the 2000 Olympic trials in Canberra.

Tunstall was a little man but a heavy hitter who carved senior roles for himself at nine Olympic Games and was secretary and treasurer of the Australian Commonwealth Games Association for 30 years from 1969.

He made many enemies and even in his 80s once told me that he was planning to 'get square with those bastards' who had voted him out as the secretary and treasurer of the Amateur Boxing Union of Australia, a position he held from 1953 to 1999.

He was frequently the centre of controversy over jokes that were labelled racist and for his old-school discipline against athletes who refused to toe his line.

'I don't believe in political correctness,' he once said. 'I'm of the old tribe and if I want to say something, I say it.'

At the 1990 Auckland Commonwealth Games, he suggested New Zealand be considered the seventh and eighth states of Australia. He sparked an international incident when, as chef de mission to the 1994 Commonwealth Games in Edmonton, Canada, he threatened to send Cathy Freeman home for carrying the Aboriginal flag in her victory lap after the 400 metres final, saying all Australians had to compete under the one flag.

As a media storm erupted around him, Tunstall explained he was just enforcing the rules that applied to all athletes, adding, 'I didn't even know what the Aboriginal flag bloody looked like.'

Freeman and Tunstall reconciled, though, and filmed a tea commercial in 1998 in which Tunstall, asked by Freeman how he'd like his brew served, delivered the punchline, 'Black is fine, thanks Cathy.'

Tunstall was born in Newcastle not long after the end of World War I. He left school in Sydney at 14 to become a fitter and turner, and then a foreman in a factory that built weighbridges. He had a sandwich shop for 19 years in inner-city Sydney and then spent a decade selling insurance before quitting to sell Australian sport to the world.

Tunstall's first sporting interest was in swimming, and he met Peggy at what was then called Redleaf Pool in Sydney's Double Bay, the expensive suburb where he lived almost all his life.

Tunstall became involved in boxing by helping out on amateur nights collecting judges' cards. But he was a terrier when he got his teeth into something, and before long he was secretary of the NSW Amateur Boxing Association, a position he held for 59 years.

During that time he made headlines as much for making offensive jokes, sometimes about Indigenous people and Jews, as for his work in driving sport. But Tunstall vehemently denied being racist, saying he was friends with many Indigenous athletes, a fact confirmed by the tributes following his death.

Tunstall was the manager of the 1960 Australian Olympic boxing team to Rome, which won two bronze medals for Mackay's Ollie Taylor and Sydney's Tony Madigan.

He helped the rise of great Australian fighters such as Joey Donovan, Lionel Rose, Jeff Fenech, Jeff Harding and Daniel Geale.

Tunstall was awarded an OBE in 1979 and, in 2005, was inducted into the Sport Australia Hall of Fame. The Arthur Tunstall Trophy is presented to the best boxer at each Australian Championships.

Following Tunstall's death in 2016 just shy of his 94th birthday, Australian Olympic Committee president John Coates said that Tunstall 'was at the forefront of the old school of voluntary sports administrators who did so much to create the Australian sports industry as we know it today'.

I had lunch occasionally with Arthur beside the water at Double Bay near where he met Peggy way back in 1941.

The last time was when he was closing in on his 90th birthday. He told me the secret to his long life was a good wife and sheer stubbornness.

He said that every morning as he creaked out of bed, he would put on his glasses, shuffle to the mirror, tell himself he was still a 'good sort' and repeat the mantra that had sustained him through countless battles. 'I say, "Arthur, today's another challenge, old son, and the bastards aren't going to beat you."'

THE EIGHTIES BOOM

Barry Michael and the Melbourne Wars

Barry Michael may have been the toughest boxer Australia produced, and in 60 professional fights he was never knocked off his feet.

He took gamesmanship to the extreme in his two biggest fights.

In stifling heat as Ash Wednesday fires roared around Melbourne in 1983, Michael constantly taunted his severely weight-drained arch foe Frank Ropis, asking him after every blow to Ropis's emaciated body: 'That one hurt, didn't it, Frank, that one too?'

'By the middle of the fight, Frank was completely rattled,' Michael told me. 'He was virtually frothing at the mouth with anger and missing wildly.'

Against Lester Ellis two years later, Michael was hit early in the battle by a huge left uppercut and right hand that broke his nose.

Ellis told me: 'All Barry said was, "My mother punches harder than that. Don't waste all your energy son, there's still 12 rounds to go."'

Throughout his career, Michael faced some of the hardest hitters of his generation, and although he was never off his feet, he had his eardrum busted in Guyana and suffered bad cuts in Indonesia and the Philippines. 'I'm substantially deaf on the left side, deaf on the right side, I've had plastic surgery over both eyes, 300 stitches over both eyes, my nose was busted four times and I had a broken left hand,' he said later, before adding with a wry laugh: 'But other than that I came out of boxing pretty well.'

Born Barry Michael Swettenham in Watford, London, in 1955, he took an arduous path to boxing fame, fighting for his life for years in places he says you wouldn't take a dog. Barry's beloved father, Len Swettenham, was his trainer, and was a realist when it came to the 'hurt business'. Boxing was all about exchanging brain cells for money, Len told me once, and the role of the men in a fighter's corner was to make sure not too many brain cells were lost in the exchange.

Michael migrated to Australia with his parents in 1957, and turned pro in 1973, beating good local fighters early in his career such as Andy Broome and Keith Ball before losing over 15 rounds to Billy Moeller for the Commonwealth junior-lightweight title in Orange, New South Wales, in 1976.

Two years later he was outpointed by Jeff Malcolm in Melbourne, but later in 1978 at Coonabarabran, New South Wales, he outpointed Billy Mulholland over 15 rounds for the Australian lightweight title.

It was an unhappy end to the year when he suffered a burst eardrum against world title contender Lennox Blackmoore in Guyana, but Michael came back to Melbourne to stop slick South African-born Blakeney 'Kid' Matthews.

A 15th-round stoppage of old foe Jimmy Brown followed in 1980, and in 1981 Michael gutsed out a 10-round decision over American bank robber Al 'Earthquake' Carter in a breathtaking scrap.

In 1982 Claude Noel scored a decision over Michael in a Commonwealth lightweight title bout in Melbourne, but the next year Michael took on Frank Ropis, who, apart from a disputed disqualification against Jeff Malcolm, had gone unbeaten in more than eight years.

The fight took place on 16 February 1983 in 46-degree heat with smoke from the raging Ash Wednesday bushfires blowing through the Melbourne Town Hall.

Michael and Ropis were the two most dangerous fighters Melbourne had seen for a long time, and while the city may have missed out on seeing the much-anticipated battle between Lionel Rose and Johnny Famechon, Michael–Ropis was the next best thing.

Michael was a natural 61 kilograms (135 lb) lightweight and Ropis a 66.5 kilograms (147 lb) welterweight. They had agreed to fight on compromise terms with a 63-kilogram limit in a fight billed as being for the Australasian light-welterweight title.

Ropis was the spiritual brother of Frank Flannery, a non-stop brawling puncher who had wins over big men such as Baby Cassius Austin, Hector Thompson and Dave Sarago.

Michael built up physically for the bout while Ropis came down in weight. Ultimately that weight reduction, the fierce heat, and the indomitable will of Michael all took their toll.

Howard Leigh, Melbourne's dapper ring announcer for decades, recalled that Ropis tried to lose too much weight too close to the fight and came into the ring like 'a walking skeleton'.

Frank landed some bombs in the middle rounds, but he wilted in the closing stages and was out on his feet at the end of ten rounds. Seconds into Round 11, referee Johnny Famechon stopped the fight.

Two years later Michael scored a one-sided 12-round decision over the Jack Rennie-trained Graeme Brooke in a Commonwealth lightweight title bout in Melbourne, then signed to face his young protégé Lester Ellis in Melbourne.

Lester had stunned Australian boxing by becoming the IBF world champion in February 1985 after just two years as a pro boxer.

Michael, who had spent 12 years as a pro, was understandably envious of this young blow-in. Michael would often travel to different Melbourne gyms to spar with all the young amateurs, and Lester was one of half a dozen youngsters Michael had sparred with years earlier. 'Lester was 12 and I was 22 and he attacked me with everything he had,' Michael told me later. 'Even back then he said he was going to be a world champion.'

They agreed to fight on 12 July 1985 at Melbourne's Festival Hall for the IBF junior-lightweight title at 59 kilograms (130 lb). Michael was now aged 30, and Lester 20.

The only hitch was that Michael hadn't been that light in almost a decade.

As far as the Ellis camp was concerned, Michael was 'an old fossil' and could not possibly make the weight.

If by some miracle of the steam baths and starvation he did, Ellis believed he would only have to show up and go through the motions against a wasted cadaver.

But, as always, Michael was one step ahead of his opponent.

Sports nutritionists devised a low-calorie, high-energy diet that peeled off the pounds but kept the strength in a body that was becoming more streamlined with every stick of celery.

Meanwhile, the bitterness between the two camps festered. Michael's friend and one-time trainer, American Dana Goodson, chose to work with Lester for the fight, telling the media that the young 'Master Blaster' would shut Michael's big mouth for good.

Although Lester was the world champion, Michael told him before the fight: 'Lester, I taught you everything you know but I didn't teach you everything that I know.'

As referee Gus Mercurio gave the fighters their instructions in centre ring, Michael kept up the banter, questioning Lester's manhood and provoking the boy champion into a rage at the opening bell.

Michael was badly hurt from a flurry of punches early in the fight and had his nose broken, but all the while he kept telling Lester that he was a boy fighting a man.

'The right hand he hit me with in the third round seriously hurt me,' Michael recalled. 'He put me in what they call the "half-dream room". It's like an explosion in your head. Blackness and stars with pins and needles in my feet. I couldn't feel my legs for a few seconds, and finally got hold of him and I said to him, "Lester, if that's the best you can do you might as well forget it."'

For round after round Michael rode Ellis's hardest punches and roughed him up in close with constant, short cuffing punches.

After 15 rounds the winner and new world champion was Barry Michael.

His years of struggle finally rewarded, Michael leapt about the ring with sheer joy on an imaginary pogo stick and bounded into the arms of his corner team Ray Styles, Leo Berry and Leo McDonald.

The win was the crowning achievement for Barry's long and wounding road in boxing.

But there was more pain ahead. Michael stopped Korean Jin-Shik Choi at a football ground in Darwin to retain the title but the promoter disappeared overseas to parts unknown with Michael's purse.

In 1986 he stopped American Mark Fernandez to retain the crown and then gained revenge over Britain's Najib Daho over 15 rounds in Manchester.

Then Michael really copped a hiding.

Melbourne crime boss Alphonse Gangitano was a silent partner in the promotion of Lester Ellis's fights and there was ill feeling towards Michael for not giving Lester a rematch.

At Lazar's nightclub in Melbourne, Gangitano's henchmen surrounded Michael, and the gangster broke the boxer's nose with what was most likely a glass ashtray.

The club's security dragged Michael through the crowd and to safety.

Four months later, Michael defended his world title against the brilliant American Rocky Lockridge in Windsor, outside London. Michael's training had been ruined by the broken nose and Lockridge stopped him in eight rounds, prompting the Australian's retirement after 14 years as a pro fighter.

While Lockridge was overtaken by drug addiction, homelessness and an early death back in America, Barry remains one of Australia's most respected boxing commentators.

And he can still boast that no boxer ever knocked him off his feet.

Master Blaster: A Young Gun on Fire

Lester Ellis blazed white hot in Australian boxing until Barry Michael snuffed out his flame. Born in Blackpool, England, in 1965, Ellis earned his first pay cheque scraping maggots from dead cows at a Melbourne abattoir.

In his fighting prime he was a gem flawed and floored, a scrawny piece of sad-eyed savagery whose huge heart and stockwhip left rip saw him peak in early 1985 as the 19-year-old IBF junior-lightweight champion.

Five months later, he survived his gruelling 15-round loss to his one-time hero Michael to win more big fights, but his best days were already over.

Ellis's life had been painful from a young age. 'I used to have hang-ups over my mother, bad hang-ups,' he once said. She ran off 'when I was five with Dad's best mate'. He had no interest in boxing until he heard the fuss about a new movie called *Rocky* and stole some bottles from a local shop to scrounge enough money for a movie ticket. 'I came out and I thought, *Bloody hell, how good was that?* After seeing that movie the demon came out in me. 'I said to my brother Keith, "I'm doing that. I am going to be a world champion."'

Ellis was a pale, skinny, sickly-looking kid weighing not much more than 30 kilograms when he started training with Matt Quinn, an RAAF veteran from the Vietnam War, in his garage gym at West Sunshine in Melbourne's western suburbs. He became a brilliant junior champion and made his professional debut in 1983.

In his first 13 pro fights, Lester beat some top Aussie talent in Roy Hughes, Brian Roberts, Gary Williams, Kirk Blair, Dennis Talbot, Norm Stevens and British champion Steve Sims, his 12th opponent and the first to hear the final bell.

In November 1984, Lester won the Commonwealth super-featherweight title with a split decision against John Sichula of Zambia at Melbourne's Festival Hall, where his next few big fights were held.

The win qualified him for a shot at the new IBF champion with the deadly name Hwan Kil Yuh.

The Korean was a rugged and relentless southpaw whose best weapon was his bald, butting head. Ellis was so nervous he didn't sleep for 36 hours before the fight.

'But I was a lot faster,' Ellis told me. 'Still, he kept banging me with his head and I needed 15 stitches after the fight. I had big gashes on my cheek and three big gashes over my eyes, so I was a bit of a mess.'

Ellis won a split decision – the Korean judge predictably voting for the Korean – and boxing was suddenly a big sport in Australia again.

'It was a great fight, but I was in bed for five days after that one,' Ellis told me.

'My world changed very quickly. I came home on the night after I beat the Korean and there were 10,000 people in the street. Kids painted "Lester Ellis World Champion" in shaving cream on the bitumen.

'How do you teach a young man of 19 how to handle success? One minute I have $50 in my pocket and the next minute I got $200,000.'

At the height of his fame, Ellis told the journalist Tess Lawrence: 'I don't really like fighting. When I first started, I [did] it to become fit. Now it's a full-time job. See, I got no alternatives. I can't do nothing else. Oh yeah, I scraped maggots off cow skins in the abattoir – but only because I was getting $100 a day for it. Boxing is the only thing I'm good at. The only thing. At school I was hopeless. Even at other sports. I was 16th man at cricket. Always came last in the bloody races. Boxing is the only thing in my life I won a trophy for.'

Two months after winning the world title, Ellis retained it in Round 13 of a savage Melbourne brawl with a Filipino volcano named Rod Sequenan on the same night Jeff Fenech won his first world title in Sydney.

But Barry Michael soon shattered the crown on Ellis's head and put a crack in his confidence for the rest of his career.

'He was an idol to me,' Lester said. 'I looked up to Barry. I never dreamed when I was a kid sparring him at the age of 12 he would be fighting me eight years later for my world title.

'He talked to me non-stop during the fight, trying to break my confidence.

'By the tenth, Barry's ear was hanging off and his nose was hanging off but I couldn't drop him.'

Lester recovered physically from the fight but the psychological scars remained. And they were deep.

Later in 1985, he was stopped in four in a rematch with John Sichula but came back to beat decent opposition in Rafael Solis and his rugged one-time sparring partner Tony Miller, a Jack Rennie-trained tough guy who battled other top Aussies including Jeff Fenech, Paul Nasari, Renato Cornett, Paul Ferreri, Jim Bowen and Carl Zappia.

Ellis then beat former world lightweight champ Ernesto España of Venezuela and stopped top Aussies Dale Artango (for the national lightweight title) and Pat Leglise (for the light-welter crown) before winning the Commonwealth light-welterweight title against Englishman Tony Laing in Adelaide in 1988.

Ellis lost that title by stoppage to Steve Larrimore of the Bahamas the following year and quit after six rounds against Argentina's Alberto Cortes, complaining of blurred vision.

He then lost to rising local star Attila Fogas and was outpointed by America's former world featherweight champ Calvin Grove in 1993.

In a 1996 rematch, Grove poleaxed him in four rounds. That should have been Ellis's last fight, but six years later he came out of retirement to challenge the much bigger and much younger Anthony Mundine. He was stopped in three ridiculous rounds.

Lester battled with alcoholism later in life but he beat it, and with the support of his long-suffering wife and family he remains an icon in the sport, forever the 19-year-old whirlwind who shook up the world.

Jeff Fenech and Johnny Lewis: The Drive to Succeed

Jeff Fenech was a wild street kid and a promising young rugby league player when he first went to the Newtown Police Boys Club in 1981.

Johnny Lewis, a signwriter for the local council, had been training fighters there for 20 years.

When Fenech walked into the gym, not particularly interested in boxing but looking for a friend, Lewis liked what he saw. 'I mentioned to one of the boxers I was training named Mark Cribb that we needed some sparring and straight away this kid, Jeff, put his hand up and volunteered,' Lewis said later.

'I said, "Mate, you can't just come in and spar these blokes," and he said, "No, I'll give it a go," and I thought, *Gee, this kid's cocky.* And it all started from there.'

Lewis had been training boxers in the big old gym on Erskineville Road since the early 1960s. He had started out there as a fighter in the previous decade when Jack Blom and Snowy MacFadyen were the trainers.

'In those days we had some great boxers training at Newtown – Billy and Danny Males, Fred Casey, and Jackie Bruce,' Lewis recalled.

'After I was there 18 months, Jack and Snowy left the gym and Dick O'Connor took over. He was probably the greatest trainer I've ever been associated with. I never lost a fight with Dick in my corner, and he trained some real good boxers, including David Floyd.

'When I was 17, some illness cropped up in Dick's family and he left the gym. He told me he'd be back in four weeks but he never returned. Since I was the oldest kid, they made me the trainer, and that's how my career as a boxing coach really started.'

Lewis had been teaching boxing for 20 years when Fenech arrived at his gym. 'I watched him for a few days and I thought, *God strewth, this kid could be anything.* You only had to show him something once and he could do it. He was so strong for his size and he had this incredible will to be the best. It was that tremendous drive that separated him from the others. You could see it in his eyes. You could see it the way he punched the bags or chased after a bloke in the ring. He just wouldn't settle for being ordinary. He had to be number one. If a kid hit him, he hit him back three times, four times. He never let anyone gain the upper hand. He was a natural. Anybody could have told you he was going to be a great fighter.'

Encouraged by Lewis and local policeman Pat Jarvis, a leading rugby league player for St George, Fenech was an instant hit in his new sport.

He quickly became the Australian amateur flyweight (51 kg) champion. Then, in what would be Lewis's proudest moment, Fenech was chosen as captain for the Australian boxing team at the Los Angeles Olympics in 1984.

Fenech won his first two Olympic fights but, in a quarter-final, was denied a medal by a controversial decision in favour of Yugoslavia's Redžep Redžepovski, the eventual silver medallist.

Fenech immediately turned pro, declaring that if he couldn't win an Olympic medal, he'd win a world title. Johnny Lewis asked me to help him in the corner for his fighters and Fenech took us on one of the most thrilling rides ever in Australian sport. His results were spectacular. Despite asthma and brittle hands that were damaged in almost every fight, he steamrolled opponents. Fenech didn't win close decisions – he crushed the opposition.

Fenech's manager was an urbane young lawyer and sports fan named Colin Love who would later become the head of the Australian Rugby League.

On a Saturday morning in 1985 Colin turned up to our Newtown boxing club with his friend Bill Mordey, a former sportswriter. They were in Bill's canary-yellow Mercedes.

Bill had big plans to become a fight promoter and he saw Fenech as the foundation upon which he could build his empire. Fenech didn't disappoint. Sparring his friend Peter Mitrevski, a three-time Australian champion, and fellow Olympian Shane Knox, Fenech made boxing history in less than three-and-a-half years and 19 pro fights. He became the first boxer anywhere in the world to win three world titles while undefeated. In 2022 the WBC declared that he should have been awarded a fourth world title, although his battle with Azumah Nelson in Las Vegas in 1991 for that belt was declared a draw by ringside officials.

In just his seventh pro fight, the day after Anzac Day, 1985, Fenech won his first world championship, knocking out Japan's Satoshi Shingaki at Sydney's Hordern Pavilion.

Fenech then manhandled American champion Jerome Coffee and overwhelmed rock-tough Daniel Zaragoza of Mexico. Despite extreme weight loss, he hammered the Los Angeles Olympic gold medallist Steve McCrory in 1986 to prove he could have won the gold medal if he'd been given the chance two years earlier.

Fenech overpowered Melbourne's Tony Miller and was then matched with Thai playboy Samart Payakaroon in Sydney in 1987 for the WBC super-bantamweight title.

Mordey smoked 120 cigarettes on the day of the fight. It was one of those days and Payakaroon was one of those opponents: the kind of guy who could have ended Fenech's dream run with one big left from his southpaw arsenal. Fenech was fighting to become the first Australian to win world titles at two different weights and the WBC sent out one of its best referees, Arthur Mercante, who 16 years earlier had been the third man in the ring when Joe Frazier beat Muhammad Ali.

Suave, handsome and cocky, WBC super-bantamweight champ Payakaroon was considered one of the all-time greats in Muay Thai kick-boxing before becoming an undefeated world boxing champion. He had a big punch and fast feet, with moves that Lewis hadn't seen since Johnny Famechon in his heyday. The Thai also had smart managers who had cancelled the Fenech fight once and then squeezed another $40,000 out of Mordey. The Thais were so confident that they wagered Payakaroon's entire purse of US$175,000 on victory.

I watched Payakaroon sparring throughout his preparation and one night not long before the bout I spotted him at his favourite Thai restaurant in Sydney, cooking himself a stir fry, a cigarette dangling from his bottom lip.

Payakaroon came out 'smokin'' in the fight too, which took place before a sold-out crowd of 12,000 at the Sydney Entertainment Centre.

It was a thriller while it lasted. Fenech hit the canvas for the first time in his career from a fast right in the opening round and, emboldened, Payakaroon landed a big uppercut as Fenech tried to swarm all over him in the second.

In the third, Fenech backed the heavy-hitting world champ against the ropes and while Payakaroon swayed away in all directions to protect his pretty face, Fenech applied a blowtorch to the Thai's ribs with such fiery combinations that Mercante appeared ready to stop the fight. Then the bell rang.

In Round 4, Payakaroon planted his feet and decided to fight Fenech at his own game. Bombs away. Three, four sizzling left crosses blasted out as the Thai's broad back shuddered from the force. But the punches hit glove, not chin, and before long Fenech, the raging bull, was goring the handsome matador again.

Fenech bullied the Thai into the ropes once more and unloaded two huge rights to Payakaroon's temple that made all the strength in his legs disappear. As the world champ fell glassy-eyed towards the canvas, Fenech smashed his spinning head with another uppercut to make sure Payakaroon didn't get up for a long time.

Payakaroon swallowed his tongue but Mercante stopped him from choking just as he did when Floyd Patterson dropped Ingemar Johansson in their world heavyweight title fight 25 years earlier.

As Payakaroon was being carried from the ring after their fight, Fenech seized the microphone and told the crowd, 'I love youse all. With 12,000 of the most beautifullest people in the world cheering me on, it's hard to feel pain.'

Fenech had broken his opponent's heart and then the English language.

The day after the fight a public relations company offered him some free advice on speech making. 'I don't need no elocution lessons,' Fenech told them. 'The people love me because I'm Jeff Fenech.'

After the fight, Payakaroon had been taken to St Vincent's Hospital for observation before being given the all-clear. But he was a nervous man – there were rumours that underworld figures in Thailand had hired a contract killer to put a bullet between his dark, brooding eyes. As he waited at Sydney airport to board a flight home he chain-smoked cigarettes. And when he arrived at Bangkok airport, he found himself surrounded by angry punters who had lost a small fortune backing him. Even farm labourers from his province were at the airport to demand how much he'd been paid to throw the fight.

Payakaroon shaved his head, donned sacred robes and entered a Buddhist monastery, where he stayed until the coast was clear.

Fenech defended his new world title against swift American Greg Richardson and the savage Mexican legend Carlos Zárate, who had beaten Melbourne's Paul Ferreri more than a decade earlier. In 1988, he became a three-time world champion by walking through the huge blows of Puerto Rican Victor Callejas.

The defining fight of his career was his 12-rounder with Ghana's 'Mighty Warrior' Azumah Nelson in Las Vegas in 1991. The match was judged a draw, despite most experts believing that Fenech had won convincingly. Shattered by the result and having lost some of his edge because of the controversy, he was sensationally stopped by Nelson in a rematch at Princes Park in Melbourne in 1992 before 38,000 people, then the largest live crowd ever for an Australian fight. Fenech recovered to fight Philip Holiday five years later for the world lightweight title, but his heart wasn't in it anymore, and he was stopped in two rounds.

Fenech and Nelson went through the motions once more in 2008. Nelson was a month shy of his 50th birthday and Fenech, who won a close ten-round decision, was 44.

In 2022 the WBC declared that Fenech should have been given the decision against Nelson in Las Vegas 31 years earlier and presented him with a fourth world-title belt, though the draw remains in the record books.

Becoming a renowned trainer, Fenech took Vic Darchinyan and Danny Green to world titles and trained a young Daniel Geale. At various times, he also piloted the career of Mike Tyson, as well as Australian world-title challengers including Hussein Hussein, his brother Nedal Hussein, Shannan Taylor, Glen Kelly, Lovemore Ndou, Sakio Bika and Nader Hamdan.

Break-even Bill and his Biggest Punt

With a transistor radio often pressed against one ear to catch the latest race results and a cigarette in his mouth, Bill Mordey was perhaps Australia's greatest ever fight promoter.

He was a character of laconic wit and roguish charm, a man who could have been played by Chips Rafferty and whose life read like something from the pen of Damon Runyon.

A self-confessed mug-lair since childhood, 'Break-even Bill' became one of the leading figures of Australian sport, and neither Henry Lawson nor Banjo Paterson could have told a better yarn as he held court, one hand clasped around a cigarette, the other nursing a bourbon and Coke.

Mordey wrote about rugby league, tennis, boxing and horse racing for more than 20 years as a leading sportswriter with Sydney's afternoon tabloid, *The Daily Mirror*, and he went on to become a media adviser to the New South Wales Rugby League.

But the fight game was always his great love and he decided to become a promoter after attending a bout I'd staged at Belmore Sports Ground in 1984 in conjunction with Australian Rugby League boss Colin Love, Bulldogs chief Peter Moore and Johnny Lewis.

That fight saw Bulldogs hooker Billy Johnstone battle Australian middleweight champ Ritchie Roberts before a crowd of more than 4000.

It was a thriller on a stinking hot summer afternoon. Billy had won just about every round when the heat got to him. He went cuckoo, and in Round 12 he charged Roberts headfirst like he was in a Spanish bullring. Roberts hit the canvas. Referee Billy Males had no option but to disqualify Billy who, broken-hearted at the lost opportunity, never fought again.

Mordey was hooked on the possibilities of big-time boxing in Sydney, though, and within a year he had bankrolled Jeff Fenech to the first of three world titles.

Break-even Bill succeeded Hugh D McIntosh as Australia's most successful fight entrepreneur, drawing what was then an Australian record crowd of 38,000 in drizzling rain to Melbourne's Princes Park to see Fenech fight Azumah Nelson in 1992.

Under his guidance, Jeff Harding and Kostya Tszyu also won world titles and he promoted other Australian boxing stars, including Joe Bugner, the Waters brothers, Lovemore Ndou, Shannan Taylor and Lester Ellis.

Bill was born at Campsie, in Sydney's inner west in 1936. His dad died when Bill was seven and he was raised by his mum, Constance Maude, better known as Maudie Mordey. His early days were spent helping her work as a seamstress, sewing collars onto shirts.

When his mum could afford it, she gave Bill threepence to go to the Burwood Police Boys Club to learn boxing, but he told me his only bout was declared a draw when he and his opponent were too tired to hit each other in Round 3.

Bill was just 13 when he had his first punt, wagering five shillings on a horse in the Melbourne Cup. One of his cousins declared the horse unbeatable. It wasn't.

His first foray into gambling ended when the SP bookie – his aunt – gave Bill his money back. Over the next 40 years most of the bookies Bill battled weren't so forgiving, yet when he was working at the *Mirror* in the mid 1960s he won 10,000 quid – the equivalent of eight years' pay – on a horse called Best Card, owned by a syndicate that included a couple of Bill's uncles and Sydney Stadium boss Harry Miller, as well as Joe Taylor, the former pug and king of Sydney's illegal casinos.

Bill's uncle Jimmy Dundee fought Vic Patrick twice and took Bill to see his first fight at Sydney Stadium, where Hockey Bennell was headlining.

At 14 Bill left St Pat's school at Strathfield and at 15 was a racing cadet on *The Sun*. He said paying him to go to the races was like handing a grenade to a baby.

Some of his friends called him 'Blue Gum' after the tall, thin tree, but he also earned another nickname during his career. As a punter and later a promoter, millions of dollars passed through Bill's hands but despite that, he always maintained he only wanted one thing. To Break Even.

Usually, when Bill said he'd only broken even on a deal it was given that he'd won big.

Bill had hoped to promote Tszyu in a fight at Red Square, but their relationship soured with the arrival of another rival promoter Vlad Warton, an oily former used car salesman.

Break-even Bill took Tszyu to court and won more than $7 million in damages for breach of contract.

After the court battle, Mordey retired to his horse stud in the upper Hunter Valley, having promoted 24 world title fights.

He died at the Mater Hospital in Newcastle in 2004 after an adverse reaction to chemotherapy. He was 67.

When Donald Trump Hired a Hitman

Donald Trump shifted uneasily in his seat as the pressure built towards bursting. It was one of the great moments in Australian sport and Trump, the man who later made political history as the 45th President of the United States, was taking mental notes under that vast orange bouffant.

It was 24 June 1989, Round 12 of the WBC light-heavyweight title fight between the 24-year-old Australian underdog Jeff Harding, a keen surfer from South Grafton, and the 35-year-old Dennis Andries, a hard-as-nails West Indian lion based in Detroit after many years in London.

At one of his early amateur tournaments, I gave the explosive Harding the nickname 'The Hitman' and it stuck for all his life.

Harding drank heavily during those early days but he won a silver medal at the 1986 Edinburgh Commonwealth Games.

Two years later, Harding outscored Apollo Sweet over ten rounds to win the vacant New South Wales cruiserweight crown. He followed it with a fifth-round knockout over Doug Sam and another early night against world-rated American Don Lee. When he'd flown into Atlantic City, he was unbeaten in 14 fights.

At the time, Trump was a brash real estate investor who had made Atlantic City the world capital of boxing thanks to his hotel and casino interests, topped by Trump Plaza, Trump Castle and the Trump Taj Mahal, then the largest casino in the world.

Big fights drew the high rollers, and in 1988 Trump had bid a record site fee of US$11 million to stage the Mike Tyson–Michael Spinks fight at the Atlantic City Convention Hall, adjacent to Trump Plaza.

It was then the biggest grossing fight of all time, even though just ten punches were landed and Tyson won in 91 seconds.

Now Trump was hosting Harding's unlikely shot at Andries, along with promoters Bob Arum and Bill Mordey. Baseball greats Ted Williams and Joe DiMaggio were ringside.

My flight into Atlantic City, 200 kilometres south of New York, was shrouded in fog. As we came into land, the heavens parted to reveal an array of skyscrapers brandishing the name 'Trump' and an immense yacht, the *Trump Princess*.

The city boasted wealth and extravagance, but it was all a con. A block behind the ritzy high-rise hotels and flashing neon was a different America of the desperate urban poor, disillusion, drugs and guns.

Trump may have been selling his gilt fantasy to the world but on fight night there was no artifice. The Harding–Andries fight was even uglier than Trump's election battle with Hillary Clinton almost 30 years later.

Even Harding's closest friends had only given him an outside chance when he'd agreed to the bout after injury forced popular former champ Donny Lalonde out of meeting Andries. Harding was such an unknown that the world titleholder initially thought he was fighting the English cruiserweight Jess Harding.

But 'The Hitman' believed in himself. In the lead-up to the fight, Harding had floored former WBC world light-heavyweight champion Matthew Saad Muhammad with a left hook while sparring in Atlantic City.

Despite news of the knockdown, Harding was still a 2–1 outsider for the title bout.

Johnny Lewis's pre-fight plan had Harding wearing down the champion and finishing strongly to take a points victory. But the plan went astray when Andries battered Harding to the canvas in the fifth.

From then on, Harding absorbed fearful punishment.

Andries's furious onslaught peaked in the tenth round and Harding was a mess by Round 11, with a flattened nose swelling up between two cut eyes. He knew he needed a knockout to win.

Before the last round Lewis told Harding: 'You'll have to dig deep, son. Give it everything you've got. Go out there and come back a world champion.'

Andries was far enough in front that he only needed to get through the last round to win on points, but in the champion's corner before the start of Round 12, his team told their exhausted man he needed a knockout to make sure of victory. It was a crucial mistake.

Like Trump in the US election, Harding threw everything into the last round against the raging favourite.

In 80 frantic seconds that could have been scripted by Sylvester Stallone, Harding tore from his corner.

He threw gloved bombs non-stop until Andries collapsed and Trump and the rest of the crowd leapt to their feet.

The Englishman managed to stagger upright and beat the count, only to go down again after another flurry of blows.

This time referee Joe Cortez stopped the fight 85 seconds into the round. At the time Harding, at 79 kilograms, was the biggest man ever to win a world boxing title for Australia.

Trump sent a limousine to ferry The Hitman's team to one of his swish hotels in Manhattan. A few days later, the new world champ flew home to Sydney in triumph. Trump, however, had many more battles to fight. Despite a big loan from his wealthy father, Donald Trump's Taj Mahal went bust. He eventually pulled out of Atlantic City and the big fights left for Las Vegas.

Harding was a troubled soul at the time, and he left Johnny Lewis to train with Manny Hinton and Brian Wilmott. He lost and regained his world title against Andries, and finally left boxing after losing to the three-time world champ Mike McCallum after a spirited 12-rounder in Bismarck, North Dakota.

Harding's courage was inspirational, but for a long time his life went into freefall. With all its traps and temptations, life was, as Ernest Hemingway once said, the best left hooker he ever saw.

By his late 30s, Harding had become one of life's punching bags, surrendering to the dark forces that had plagued him for years.

He spent time in prison and in detox at a hospital in Windsor and once registered a blood alcohol reading of 0.17 when he drove his white four-wheel-drive through a red light in Redfern into the path of a marked police car, causing it to swerve across the road.

In 2004, I wrote that the saddest sight in Australian sport could be seen lumbering around the Sydney suburb of

Redfern with a stubby of beer in one hand, Eveleigh Street his boulevard of broken dreams. For anyone who remembered the doggedness Harding showed in becoming world champ, the sight of the dishevelled 'Hitman' stumbling through a boozy fog was shattering.

Nine years later, in 2013, Jeff Fenech was inducted as a 'Legend' into the Australian Boxing Hall of Fame, and I was invited to Melbourne's Crown Casino to make a speech for the occasion.

I reminded the crowd in the Palladium Room of all the times I had travelled to Melbourne with Jeff for fights in the past, when he'd pack out Rod Laver Arena and punch out some of the best boxers in the world.

Harding, seated in the crowd, recognised an old friend and leapt from his perch to throw his arms around the widow of Lionel Rose. Like Rose, Harding had known fanfare and failure and lived rough for a while on park benches. But now declaring himself sober, 'the Hitman' had dragged himself back from life's abyss.

And on that night at the Crown, when Australian boxing's greatest champs gathered to celebrate the courage of everyone who ever laced on a glove, it was a moving sight to see Harding winning his greatest fight of all.

Aussie Joe and the Biggest Fight in Britain

In the early 1980s, Joe Bugner and wife Marlene relocated from Hollywood to Australia, the country of Marlene's birth. They enjoyed the trappings of celebrity in Sydney's high society but that lifestyle did not come cheap. To survive at the big end of town, Joe had to get back into the business of bloody noses and broken jaws.

In 1986, after a two-year absence from the ring, Bugner returned to the fight game in Sydney, aged 36 and a half. He beat

Oklahoma's James Tillis, the first man to go the distance with Mike Tyson, and then defeated David Bey, who had challenged for the world heavyweight title.

In Sydney in July 1987 he squared off against another former world champ, Greg Page, in the biggest heavyweight fight in Sydney since Jack Johnson beat Tommy Burns at Sydney Stadium almost 80 years before.

Page was from Muhammad Ali's hometown of Louisville, Kentucky, and his trainer was Richie Giachetti, a squat man with dark curly hair, a thick moustache and a fat cigar drooping from a mouth that was constantly cursing. Giachetti also trained the great heavyweight Larry Holmes and had an extensive rap sheet with the FBI as a gangland arsonist known as 'Richie the Torch'.

Page was rattled by Bugner's pre-fight taunts and showmanship that came straight from the Muhammad Ali playbook, and the big American banned media from his training sessions. Bugner invited all comers to see him slugging it out in sparring with the heavily tattooed Melbourne slaughterman Dave Russell.

'Aussie Joe' underwent a naturalisation ceremony in centre ring at the Sydney Entertainment Centre minutes before the opening bell against Page. He was all smiles after the ceremony, but it looked like the 37-year-old embarking on the fifth comeback of his career would be in for a tough fight, as the fleet-footed Page took the first round. From then on, however, Bugner was in control, winning a comfortable decision to close in on a multi-million-dollar world title fight with Tyson.

Meanwhile, ambitious 39-year-old Barry Hearn, who had made his name promoting British snooker, wanted to stage the biggest and richest boxing event ever held in Britain.

During a meal at a Chinese restaurant, Hearns's wife, Susan, was highly critical of his attempts to become a big-time fight promoter. This inspired Hearns to announce that he was going to try and make a fight between Joe Bugner and Frank Bruno, England's most popular boxer.

'As a fight fan I knew it was the best conflict,' Hearn said. 'You had the fan favourite and the villain of the piece, the guy who had gone off to Australia and become Aussie Joe, coming back to fight our beloved Frank Bruno.

'I was in the Chinese restaurant and I dialled directly to Australia and spoke with Joe from the restaurant. I told him of my plan. He said, "Well, that's gonna cost you a lot of money, Barry."'

'I said, "Well, Joe, I've done some research and I think for your last fight you were paid only $20,000. I'll pay you £250,000."' (At the time, £250,000 was more than A$600,000.)

'The line went quiet and then Joe said in his squeaky Australian voice: "What plane did you want me on, Barry?"'

The bout was set for the Tottenham Hotspur's stadium, White Hart Lane, for 24 October 1987. Bugner had just a month to get ready, an unusually short preparation, but it was a big outdoor fight and it had to take place before the bite of winter set in. It represented the biggest payday of Joe's life and he needed the cash.

I travelled to Britain to go in Joe's corner. We all stayed in a hotel near Buckingham Palace and Joe did everything he could to sell tickets, promoting the Australia–England rivalry, carrying a stuffed crocodile over his shoulder wherever he went in a nod to the recently released movie *Crocodile Dundee*, and beaming out from under a wide-brim Akubra hat at press conferences.

Court officials were also trying to serve summonses claiming alimony for Joe's first wife, and reporters and photographers were on 24-hour vigils outside the hotel, waiting for any glimpse of Joe and the glamorous Marlene, and ferreting around for any scandal they could drum up.

'I'll be fighting Frank Bruno and Fleet Street all on the one night and I'll give them a terrible time to remember,' Joe said. 'This is the greatest opportunity of my career because at the age of 37 I finally have the chance to shut the mouths of my many critics. Frank doesn't know enough to beat a crafty old dog like me.'

A fleet of police-escorted limousines took Joe and his team to the stadium and before long Jeff Fenech and I were in Bruno's dressing-room, supervising the taping of his hands, which were the size of dinner plates.

Bruno had built his reputation on being a loveable, humble sportsman, but on this night he was all menace and malevolence. The veins in his neck were bulging with rage and his nostrils were flaring with the scent of battle. He knew that his whole future was on the line against a man who had fought the very best of boxing for the last 20 years.

Barry Hearn visited Frank Bruno's room and thought it was as cold and unwelcoming as a morgue. Bruno was deep in thought and no one would dare say a word to him.

He then headed off to Joe's room. As he approached he could hear music playing and when he opened the door Joe was holding up two dressing gowns and asking Marlene which one he'd look better in. Joe had been in big fights so many times around the world he wasn't the slightest bit worried about the enormity of this occasion.

There were 37,000 people there that night paying £3 million in gate receipts and the fight delivered the biggest audience for televised boxing for many years.

The ringside area was packed with celebrities, including American actors Demi Moore and her husband, Bruce Willis, then Hollywood's golden couple. Willis predicted a Bugner victory and said he had once seen Bugner hit Muhammad Ali with the force of a Pontiac car.

Joe eventually chose a white satin gown with an Aussie wattle motif, and he marched to the ring waving the Aussie flag.

His confidence didn't go down well with the pro-Bruno crowd and Joe was jeered into the ring like Mel Gibson marching to his execution in *Braveheart*.

Before the opening bell, Johnny Lewis told Joe to unleash his huge right hand the first chance he got.

Joe came out swinging in the first round, the steam of his breath like clouds of smoke on that freezing night.

But Joe was 37 and Bruno 25, and the difference was obvious early.

Bruno's persistence, his powerful left jab, his tremendous physical condition, and his youth were too difficult to overcome. Nevertheless, Joe shook Bruno in the first round, hurt him in the second with the left hook, and at one stage made Bruno miss outrageously with a looping swing. But soon reality began to catch Aussie Joe.

In Round 8, Bruno landed a thumping left hook and a solid right cross and Joe slumped into a sitting position on the bottom rope in Bruno's corner. Referee John Coyle stood by as Bruno rained punches onto the top of Joe's head, at one stage thumping him like he was trying to drive in a fence post.

Lewis had promised Marlene that he would not allow her husband to get badly hurt, and he threw in the towel at the end of Round 8.

Still, Joe refused to concede, even arguing with Lewis in his corner when the trainer signalled the finish.

Joe never got to taste the victory champagne that was kept for him. Sure enough, the rest of us opened the bottles because they were too good to waste but Joe's doctor told the beaten fighter to lay off the bubbly for a while, given the hits he'd taken.

Joe's glory days were over, even though he continued to fight, whenever the bank balance dipped, until he was almost 50. While living on the Gold Coast, he beat Aussie heavyweights Vince Cervi, Bob Mirovic and Colin Wilson.

In his penultimate fight, Joe won the minor World Boxing Federation (WBF) heavyweight title by beating the big American James 'Bonecrusher' Smith, who had once gone 15 rounds with Tyson.

In his later years Joe was moved into a nursing home as the great memories of his career began to fade, but he remained ever smiling and a good and happy man at heart.

Being involved with him and his career was one of the highlights of my life, and not just for me. Joe was once rated only below Ali, Frazier and Foreman in the world rankings, and he showed immense humility in his comeback in the late 1980s, training beside, and inspiring, a group of eager amateurs at the Newtown Police Boys Club.

He displayed so much generosity, humility, friendship and dedication that Johnny Lewis was moved to call him 'one of the finest human beings I've ever known'.

'Joe was too much of a nice guy in his fighting career,' Johnny told me. 'If he'd had the same ruthlessness of a young Jeff Fenech he would have been world champ – even with Ali, Frazier and Foreman on the scene.'

There was to be another big hit for Joe in the postscript to the Bruno fight.

Lewis had been worried to the point of paranoia about hair loss among his boxing team ever since his own follicles began fleeing down the shower drain a decade earlier. Johnny and I shared a hotel room in London, and he was almost as concerned about the state of our scalps as he was about Joe's fitness.

Johnny began issuing dire warnings to everyone else on Joe's team about the insidiousness of male pattern baldness. On one occasion, we were watching the BBC news after one of Joe's final training sessions at the Lonsdale gym in Carnaby Street and Johnny asked if I'd ever considered employing a comb-over.

After the fight was stopped and after Joe limped back dejectedly to his corner with 37,000 Brits jeering him and cheering for Bruno, Lewis told his dismayed corner team: 'I guess Frank was just too big, too mobile and too young tonight.'

But he left his gravest announcement for last.

'And another thing I noticed in the fight ... Joe's getting very thin on top.'

Happily for Bugner, almost four decades later, he still has much more hair than his old mentor.

Troubled Waters

Troy, Guy and Dean Waters learned to fight on their mad, bad father's isolated property in Kulnura, in the hinterland of the New South Wales Central Coast. When I first visited the property in 1983, after Troy and Dean had won national amateur titles and were in contention for the 1984 Olympics, more than 100 stray dogs were living there. At the time, Troy, the youngest, was a welterweight, Dean, the oldest brother, a heavyweight, and middle brother Guy appropriately a middleweight.

The Waters brothers were all born in England and had been coached from infancy by their father, Cec, an eccentric little man in a beanie with a commanding presence. Cec presented himself publicly as a principled no-nonsense disciplinarian, but in reality he was a ruthless pimp and sex fiend, who later ordered the cold-blooded killing of his wife's lover.

In a ramshackle farmhouse straight out of a rustic comedy, with a boxing ring in the middle of a horse paddock, Cec taught his boys to be respectful to other people and not to swear, drink alcohol, eat meat or hang around with loose women. It was all too good to be true.

The son of a wife-beating alcoholic, Cec was a cocky bantamweight. He had enlisted in the British army at 15 and became a good scrapper, having much more success with his fists than he did with women. He once told me: 'My father's advice about women has always stuck by me. He said, if you ever get a good woman, shoot her before she turns bad so she'll have died a good woman.'

Cec underwent his first murder investigation when his third wife disappeared while the family were still living in England. Neighbours suspected he had killed her and bricked up her body in a chimney. The case made the front page of England's *News of the World*, but the missing wife later surfaced to say she had only run away.

The publicity for the case ruined Cec's driving school business and he and his three boys and daughter, Tracey, emigrated to Australia in 1972, arriving with just $7 between them.

Cec eventually settled on the 10-hectare property at Kulnura, an hour's drive north of Sydney, a place with a hillbilly feel. The house was riddled with dog and cat faeces, but Cec said he liked it because it was far enough away from the temptations of the concrete jungle to keep his family safe.

Cec fashioned a boxing ring in a paddock and taught his boys how to hold their hands high and hit without being hit. 'Boxing is the noble art of self-defence,' he told me on my first visit there. 'I tell my boys a boxer is like a Roman soldier. He fights from behind his shield and he jabs out at the enemy with a spear in his left hand. Everything is built around that: a tight defence and a good jab.'

While he threatened to kill his children if they turned out to be gay, Cec had a number of sexual relationships with men when he spent time in British prisons, but that detail would only emerge decades later as his world unravelled. He also had parts in some British crime movies and made his children go on holidays with him to nudist camps.

Cec took plenty of knocks in life and inside his twisted head was a volcano of rage. 'When Troy was little we went running in a London park,' he once said. 'It was winter and there was a lot of snow. I just tripped him. He looked up at me and there were tears in his eyes. He said: "Why did you trip me, Daddy?" I said: "So you will pick yourself up. You've got to learn to pick yourself up. No one else will do it for you."'

Given they were raised by a domineering father who brutalised them from infancy, it's a wonder the brothers ever achieved anything worthwhile. But they did. And nothing the boys endured in their fights would be as brutal as their upbringing.

The youngest, Troy, had a powerful right-hand punch built by the shot-put in junior athletics. He used it to cut through Aussie fighters such as John Piggott, Graeme Looker and New South Wales light-middle champ Tony Campbell.

In 1986, after just five pro fights, Troy travelled to Seoul, South Korea, to drop a close decision to future world champ In Chul Baek, but he captured the Australian light-middleweight title when he outpointed world-class Paul Toweel, nephew of world champ Vic.

A fourth-round stoppage over Lloyd Hibbert at Hobart's Wrest Point Casino in 1987 gave Troy the Commonwealth title.

His first world title shot came against IBF champ Gianfranco Rosi in Saint-Vincent, Italy, but the elusive Italian won on points.

Waters then beat good locals Ronald Doo, Chris Seng and Craig Trotter before challenging Terry Norris for the WBC crown in San Diego in 1993.

Norris was considered one of the world's best, pound for pound, after beating Sugar Ray Leonard, Donald Curry and Meldrick Taylor, but Waters had him on the canvas before losing because of cuts over both eyes in what *Ring* magazine judged the Fight of the Year.

Troy had escaped his father's clutches by then and one of the men in his corner was Billy Moore, son of the great Archie, who had maintained his love for all things Australian into old age.

Troy followed that thriller with a stoppage of Olympic gold medallist Robert Wangila, and a year later he gave Simon Brown the fight of his life before dropping a 12-round majority decision in another WBC title bout in Las Vegas.

He outpointed the former world welterweight champ Jorge Vaca and the WBO middleweight title challenger Lonnie Beasley, but in 1997 was stopped in the opening round by Felix Trinidad at Madison Square Garden, New York.

Troy retired the next year and settled on the Central Coast with a lovely wife and two children to enjoy the happy family life that his father had denied him.

Middle brother Guy Waters became a tremendous boxing stylist with a superb left jab and solid defence.

He lost to Victorian Brendon Cannon for a place at the 1984 Olympics and his pro career started dreadfully when he was overpowered in two rounds by paratrooper Geoff Peate, who was 10 kilograms heavier.

But in 1986 Guy beat world title challenger Emmanuel Otti before outboxing world-class Gary Hubble at Sydney's Hordern Pavilion eight months later.

Six more wins down the track, he then handed out a boxing lesson to Canadian Willie Featherstone for the Commonwealth crown, pounded Britain's Roy Skeldon, Italian-based Ugandan Yawe Davis and another Canadian, Dave Fiddler, to earn a crack at the WBC light-heavyweight title that Dennis Andries had just regained from Jeff Harding.

I called the fight for Sky TV with the veteran Melbourne broadcaster Ron Casey and Guy boxed brilliantly for the first ten rounds at the Memorial Drive Tennis Centre in Adelaide in 1991.

Andries, though, dominated the closing stages to win a close decision.

Still, the quiet, unassuming Guy Waters had made a big noise on the world scene. He won a split decision over former WBA champ Leslie Stewart in Melbourne and in 1993 travelled to Minot, North Dakota, to lose a 12-round decision against WBA champ Virgil Hill. Guy was still good enough to challenge the much bigger Juan Carlos Gomez for the WBC cruiserweight title in Hamburg in 1998.

Dropping 10 kilograms to super-middleweight, Guy dominated Japan's Yoshinori Nishizawa for the Oriental and Pacific Boxing Federation (OPBF) title in 2000, but he retired the following year after stoppage losses to Englishman David Starie in Essex and Anthony Mundine in Sydney.

Dean, the oldest of the Waters brothers and a 100-kilogram tank, scored two wins over the veteran heavyweight Maile Haumono and then won the Australian heavyweight title by stopping Dave Russell beside the Murray River at Swan Hill in 1986. The next year Commonwealth heavyweight champion Horace Notice stopped him at Wembley in London and Dean sank into inactivity.

It would later emerge that Dean had other things on his mind than boxing, and on 29 June 1988, acting under orders from his father, he crept up to an isolated Central Coast farmhouse where Cec's fifth wife, Christine, was living with a local horse breaker named Alan Hall. At different times, Hall had been charged with sexual assault of a man, and drug dealing.

Cec had previously forced Christine to work as a prostitute to help bankroll his dream of raising three boxing world champions. He initially encouraged a sexual relationship between Hall and Christine because he wanted to watch, and because he saw it as payment for Hall's services in breaking some of Cec's horses.

But Cec became enraged when he lost control of the situation. Hall showed Christine affection that Cec had never shown her, and she fell in love with him. Before long she left Cec and moved in with Hall. Cec had Dean burn down Hall's house.

'It was a bizarre scenario,' Detective Chief Inspector Dennis O'Toole told the program *Crime Investigation Australia*, 'but it did happen.'

On 29 June 1988, Dean, carrying a shotgun and taking another of Cec's boxers Damon Cooper with him for back-up, crept up to the new house where Hall and Christine were living. Under his father's orders, Dean had already dug shallow graves at a nearby forest for the lovers, but at the last minute decided that he wouldn't kill his stepmother.

As Dean and Cooper lay in grass outside Hall's house, Cooper tried to run away, but Dean coaxed him into staying. Dean lured Hall outside by throwing a bucket against a wall to set Hall's dogs barking. When Hall ventured outside Dean shot him dead.

Within hours, police were combing Cec's Kulnura property. Dean and Cec were eventually charged with Hall's murder, but as Troy Waters was preparing to fly to Italy for his world title shot against Gianfranco Rosi in October 1989, the judge at their committal hearing dismissed the charges due to insufficient evidence.

While Dean had continually clammed up in police interrogations, he endured deep remorse and sleepless nights. He had taken a life and knew he could never give it back and it almost pushed him to suicide. Dean moved to Melbourne and became involved in the drug scene. His conscience was so troubled he finally confessed all in graphic detail to a Central Coast religious minister, Pastor Kevin Brett. Pastor Brett told Dean that he would never know peace until he went to the police.

Dean finally told the truth to Detective O'Toole in 1996, though he had lied about the crime for so long it was difficult for him to get the words out.

Cec was arrested but maintained his innocence, arguing vehemently that it was all a conspiracy. Not long after, Cec died of a heart attack aged 70, before he could be tried for murder.

However, Dean's offsider in the murder, Damon Cooper, turned himself in, and in 1997 he was sentenced to 18 years' jail for manslaughter, despite the fact he hadn't shot anyone. A subsequent appeal and plea to the governor for clemency were rejected.

Waters's lawyer, Manny Conditsis, said his client would be defending the charge of murder on the grounds of diminished responsibility but was prepared to plead guilty to manslaughter. The Crown chose to pursue a murder charge instead, as the evidence was clear cut.

Dean faced Newcastle Court with a legal team that established a case in minute detail that Dean had committed the crime while under the control of a tyrannical father who had brainwashed him.

Three psychologists, including the Crown's, said he was suffering from 'an abnormality of the mind' when he committed the crime.

Dean's sister, Tracey, detailed their years of abuse from Cec, which included forbidding the children to use the toilet at night, making them use a bucket in the lounge room instead. At times, when Dean had to urinate, Cec would unzip his fly and take out his penis, tucking it away again when he was finished. He was still doing that when Dean was 25 and the Australian heavyweight champion. Cec regularly beat the children with a rubber hose even when they were adults. He would follow them in a car when they did roadwork, bumping into them if they started to lag.

Some of the jury cried at these horror stories, and they took just 40 minutes to deliver a verdict of not guilty. Dean sobbed.

Detective O'Toole told *Crime Investigations Australia* that he was 'stunned' by the verdict and that it took him some time to comprehend it. 'It's pretty difficult to accept that the person who actually caused the death of another person walks free while his accomplice, who didn't cause any damage to the deceased at all, gets [18 years'] jail. I find that difficult,' he said.

Damon Cooper was finally released from prison in 2009 after serving 12 years.

* * *

In the years after his retirement from boxing, Troy Waters overcame the trauma of his tyrannical father's control and built a life for himself, his lovely wife, Michelle, and his children, Nate and Shontae.

Having endured so much sadness in his own childhood he was determined to make his own family life one of joy.

He was doing that in July 2014 when a prolonged feeling of lethargy sent him to his local doctor.

Troy had remained super-fit, even though he'd hung up the gloves. For one of the first times in his life, he didn't see the blow coming: acute myeloid leukaemia.

Troy was just 49 when he told *The Daily Telegraph*: 'It does my head in. I see people down at the pub drinking and smoking and nothing happens, they're all as solid as a rock. You supposedly live a healthy life and this stuff happens.'

Troy bravely endured months in hospital and grim battles with chemotherapy.

Brother Dean provided bone marrow for a transplant, but sadly Troy Waters died in 2018 aged just 53.

An Unsung Hero

Renato Cornett was a teammate of Jeff Fenech's at the Los Angeles Olympics and one of the most talented fighters in Australia for the best part of 20 years. And yet his 200-odd amateur and pro fights were contested in relative anonymity. He always had problems with southpaws, but his two world title fights were thousands of miles from home against cagey left-handers.

In Cornett's last world title fight, in December 1999, he challenged Paul Spadafora, a veteran of 100 back-alley brawls and at least one gun battle on the streets of Pittsburgh. Cornett held his own, but in the 11th round, the skin on his face, tenderised by years of working in the sun, opened up as though Spadafora was wielding a broken bottle instead of boxing gloves.

'The life of a fighter certainly isn't easy,' Cornett told me a few weeks after the fight, still sweating from a two-hour training session in the gym that followed a ten-hour working day as a concreter.

'But this is the life I've chosen. I might not have had the recognition or the opportunities that went to other fighters over the years but I've always given my best.'

Born in Varazdin, Croatia, Cornett was 15 and in his words 'a scrawny dude' when he first took boxing lessons after being beaten up by a girl at Woodridge High School in Brisbane.

In all he had 154 amateur fights.

At the Olympics, he suffered an almost identical fate to Fenech, as the victim of a controversial decision, but while his better-known teammate from Marrickville was met at Sydney Airport by the flash guns and microphones of a media scrum, the only people to welcome Cornett home were wearing customs uniforms.

Cornett turned pro in 1986 and beat veteran Brian Roberts, Craig Pevy, Percy Israel and Kirk Blair before outpointing rugged Tony Miller in 1988 for the Australian super-featherweight crown at Parramatta. He survived a savage skirmish with Mexican Bruno Rabanales and then stopped Brazilian Francisco Tomas da Cruz, who had fought Julio César Chávez for the WBC title.

In 1993, Cornett travelled to Copenhagen to face Denmark's WBO champion Jimmi Bredahl but lost over 12 rounds. Bredahl lost his world title to a young Oscar De La Hoya the following year.

Cornett went undefeated over the next six years, beating Lincoln Stewart for the IBF Pan Pacific lightweight title, until he faced Spadafora for the IBF crown in Pittsburgh.

Despite the defeat he earned the respect of everyone watching, with one reporter calling him 'a tough piece of Aussie mutton'.

Cornett retired after his next bout, a ninth-round stoppage against Lovemore Ndou.

Another Olympic teammate, Shane 'The Hammer' Knox, compiled 16 wins in 16 pro fights before retiring to become a coach.

Spike's Silver Lining

The Lithgow Bash, Grahame 'Spike' Cheney, won a silver medal for Australia at the Seoul Olympics, the best performance by an Aussie Olympian since Snowy Baker 80 years before.

At the time, Spike lived with his parents, Bruce and Carol, in Sheedys Gully and was trained by Lithgow mainstay John Bolt, who also helped develop other star fighters Rick Timperi and Wayne Young. Timperi, who also trained with Johnny Lewis, fought for Australia at three Olympics and was part of a great era of Australian amateur fighters that included such boxers as Brian Williams, Greg Eadie, Justann Crawford, Jamien Wright, Richie Rowles, Justin Rowsell, Lee Trautsch, Lynden Hosking, and John and Glen Sutherland. Rowsell had a great professional career with 31 wins in 33 fights and Johnny Lewis regarded him as one of the slickest boxers he ever saw.

Spike Cheney was simply brilliant in Seoul and on the way to the final of the light-welterweight division he beat the slick American Todd Foster and Ghana's Ike Quartey, who as a professional held the world welterweight title for four years.

In the final, Spike lost to Soviet veteran Vyacheslav Yanovskiy but outpointed him in a rematch at Homebush in Sydney a few months later. He won a bronze medal at the 1990 Commonwealth Games and turned professional, though a series of personal problems and illnesses meant he was fighting more than just opponents in the ring.

He won his first five pro fights and in his sixth, in the main supporting bout to Jeff Fenech's rematch with Azumah Nelson at Princes Park in Melbourne, he dominated Argentinean Alberto Cortes, who held a big win over Lester Ellis.

Spike quit against Alex Tui at the Hordern Pavilion in Sydney in 1993, blaming the loss on chronic fatigue, but he came back to win a rematch and outpoint Stefan Scriggins, who had fought at the 1992 Olympics in Barcelona.

Spike lost to Leo Young Jr in Melbourne but manhandled Guyanese world title challenger Terrence Alli, before retiring from the sport in 1996 after losing in four rounds to Russian Viktor Baranov.

The years that followed that were not kind to Spike. Peter Kogoy reported in *The Sun-Herald* newspaper in 1998 that Spike was fighting 'a mental disease that has caused him to withdraw from the real world and has resulted in massive mood swings'.

Many years later Spike lost both his parents – his mother, Carol, was killed in a car accident – and it became harder and harder for him to fight his demons.

Yet it always gladdens the hearts of those who saw him fight at the Olympics to hear reports that he is doing well. Bill Mordey rated Spike in the same class as world champs Jeff Fenech and Jeff Harding.

Queensland's Darren Obah was one of Spike Cheney's teammates at the Seoul Olympics where he made it to the third round before being outpointed by Frenchman Laurent Boudouani, a future WBA light-middleweight champion.

Despite a loss to Ernie Artango in a challenge for the Australian middleweight title in 1994 in Caloundra, Obah fought for the WBA interim world middleweight title against Julio César Green in Madison Square Garden in 1999. A loss to Anthony Mundine in 2002 signalled the end of Obah's time at the top in Australia.

Kostya Tszyu: From Russia with Gloves

Kostya Tszyu's father, Boris, might have made it as an Olympic wrestler, but opportunity never came calling at the one bleak room where he lived with his wife and children. Boris had the speed, strength and athleticism of his hyperactive son, but rather than pursue his dream of sporting success, he concentrated on putting bread on the rickety table at Flat 64, 8 Korolenko House, in Lobva, a suburb of Serov.

Boris, whose grandfather migrated from Korea at the beginning of the 20th century, lived most of his life in the grimy industrial city at the base of the Ural Mountains, where the winds of Siberia were as chilling as the Stalinist regime he endured during his formative years. Amid the privations and perils of Communist Russia, however, Boris sparked in his son the desire to burst free from his concrete surrounds. Kostya grew up in a small two-bedroom apartment that the Tszyus shared with another family. Boris and his wife Valentina had a bed; Kostya and his sister Olga slept on the floor. The families generally washed at a bathouse down the street. When, in 1995, Tszyu brought his parents from Russia to live with him and his future wife, Natasha, in a modest suburban home in the Sydney suburb of Sans Souci, his parents were amazed that a country of such beauty and wealth existed.

By then, Kostya was already on the road to greatness. He had fought for the Soviet Union at the 1988 Seoul Olympics and won the world amateur title in Sydney in 1991, beating American Vernon Forrest in the light-welterweight final. It was 35 degrees in Sydney on the day Tszyu became world champion, and 35 below zero when he returned to Serov. He leapt at the chance to turn pro in sunny Australia with Bill Mordey's backing.

Tszyu had hired Johnny Lewis as his trainer, and soon found himself up against fellow Seoul Olympian Darrell Hiles on the undercard to Fenech's second fight with Azumah Nelson in Melbourne.

Lewis told Tszyu that it was important he win the first round.

Tszyu had mastered the short, savage right cross but his English was still rudimentary. Seconds into the fight, the little pig-tailed Russian had knocked Hiles out.

Apparently Tszyu thought Lewis had told him: 'You must win IN the first round.'

In just his fourth pro bout, Tszyu battered former world featherweight king Juan Laporte and, in his sixth, knocked out future world champion Sammy Fuentes in only 54 seconds. He took just two rounds to smash Steve Larrimore, who had stopped Lester Ellis.

In 1993, Tszyu outpointed former world champion Livingstone Bramble and, a few months later, in one of his toughest fights, he outpointed Olympic silver medallist Héctor López. He won the IBF junior-welterweight title in 1995, stopping Jake Rodriguez in six rounds.

Tszyu suffered a stunning upset loss in 1997 to veteran Vince Phillips, which he blamed on a blood disorder. But he fought back, and along the way stopped slick Calvin Grove and the mighty Mexican Julio Cesar Chavez. In 2001 he was being outboxed by cocky Zab Judah in Las Vegas when a Tszyu right hand flattened the American and left him wondering what bus had just run him down. By 2003 Tszyu held all three major world-title belts – the IBF, WBA and WBC.

A year later Tszyu was too modest to shout 'I am the greatest' after crushing Sharmba Mitchell in three brutal rounds at Glendale Arena in Phoenix, Arizona, in their second fight. But just about everyone else was proclaiming him one of the greatest junior-welterweights of all time.

Despite having been out of the ring injured for 22 months, the 35-year-old Tszyu decked Mitchell four times in three rounds for one of the most devastating victories of his career.

Written off by the American critics as too old and slow for the fast-moving American southpaw, Tszyu stalked his challenger methodically before landing a huge right hand midway through Round 2 that set up the sudden end to their rematch.

Referee Raul Caiz stopped the fight with 12 seconds remaining in Round 3.

'They'll still be talking about Kostya Tszyu in 300 years,' Johnny Lewis said. 'Only a super athlete can come back from nearly two years out of the game, take on the next best junior-welterweight in the world and absolutely crush him.'

Mitchell could see the right hand coming in Round 2, but Tszyu was so precise with the punch, so pin-point perfect with its execution, that for Mitchell it was like trying to dodge the bullet of a Russian sniper at close range. It was also Kostya's last win after almost a decade at the top during which he engaged in 18 world title fights.

THE LATER ROUNDS

Anthony Mundine: The Mouth that Roared

Along with 6000 other people I saw Anthony 'The Man' Mundine fight for the first time in 2000. He had sensationally walked out of the St George Illawarra Dragons rugby league side mid-season, foregoing a contract worth $600,000 a year to make his professional boxing debut against Kiwi Gerrard Zohs at the Sydney Entertainment Centre.

Mundine was a sensational footballer, performing stunning backflips after scoring tries. But he was known for his big mouth as much as his fast feet, making all manner of claims about how he was a better player than many of the game's greats, and that he was being held back by racism.

When he was a boy, Anthony's father, Tony, the great middleweight of the 1970s, would take Anthony through the seedier parts of Sydney to show him the addicts and deadbeats. Tony would tell his son that their sad state was the dividend for an investment in drugs and alcohol.

The younger Mundine followed his father's example of never drinking or smoking, and he reaped the results.

Anthony's pro boxing debut was a success, as he showed speed and power to win by a fourth-round knockout. But his talk of becoming a world champ seemed like a pipedream. Still, in 2001 he was awarded a hotly disputed 12-round split decision over the experienced and cagey Sam Soliman at Wollongong in an IBF Pan Pacific super-middleweight title bout.

Then Anthony showed his real potential with a crushing knockout of Guy Waters. Before I knew it I was in Dortmund, Germany, with my great mate Ray Wheatley, who had helped organise Mundine's fight for the IBF world super-middleweight title.

With just ten pro fights behind him, Mundine was ready to challenge Germany's undefeated world champ Sven Ottke, a three-time Olympian who had engaged in almost 350 amateur fights.

Ottke had competed alongside Kostya Tszyu at the 1988 Olympics in Seoul and by the time he faced Mundine at Dortmund's Westphalia Hall, he was Germany's favourite boxer.

A mild-mannered family man, Ottke's many sponsorships included a deal worth $400,000 a year to advertise condoms. Going into the fight, Mundine said he hadn't had sex for ten weeks to focus his mind and body.

At the weigh-in a day before the bout, Mundine looked fitter, stronger and fiercer than the 34-year-old German. But Ottke, the smaller and physically less impressive specimen, was adamant that size didn't count. 'Boxing is not about size but technique,' Ottke told me. 'I believe that Mundine's muscles will not help him against me. I am eight years older than him and that means more experience and better technique.'

The Aussie upstart said he had been working on a special right uppercut and had the superior speed and power to negate Ottke's slippery skills and radar left jab.

While Mundine looked the more powerful man at the weigh-in, held amid other powerful speed machines at Dortmund's leading BMW dealership, he had also gone down big with the promoters of the fight, the Sauerland Group in Germany. Eckhard Klein, the young promoter, said Mundine's outspoken manner and confident swagger had been a tonic for German boxing and the nation's sporting fans during a particularly gloomy winter.

As it turned out, six million Germans tuned in to see the brash former rugby league star take on their home favourite on free-to-air television.

I watched the fight while perched on the ringside apron alongside Sam Soliman and the esteemed British official Mickey Vann.

Mundine had told reporters that he had no fear of Ottke because the German 'punched like a woman', but Ottke's trainer, Ulli Wegner, had predicted that Mundine's muddled head would be bouncing around all night like one of those dashboard dachshunds as Ottke used it for target practice.

Mundine had always been a surprise packet, and for the first six rounds Ottke was made to look second rate as Mundine seemed faster, stronger and more dangerous.

Mickey Vann leaned over to me and said, 'Look's like your Aussie is out in front.'

Alas for The Man, common sense prevailed, and in the tenth round the natural order was restored. Sensing that the inexperienced Mundine was weary from darting about the ring like a stinging butterfly, Ottke went for the kill, landing a right to the temple that dropped Mundine like a dead man.

It was only Ottke's fifth knockout in 25 pro fights, and after the sudden end to a desperately close fight, the crowd of 6500 at the Westphalia Hall erupted with joy.

Mundine took ten minutes to get back to his feet, and all the while his mother Lyn was crying herself sick. Having seen her husband knocked rotten several times, she now had to endure the misery of a son badly damaged by another man's fists.

Mundine put up a gutsy effort against Ottke and continued the stoicism after the fight when German medics wanted to carry him from the arena on a stretcher.

The stretcher was standard procedure for concussion victims in that part of the world and the locals were adamant Mundine was going to be carried out on his back, whether he liked it or not. But Mundine refused to get on.

Officials brought the ambulance to a back entrance of the arena so that the shattered fighter would not have to be carried out in public.

Still, Mundine would have none of it, instead walking to the ambulance with his personal physician and cornerman Dr Martin Raftery for the drive to the hospital, Klinik Nord, where he was to be kept for observation.

Mundine told the German medical team that he didn't want to leave the stadium looking like a loser. 'The Man' wanted to walk out like a man.

Sven Ottke retired three years later having never lost in 34 fights, one of the few world champions to leave the game undefeated. Still, he admitted that the battle with Anthony Mundine was the toughest of his career, and that Mundine was the fastest and most dangerous boxer he ever faced.

Danny Green All Go

Anthony Mundine will forever be linked with Danny Green in Australian boxing history as their two fights, 11 years apart, were two of the biggest-grossing bouts this country has seen.

Both went the distance. Mundine won the first at the Sydney Football Stadium in 2006, Green the second at Adelaide Oval in 2017.

I first mooted a fight between them after Green came close to beating Russia's Aleksandr Lebziak at the Sydney Olympics in 2000 (Lebziak went on to win the gold medal), and Mundine made his much-publicised professional debut the same year.

I'd initially met Danny in a dressing-room at a community club at Broadbeach on the Gold Coast in April 2000, a few months before his Sydney Olympics bout. In those days he was a Perth carpenter, and he had all the composure of an old wooden house that was falling apart as he sat, exhausted and demoralised, head slumped in his swollen hands.

He had just been beaten 10–9 by Maroubra fitness fanatic Jason DeLisle for the 2000 Australian amateur light-heavyweight title. DeLisle was a tough and determined fighter, brilliantly trained by Dino Billinghurst to challenge for the IBF light-heavyweight title six years later.

After the loss at Broadbeach, Green was wondering if all the blood, sweat, tears and broken bones were really worth it, only to end up as small type in the results section of the next day's papers.

While still an amateur boxer, Green's nose had been broken four times, along with his eye socket. His hands should have had been tattooed with the warning 'fragile', such was the frequency with which they shattered on impact. But boxing had taught him to bite down hard on the mouthguard and soak up whatever those impostors Triumph and Disaster threw at him.

He learned from the loss and came back to compete in the Olympic Games before joining the pro ranks in 2001, and he went on to beat DeLisle twice.

In 2003, though, Green was again a forlorn figure, flopped in the foyer of the Dorint Parkhotel in Bad Neuenahr, Germany, the morning after being disqualified in a world title fight he'd been winning against local hero Markus Beyer. He had battered Beyer for five cruel rounds under a giant marquee at the Nürburgring motor racing track, only to have victory controversially torn from him by a German doctor and an American referee amid wild scenes.

Green had taken the Beyer fight for just $45,000 but had been promised more than $1 million for his first defence against Canadian Eric Lucas in Montreal planned for later in the year, and an even bigger purse for a unification title fight with Mundine's conqueror Sven Ottke.

From Round 1, Green had belted Beyer, telling Jeff Fenech, his trainer in the corner, that he had a much tougher time in the gym against his sparring partner and fellow Sydney Olympian Paul Miller than he did fighting the WBC champion.

With 50 seconds remaining in the opening round, Beyer hit the canvas from a looping right hand. He rose to his feet looking deathly afraid of the Australian's power.

In the closing stages of Round 2, Beyer was down again from a right uppercut, and at the end of the round he had a cut over his right eye that the referee ruled was from an accidental clash of heads. Even though the referee said the headbutt was accidental, he took a point off Green.

By the end of the fourth round, Beyer was cut above and below his right eye, and in Round 5, both men were covered in the German's blood and so was the grey suit I was wearing.

Then Green shoved his forehead into Beyer's face again. Now Green had lost three points for headbutts, but was still ahead on all three judges' cards.

Green dropped Beyer twice and had the badly cut southpaw world champion on the brink of defeat when the Australian was disqualified at the end of the fifth round for an intentional headbutt.

Initially, referee Bill Clancy instructed the judges to take two points from Green for the headbutt at the end of the fifth round, but after ten minutes of discussion between the German doctor, Professor Walter Wagner, and WBC officials, the doctor ruled Beyer could not continue because of the cut, and Green was disqualified.

The Australians were furious because Beyer already had cuts around his right eye that threatened the early finish to the fight when Green slammed his head into the German's face at the end of Round 5.

'I beat Beyer convincingly in all five rounds and the only way the Germans could keep the world title was to pull a stunt like this,' Green told me after the fight.

'When they declared Beyer was still the champion, he was hanging his head in shame when I went over to shake his hand. It hurts so much because just a few more minutes and I would have been coming home to Sydney with the WBC belt.'

Green threatened terrible retribution if he ever got Beyer in the ring again, but despite his confidence that he had Beyer's measure, the German learned from that shellacking and in their rematch two years later he won a points decision.

Back in Australia after that rematch, Green was at the lowest point in his life, his dreams and aspirations crushed in a very public humiliation. He gave himself a morale boost with two wins in Perth over American James Crawford and Mexican Quirino Garcia. But what really lifted his spirits was when Danny headed off into the desert of central Australia on a voyage of self-discovery.

He packed up the rumbling black beast that was his Falcon GT muscle car and set off from his Perth beachside apartment with his father, Mal, for a high-speed odyssey to Sydney and his first fight with Mundine.

The drive was one of the great experiences of Danny Green's life. To cross the vast Australian outback and see what an awe-inspiring country we live in was an emotional experience.

Not that the journey didn't have its hazards. 'Before we left, Mum had made about 15 rounds of curried-egg sandwiches for the trip,' Green said. 'There was so much methane being produced in that vehicle it's amazing that we ever had to refuel.'

It was just on sunset on the first day of their drive out near Caiguna, where the Nullarbor Highway disappears over the horizon for 140 kilometres without a bend, that the two travellers pulled the GT over and jumped out for a breath of fresh air.

Mal Green told me that Danny stood in the stillness for half an hour, spellbound by a wedgetail eagle soaring high and free on the desert thermals. 'There was no traffic, no sound, nothing, just this beautiful stillness and this eagle flying high.'

Danny knew that travelling with Mal would put his head straight. Mal was Danny's idol and exemplar, a dry good-humoured bush battler who taught his son about mateship, loyalty and the determination he had learned trying to survive on a dusty farm in the West Australian wheat belt.

Mal's parents had died when he was 15 and he and his brothers and sisters worked the land themselves, supporting and helping each other to make it through.

But after three years of successive drought in the early 1970s, Mal moved with his wife, Maria, and their young family to Perth, where Danny was born in 1973.

Mal got a job flipping burgers at Hungry Jack's, working his way up the ranks until he became a big cheese in the burger business and such good friends with the boss, Jack Cowan, that Cowan lent Danny his 50-million-dollar yacht for a cruise on the Adriatic in 2003.

Mal had played Aussie rules in the bush and started coaching kids when he came to Perth. His assistant was Louie Manolikos, whose plucky son Justin played centre and later became Danny's manager.

At the Marist club in Perth, Mal coached Danny to three premierships from the age of eight to 16.

'He was never going to make a top AFL player,' Mal said. 'But there was no harder trier in his team. He wasn't the captain, but he was a leader in the example he showed in his determination as a rover.

'There was always the humour to put people at ease but when the job had to be done he would knuckle down and give it everything.'

Surfing off Perth's Scarborough beach kept the young Green fit for football, and at 18 he followed older brother Brendan, who'd been drafted to the Eagles, to the carport boxing gym of Burmese immigrant Pat Devellerez for extra training.

That was when Danny fell in love with boxing.

He was always boxing's biggest joker. By the time he fought Mundine in 2006, Danny was 76 kilograms of tattoos, toughness and tenacity, but he was also the sport's clown prince, with as many punchlines as relentless punches.

'I'm a better fighter than Mundine,' he said in the lead-up to the bout, 'and I'm funnier, too. My jokes leave his for dead.'

Before the first Beyer fight back in 2003, Green had told wide-eyed reporters in Germany that he was a tank commander away from boxing and, with a straight face, announced to a press conference in Montreal that he prepared for fights by wrestling a pet crocodile in his backyard.

He let off a stink bomb in the middle of a group of Penrith Panthers rugby league players at a fight night in Sydney and once, when Mundine told a Sydney radio station he was the cream of the boxing crop, Green rang in as a talkback caller to tell Mundine he wasn't the cream, just the cream puff.

But when it came to competition – any competition – Green was deadly serious. As an amateur boxer, representing his country without pay, he'd worked sporadically as a carpenter, often surviving off what his wife, Nina, a former swimming champion, made working in a lunch bar and managing a hostel.

When he and Nina first came to Sydney to make a career from boxing in 2001, they'd put a microwave oven and a few household goods in their old Mitsubishi Magna and headed east. The couple lived in a flat beside the railway tracks at Ashfield, before moving back to Perth a couple of years later.

In Sydney, his sponsor, Steve Bowden, a former Newtown rugby league enforcer, offered Green the use of his $750,000 Bentley Continental but Green told him it was a dangerous thing to offer a pure bogan. 'I said I couldn't do it to him,' Green told me. 'I'd take the traction control off and start doing doughnuts.'

After Green and his father drove across the desert to begin training for the Mundine fight, Danny knew they'd be facing an opponent full of confidence.

In 2003 Mundine brought American Antwun Echols to Sydney to capture the vacant WBA super-middleweight title by decision, becoming a world champion, something that always eluded Mundine's father Tony. He then climbed off the canvas to retain the title against Japan's Yoshinori Nishizawa. In his next fight, however, Mundine lost the WBA crown when he was knocked down early and outpointed by Puerto Rican Manny Siaca. He was then overpowered in 12 rounds by Siaca's conqueror, Mikkel Kessler of Denmark. But Mundine still believed he would be too quick for his great Aussie rival.

He was. Green had given himself a mohawk haircut, but it was Mundine cutting loose throughout the bout, with superior combinations to win a points decision over 12 rounds before a crowd of 28,000 at Aussie Stadium. Pay-per-view revenue made it the richest fight ever held in Australia; estimates of Mundine's payday were as high as $8 million.

Green dusted himself off and went on a surfing holiday at Yallingup, south of Perth. While there, a frantic man came running up from the beach. Someone was drowning.

'Before I knew it, Danny had run to get a surfboard and raced out into the ocean to save him,' Yallingup Beach Holiday Park manager Vicki Samuels told me. 'If Danny hadn't dived into the ocean the young man would have drowned for sure.'

Green shrugged his shoulders. 'Anyone who is a good swimmer would have done the same thing,' he said. 'The bloke was in a bad way when I got there. The undertow kept dragging him down and he told me later he'd already said his prayers and was ready to die. Saving a life was a lot more important than anything I ever did in the ring.'

Green was dragging the distressed man back to shore when the bloke suddenly saw the light. He was dazed and confused, the situation so surreal he was sure he was hallucinating as the heavy waves hit him from all sides. 'Mate, aren't you Danny Green?' he exclaimed. 'I've seen you fight on television.'

The Fastest Man in the World

Roy Jones Jr was one of the best fighters in the world for more than a decade. At his peak he was one of the fastest and most brilliant boxers I ever saw.

I watched him live for the first time at the American Airlines Arena in Miami, sitting ringside between Ray Wheatley and Jones's long-time rival, Antonio Tarver. Jones was up against undefeated Australian Glen Kelly.

The bookies said Kelly had about as much chance as a three-legged horse in the Melbourne Cup, but the magnificently muscled Sydney fighter known as 'Kunga' had trained hard to prove them wrong.

The IBF's top light-heavyweight contender – a former garbo from Little Bay in Sydney – was trying to take the world light-heavyweight title from Jones, a man whose passions in life included cock-fighting, acting, rap singing, hunting big game with a bow and arrow and squashing world-title challengers like grapes.

Kelly received A$1.5 million for the fight but probably took home less than half of that after agents' fees, taxes and expenses were taken out.

Jones received A$6 million, but anyone who thought about taking a cent of it would regret doing so.

Kelly would be marrying long-time fiancée Tracy in a Las Vegas wedding chapel a week after the fight and wanted the ceremony to be a double celebration.

He'd spent four years collecting garbage for Waverley Council and knew he'd have to work harder than ever if he was to out-hustle Jones, a boxer who had outclassed everyone in the pro ranks since being voted the best boxer of the 1988 Olympics.

Before the fight, Kelly's trainer, Jeff Fenech, told me that Jones was unquestionably the best fighter in the world at that time, regardless of weight classes.

Jones, whose rap music was proving a huge hit in America, was quick to agree. 'No one has ever given me a close fight,' said the man whose only defeat in the pro ranks until that time was a disqualification for punching an opponent on the canvas. In a rematch he'd knocked out that opponent in one round.

Jones pulled an eclectic crowd for the fight against Kelly. OJ Simpson joined rap singers Bun B, Pimp C, UGK and Scarface at ringside along with baseball's home-run king Barry Bonds.

The world champ spent six rounds playing cat and mouse with Kelly, then in the seventh he put both hands behind his back, lured the Australian into range and knocked him out with a looping right behind the ear.

Two months later, Jones was in Sydney appearing in the movie *The Matrix Reloaded*. He turned up for a photoshoot I'd organised outside the Sydney Opera House wearing baggy old jeans, a loose T-shirt that hid the multi-million-dollar body, and a baseball cap turned back to front. He was totally anonymous as he dangled a fishing line off the end of Bennelong Point at the bottom of the Sydney Opera House stairs.

On his 35-hectare ranch in Pensacola, Florida, down in the backwoods near the Alabama border, Roy Jr had a team of pit bull terriers, 1500 roosters trained to kill, a bow and arrow he used to hunt deer and .270 and 30–30 rifles with which he shot anything he damn well wanted.

He had also won the world middleweight (72 kg), super-middleweight (76 kg), light-heavyweight (79.5 kg) and heavyweight (unlimited) titles and was destined to be measured in decades to come alongside the likes of Muhammad Ali and Sugar Ray Robinson.

Roy had grown up in a caravan in backwoods country. While other kids in his neighbourhood played games and watched *The Brady Bunch* after school, Roy's old man made him train in a boxing ring he'd fashioned in a field and hit him with sticks and belts. There Roy would stay for five or six hours every day until his little arms could hardly move. On weekends he trained double time.

As a kid, Roy had thought often about shooting his father, but he patched things up with the grizzled Vietnam vet who'd set him on his path to boxing greatness with a boot in the backside and a rubber hose across his legs.

'I had a harsh upbringing,' he conceded. 'But looking back, all the overtime he made me put in as a kid is why I'm now so far in front of everyone.'

Roy was at his peak then.

A few years later, on 2 December 2009, at the Acer Arena in Sydney, Danny Green stopped him in the first round in one of the best performances ever by an Australian fighter.

Golden Chance that Slipped Away

Kevin 'Bones' Kelly, Glen Kelly's brother, was a 30–1 underdog when he knocked down defending WBA champion David Reid in Atlantic City in 1999, only to lose a close decision.

An unheralded wharfie from La Perouse, Kelly had reduced America's only Olympic gold medallist from the Atlanta Games to 70 stunned kilograms of frozen fighter in Round 5 of their junior-middleweight title fight beside the boardwalk.

It was the best moment of Kelly's sporting life, which had begun at age four, grazing his knees in the Souths Juniors rugby league competition.

And it didn't get any better than this – because David Reid got back up. Kelly, perhaps overawed by the occasion, let the title slip through his fingers as Reid went on to post a controversial points victory.

It was such a close decision that after the fight American TV commentator Rich Moratta said it could have gone either way and that the Aussie had exposed all the flaws in the world champ's technique with his fluent jab and shifty footwork.

Trained by George Reno and Dino Billinghurst, Kelly had turned pro in 1992 but had a mixed start to his career, beating Les Fear but losing to Brad Mayo, David Clencie, Brian Williams and Peter Giles, and fighting a draw with Dale Artango before finally winning the Australian light-middleweight title with a decision over Williams in 1995 at Sydney's Parramatta Leagues Club.

He took the Commonwealth title in his next fight against Leo Young Jr in Adelaide but lost it by hometown decision to former world champ Chris Pyatt in Cardiff, Wales.

Kelly came back to beat Mark Picker, Paulo Pinto and Sam Soliman to earn the shot at Reid.

Kali Meehan: So Close

Promoter Don King showcased some great heavyweights – Muhammad Ali, George Foreman, Joe Frazier, Mike Tyson and Evander Holyfield among them – but the man with the electric hair once told me that even he was taken aback by the courage of Kali Meehan, big-time boxing's ring-in.

Weighing 105 kilograms and 195 centimetres tall, Meehan played for the Central Coast rugby league team when he wasn't boxing.

He had become a forgotten force in world boxing but his career was resurrected as a sparring partner for King's fighters.

Then, out of nowhere, he secured a shot against WBO champ Lamon Brewster in Las Vegas on 4 September 2004, going down in a hotly disputed split decision after having Brewster out on his feet in the eighth round.

Meehan had staggered Brewster in Round 8 with a left-right combination to the head that forced the champion back into the challenger's corner. He then connected with six or seven hard right hands to the head, then went downstairs, scoring with several good body shots.

Brewster collapsed on the ropes twice, and referee Jay Nady looked set to halt the bout.

But Meehan could not deliver the knockout shot.

'Many people thought he beat Lamon Brewster, but Kali didn't get the decision because he didn't have the killer instinct,' Don King told me. 'They knew each other and were friends. Kali liked the guy too much.'

If one of the judges, Dave Moretti, had given the final round to Meehan, the Aussie would have created boxing history and caused one of the biggest upsets in the sport.

Brewster won the 12th round on two of the three scorecards to pull out a split decision.

The crowd loudly booed the scoring.

Meehan was the first Australian in 98 years to box for the biggest prize in the toughest sport of all after Bill Lang collected £600 to fight Tommy Burns in 1908.

It was a stunning turnaround in fortunes for the New Zealand-born giant who started boxing in Auckland at age 13, collecting bottles from the bins at rugby games to pay his membership at the local gym.

'I've done it tough my whole life,' said Meehan, who until just a few weeks before the Brewster fight had been working doors at a nightclub before going straight to his job collecting rubbish for Drummoyne Council at 4 a.m. 'I know what it's like to go hungry and it's a terrible thing when your kids want something to eat and you have to tell them there's nothing but rice in the cupboard.'

Inspired by the great heavyweight champ Larry Holmes, Meehan had 26 amateur fights in New Zealand, battling Olympians David Tua and Paea Wolfgramm in between work in a tannery and as a garbo, bouncer and painter. He started making a name for himself as a professional on Queensland's Gold Coast backed by the astute promoter Mark Ericksen.

Two months after the Brewster fight, Meehan carried an injury into the ring at Madison Square Garden and predictably lost to American Hasim Rahman, who regained a version of the world heavyweight title in his next start.

Meehan's son Willis Meehan, 195 centimetres and 115 kilograms, won the Australian super-heavyweight amateur title at just 17, and played for the Roosters in the NRL in 2014 before being sacked for disciplinary reasons.

Sam Soliman, The Melbourne Magician

One of the finest displays of pure boxing skill I ever saw came from Melbourne's artful dodger, Sam Soliman, when he became the number-one contender for the world middleweight title by completely outclassing Dutchman Raymond Joval.

The fight took place on 18 July 2004 at the Pechanga Resort and Casino in Temecula, California, down near the Mexican border. Soliman was 30 at the time and already a veteran in the sport, but he showed that he remained one of the most elusive and evasive fighters in the world.

As he limbered up under a canvas canopy outside the Grand Ballroom at the Pechanga Casino, he was more worried about a dozen schoolkids he'd seconded to carry his vast array of championship belts into the ring for his fight. 'Hey kids, it's very hot out there,' he told them. 'I don't want any of you getting sick. If you feel hot come inside where it's cool.'

Moments later, Soliman was under the glare of the Fox Sports TV cameras fighting the number-two middleweight in the world for a piece of boxing history.

The fight started in controversy when Soliman's trainer, Dave Hedgcock, a former world kickboxing champ, insisted that Joval not wear gel or braids in the tight band of dyed gold hair that encircled his otherwise-shaved head. There were fears Joval could use the hardened hair as an extra weapon at close quarters. But in the end Joval could have brought a chainsaw into the ring and not caused Soliman much damage.

After Joval went down in Round 4, Soliman began leaping around the ring, shimmying, sashaying, showboating and doing a series of martial arts butterfly kicks to the astonishment of referee Jack Reiss.

Joval's hulking pal, three-time world champ James Toney, who has the face of a junkyard dog and a bark to match, did his best to intimidate the Australian's corner. Fresh from a knockout win over former heavyweight king Evander Holyfield, Toney was as frustrated as Joval by the hit and not-be-hit style of the mesmerising Soliman. Several times he approached Soliman's corner during the fight. 'Tell that damn Aussie to stand and fight or I'll bust him in the head,' he snapped on one occasion, prompting Soliman's trainer, Dave Hedgcock, to hurl ice at the angry accuser. But nothing the 110-kilogram monster snarled could throw Soliman off his game plan.

The ever-smiling Aussie, who was cheered ringside by his good friend, singer and actress Holly Valance, and two-time Olympic boxer Robbie Peden, won every round against Joval, decking him in Round 4 and almost stopping him in the 11th. A heavy underdog going into the fight, Soliman gained revenge for a close 12-round decision Joval took against the Australian in Amsterdam in 2001.

Soliman became the first Australian middleweight since Tony Mundine beat the legendary Emile Griffith in Paris 31 years earlier to become the number-one contender for the world middleweight title, the crown Bernard Hopkins would be defending against Oscar De La Hoya two months later in a fight that generated total purses of $50 million.

'That's the sort of guy Sammy is, said his manager, Stuart Duncan, who had transformed Soliman from a penniless pug who would take fights on short notice and lose as many as he won into a world-beating star.

'Sammy has always had this incredible ability to hit and not be hit but he just wasn't moving in the right direction. He was scratching for money and taking fights against some of the world's best on just a few days' notice.'

It would take Soliman a decade to reach the pinnacle of his career, though. He would have to battle the likes of Anthony Mundine, the brilliant American Winky Wright and the rugged Australian world champ Sakio Bika, before outpointing Germany's Felix Sturm in Krefeld, Germany, for the IBF middleweight title in 2014, to become world champ at the age of 40.

Robbie Peden, Queensland's Golden Boy

On a dark desert highway, cool wind in his hair, Robbie Peden was driving me to my hotel in California. He was flooring the accelerator on the rental car like he'd floored opponents for the previous 20 years, tossing it into corners the way he threw foes around the ring.

It was July 2004 and we were two hours south of Los Angeles, deep in the Temecula Valley where the Pechanga Indians had made their casino one of the biggest money-spinning operations in the state. Peden and his trainer, Roger Bloodworth, were there to see another Aussie, Sam Soliman, take on the world's second-ranked middleweight, Raymond Joval, and to party with their heavyweight mate James 'Lights Out' Toney.

In the fight game, Peden was everyone's buddy and he had partied everywhere from Miami to Maroochydore, Tampa Bay to Townsville. His accent was born somewhere between Wynnum-Manly in Queensland and the Mississippi Delta and he had the cocky swagger of a young man who knew a lot about winning women and flattening men.

Peden was a veteran of 145 amateur fights, fought at the Barcelona and Atlanta Olympics, and beat the classy West Indian Gairy St Clair and crack Englishman Spencer Oliver on his way to the Commonwealth Games gold in 1994. On the eve of Atlanta 1996, he outclassed the eventual gold medallist, Somluck Kamsing of Thailand, in a pre-Games tournament.

Since the Atlanta Olympics, Queensland's first world boxing champion – the son of a Scottish father and Indigenous mother – had lived in America and had scored some spectacular wins as a professional, not the least being a fifth-round knockout in Pechanga of red-hot American Nate Campbell just a few months earlier in March 2004. The American was outboxing Peden and taunting him by sticking out his unprotected chin. Campbell stuck out his chin once too often.

But as we drove through the Temecula Valley, the tough little terrier from bayside Brisbane was still a battling contender outlining the special bond he had forged with his dad, Brian, in Brisbane and trainer Roger Bloodworth, who was like a second father to him in America.

When Peden had first hit the United States looking for fights, he'd flown 30 hours from Brisbane to Virginia Beach, got off the plane and gone straight to the gym to spar Pernell Whitaker, Olympic gold medallist and four-time world champ.

Bloodworth, who'd made his name training Evander Holyfield, Fernando Vargas and Andrew Golota, wanted to test the Aussie kid's mettle. 'Robbie tried to knock Pernell out,' Bloodworth said.

'I couldn't believe his determination and drive. I knew right then that he had the right stuff.'

Almost a year after Sam Soliman rang rings around Raymond Joval at Pechanga Casino, Robbie Peden was matched with Nate Campbell for a second time, fighting in Melbourne for the same IBF junior-lightweight title once held by Aussies Lester Ellis and Barry Michael.

It was Peden's first professional bout in Australia after nearly a decade based in America. Campbell had almost broken Peden in two with a body punch the previous time they exchanged unpleasantries before the cocky American got careless.

Peden spent three weeks training in New York and another four in St Louis. Then, for five weeks at his training camp on Queensland's Sunshine Coast, Peden sparred the cream of Australia's lighter boxers – Jackson Asiku, Michael Katsidis, Naoufel Ben Rabah and Nedal 'Skinny' Hussein, the world-rated super-bantamweight he'd beaten three times in the amateurs.

Peden went into the Campbell world title fight as a $2.60 outsider, but he was in charge from the opening bell. Campbell was bleeding from the nose from the second round and by the fourth he was cut around his right eye.

Referee Johnny Wright, a rugged welterweight of the 1970s, stopped the fight seven seconds from the end of the eighth round.

Peden was paraded around the ring in triumph on the shoulders of another of his mates, the heavyweight David Tua, then New Zealand's most famous fighter. The victory came 21 years after his father first showed him how to throw a straight left.

Seven months after winning the world title in Melbourne, Peden staked it against the WBC championship of Mexican Marco Antonio Barrera, best known for ending the career of England's 'Prince' Naseem Hamed.

In America, the fight was as big as Kostya Tszyu versus Ricky Hatton, a unification fight for the world junior-lightweight championship at the MGM Grand Casino, that great green cash register at the end of the Vegas strip.

Peden claimed his big advantage was that even though they were both 31, he was much fresher than the Mexican, who by that stage had fought more wars than Alexander the Great.

But it wasn't to be. Barrera won a comfortable decision over 12 rounds.

Peden fought only once more, returning to Brisbane to fight in his hometown for the first time as a professional.

In a huge upset he was stopped in the eighth round by Filipino Ranee Ganoy.

Robbie Peden was just one of the many top Australian fighters to have boxed at an Olympic Games. The 2000 Olympics produced Danny Green, Daniel Geale, Vic Darchinyan, Sakio Bika and Michael Katsidis. From Athens four years later came leading pros Joel Brunker and Jamie Pittman, and from Beijing in 2008 came Paul Fleming, Brad 'Hollywood' Pitt and the Steve Deller–trained Todd Kidd and Jarrod Fletcher. London 2012 produced Jeff Horn and the Gareth Williams–trained Cameron Hammond and Damien Hooper. Four years later, Australia was represented in Rio by Shelley Watts, Daniel Lewis – who won his Olympic spot against Tim Tszyu – and big Jason Whateley.

Paul Briggs: Redemption Song

Paul Briggs was sexually abused as an eight-year-old boy and spent the next 21 years a victim of his own rage and self-loathing. His anger and hate fuelled the destructive fighting skills that made him a national kickboxing champion at just 15 and a world kickboxing champ four years later.

The unresolved fury also made him unmerciful in his secondary career as a drug taking, drug-dealing standover man.

He was Chopper Read with ears, packing firearms and breaking legs with a baseball bat or metal pole.

'In the space of a few brutal minutes, that rape destroyed my life, and I would never be the same little boy again,' he revealed in his painfully confronting biography *Heart, Soul, Fire*, written with Gregor Salmon.

'Every night for years I'd fear the onset of the most violent and graphic dreams. And between then and now, many, many men paid dearly for what was done to me. My pain was something I felt compelled to share.'

For his 21st birthday Briggs stayed awake for five days. 'I consumed about 25 ecstasy tablets, at least six grams of cocaine, two or three bottles of amyl nitrite, a few lines of ketamine, a pile of speed, tokes from joint after joint and drinks from bottle after bottle of vodka. In those days I didn't take drugs so much as take them on.'

Briggs became a creature so loathsome and hideous that he couldn't look at himself in the mirror. Fuelled by his unquenchable inner rage, he would steal from his lair under cover of darkness and prowl nightclubs and drug dens, wreaking havoc as a dealer and standover man.

Therapy eventually helped Briggs find forgiveness and an inner calm, but it took a long time. And, ironically, he says the peace and contentment it brought him made him an even more vicious fighting machine than he was as a skinhead standover man.

Briggs made his professional boxing debut in 1994, winning a ten-round majority decision over Ronald Doo in Brisbane but, out of shape and in the drug and crime culture, he didn't fight again for three years and then suffered a third-round stoppage to Larl Zada.

Briggs scored a fifth-round technical decision over Daniel Rowsell for the IBF Pan Pacific cruiserweight title at Tweed Heads, stopped Adrian Bellin in eight to win the Australian light-heavyweight title in Melbourne, and stopped Paul Smallman in four for the OPBF light-heavyweight title at Broadbeach.

A win over Olympian Peter Kariuki primed him for a crushing knockout in four over Glen Kelly and points victories over ex-world middleweight champion Jorge Castro of Argentina and Mexican Jesus Ruiz.

Briggs punched his way to a world light-heavyweight title fight by overpowering Croatian giant Stipe Drews at the State Sports Centre in Sydney on 15 August 2004.

The 29-year-old Gold Coast fighter showed enormous courage and composure to dominate the second half of the fight against a lanky southpaw who, at 195 centimetres, towered above him by 15 centimetres.

For the first five rounds, Briggs had difficulty coping with the Croatian's enormous reach advantage and deadly accurate right jab. But midway through the sixth, Briggs threw a punch that not only changed the whole fight, but the trajectory of his career as well.

As Drews tried to hold the charging Aussie, Briggs slammed home a left hook that travelled no more than 25 centimetres but decked Drews hard.

The previously undefeated Croatian bravely battled to his feet only to go down again as Briggs looked for the knockout. As Drews got back to his feet for the second time, he was desperate to survive. Suddenly the elegant boxer turned into a frightened animal and brought his knee hard up into Briggs's groin.

American referee Lawrence Cole resisted the temptation to disqualify Drews but took two points from the German-based giant.

Briggs stormed home to win a unanimous 12-round decision.

Drews never got over the mauling, and three years later in Perth, he was reluctant to throw a punch against Danny Green, losing his world light-heavyweight title to the Australian.

In his biggest tests, Briggs twice came up short in WBC title fights against Poland's Tomasz Adamek in Chicago, though, with Johnny Lewis in his corner, he did put Adamek on the canvas in round one of their 2006 rematch.

Adamek, a boxer as grim as Chernobyl, brawled with Briggs over 24 of the most pulsating rounds anyone could remember, with each man tearing away a piece of the other's life.

The Pole went on to dominate the heavier cruiserweight division and became a leading contender for the world heavyweight crown.

Paul Briggs had nothing left when his career ended in controversy, lasting just 29 seconds against Danny Green in Perth in 2010.

Girl Power

It has only been during the twenty-first century that Australian women have become heavily involved in the most primal of all sports.

By 1920, women were attending Australian fights without needing a disguise, but they still could not participate in the action.

At Sydney Stadium, on 30 July 1931, police banned a women's contest between Aggie Green and Jessie Hammond, and in 1933, the Pope denounced even the presence of women at a world heavyweight title fight in Rome between Primo Carnera and Paulino Uzcudun.

In 1978, however, promoter Larry Memery declared Australia's first official women's boxing match on 25 November that year 'an outstanding success'. 'Neither girl was hurt, not even a blood nose,' he said.

Dee Dee Dowton of Collingwood outpointed Kim Ross of Thornbury. Memery had staged the contest on King Island, part of Tasmania, because the Victorian government refused to grant licences to women boxers.

The new millennium saw demands for equality in the sport finally begin to be realised. Australia was first represented at the world women's amateur boxing championships in 2001 and South Australia's Desi Kontos won a bronze medal at the 2002 world championships in Antalya, Turkey.

In 2012, West Australian Naomi Fischer-Rasmussen became the first female boxer to represent Australia at the Olympics. Three other women, Kristy Harris, Shelley Watts and Kaye Scott, were chosen in Australia's 2014 boxing team for the Glasgow Commonwealth Games.

At the Hydro arena by the banks of the River Clyde, Watts, 26, a law student from Laurieton, New South Wales, entered the record books as Australia's first female Commonwealth Games boxing gold medallist, winning the 60-kilogram final by outpointing India's Laishram Devi. Her gold-medal victory, coming on the same program as fellow Australian Andrew Moloney's win in the men's 52 kilogram and Joe Goodall's super-heavyweight silver, took place in the early hours of the morning, Australian time.

'I rang my dad straight after the fight. He said all the lights in the street were on,' Watts explained. 'He said he'd run outside screaming, "Yes, yes, yes!", but everyone was already awake.'

One of the pioneers of women's professional boxing in Australia was martial arts expert Sharon Anyos. She started in karate in 1976 aged six, and, by the late 1980s, had become a globally recognised exponent of the sport, competing in major international championships.

Anyos had her first professional boxing fight in 1998 at the Carrara Basketball Stadium on the Gold Coast, stopping Cathy Jones in two rounds. Seven years later, she became Australia's first women's world champion by outpointing Marcela Eliana Acuña of Argentina at the Gold Coast Convention Centre for the WBC featherweight title. She had her last fight in 2007, compiling a career record of 14 wins and three losses.

Anyos paved the way for Melbourne's Susie Ramadan to win the IBF female bantamweight title in a ten-round decision against American Terri Lynn Cruz in Melbourne in 2011. Ramadan went on to outpoint Thailand's Usanakorn Kokietgym for the WBC bantamweight title in 2012.

In 2010, Perth's Erin McGowan won the vacant WBO female lightweight title against England's Lyndsey Scragg. Sydney's Lauryn Eagle, a well-known model and waterski champion, won the Australian women's lightweight title over Nadine Brown in 2013. The same year, Melbourne's Diana Prazak stopped Frida Wallberg for the WBC female super-featherweight title in Stockholm. Prazak retained her title against Brisbane's Shannon 'Shotgun' O'Connell on 1 March 2014 in Melbourne.

By her own admission, Prazak was 'an overweight chain smoker' throughout her twenties. She ate too much, drank often and worked too hard in her IT job.

In 2008, a friend suggested she take a group boxing class at a local gym to lose weight. Prazak recalled: 'When I walked into the gym everyone laughed at me. They said I was too fat, too old, and I was a girl, so I would never amount to anything in the sport. But I'm a very competitive person. Very stubborn.'

Prazak shed 30 kilograms in three months, entered an amateur fight and won by knockout. At 27, she began a professional career in boxing. Even though she lost her first pro fight to Sarah Howlett, within 18 months she had won a version of a world title at 59 kilograms.

She was trained by Lucia Rijker of Holland, who played the villain in the Academy Award–winning movie *Million Dollar Baby*. More recently Australians Ebanie Bridges, Louisa Hawton, Cherneka Johnson and Beck Hawker have won world women's championships.

Ali and Tyson: Requiem for the Heavyweights

In 2005, Jeff Fenech trained Mike Tyson for his last professional fight and I was in Washington DC to watch. Muhammad Ali was there too, supporting his daughter Laila, who fought on the undercard.

Ali gave me a sad little wave after the fight as he shuffled out of Washington DC's MCI Centre and back into his twilight zone. We had just watched Tyson wave the white flag, forced to surrender against Ireland's plodding but determined Kevin McBride.

It was fitting that Ali was there for the end of Tyson's career. Two decades earlier, in November 1986, Tyson crushed Ali's final conqueror Trevor Berbick to become, at just 20, the youngest heavyweight champion of the world.

Now Ali was on hand to witness the torch of humiliation pass on; one faded, broken-down champion administering last rites to another. With his vacant stare, thinning hair and uncontrollable tremors, Ali was the ghost of championships past.

After 20 years, during which he managed to blow an estimated A$400 million, Tyson, a convicted rapist, dope smoker and road rager, saw the McBride bout as a turning point: the first in a seven-fight deal designed to knockout his $55 million debt. Tyson's cut was $12 million; McBride's $360,000.

Tyson was focused and humble, despite the distractions from fans, pushers, rap stars and hustlers, all clamouring to be a part of the procession.

The Mike Tyson I met was highly intelligent, extremely articulate and a deep thinker. He was gracious with his time, stopping to shake hands with well-wishers and posing for photographs with anyone who asked. He signed so many autographs in a seven-day stretch it was surprising that he could still make a fist. But Tyson was also erratic. As someone who had spent years behind bars, and many more on antidepressants (mixed with the occasional joint) this was unsurprising. He could hold things together, but I sensed that underneath the surface was a sad man ready to implode.

Mike Tyson knew more about the history of prize-fighting than just about anyone I met in 40 years covering the sport. It was the legacy of a youth spent training with his eccentric father-figure, Cus D'Amato, in a sprawling timber mansion in the Catskill Mountains, north of New York City. D'Amato's protégés and later Tyson's managers – millionaire businessmen Jim Jacobs and Bill Cayton – owned the biggest fight-film collection in the world, and for the nine years Tyson lived in the Catskills, boxing's great old-time champs constantly danced before him.

Despite being bankrupt, Tyson said there was always a promoter willing to fly him around the world to make appearances or add his support to their shows for a million dollars' pocket money. (He was reportedly paid more than $A1.7 million to sign for a series of K-l kickboxing bouts in Japan, only to announce his retirement from K-l without so much as a kick in the shins.) And bankruptcy itself, he said, had its upside: it at least weeded out women only after him for his cash.

Tyson might have been broke, but he still lived in a world of customised Hummers delivering just a few miles to the gallon, Bentley Continentals, stretch limos and private jets.

One of Tyson's mates was so rich he literally threw money away. The night before the McBride fight, Brian Lesk, a Phoenix multi-millionaire with a Bentley and private jet, stood on the balcony of his suite at the Ritz-Carlton in Washington, tossing US$20,000 worth of cash into the street. When people screeched to a halt to pick up the loot, Lesk thought the resulting traffic chaos was hilarious. (The next day, when the butler let me in to Lesk's US$9000-a-night digs, 26 empty Cristal champagne bottles – about $17,000 worth – were waiting for collection.)

The night before that episode, I'd joined Tyson, Fenech, and Tyson's promoter Shelly Finkel for dinner at Washington's Ritz-

Carlton. Finkel had started as a showman three decades earlier, when he drew 600,000 people to the Watkins Glen motor racing track in New York to see the Grateful Dead and the Allman Brothers.

As part of the pre-fight hype, Finkel called Tyson the most recognisable face in sport. And as Tyson sat opposite me, half his face covered by a tattoo, he was hard to miss.

We ate salmon steaks from Copper River, Alaska. 'The food's great here but at these prices it should be,' Tyson told me. Having squandered as much cash as he had in his time, he'd know.

In the flesh, the 106-kilogram Tyson was every bit as menacing as he looked in the ring, though at 180 centimetres, he was much shorter than most rugby league or AFL players. We talked about the pain he'd encountered in life, and the pain he still felt over lost love.

Tyson told me one of the best times in his life was making the 1999 movie *Black and White*, in which Robert Downey Jr plays a bisexual movie-director. Downey's character fantasises about a romance with Iron Mike and tries to seduce him at a party. Tyson (playing himself) rejects the romantic advances and instead tries to drive Downey's head through the floorboards.

As our meal progressed, Tyson struck up a conversation with a middle-aged couple at an adjoining table, telling them of the peace and beauty he enjoyed living in the Catskill Mountains. Then he phoned his 15-year-old daughter, Mickey, and chastised her about a flippant phone message she'd left on his answering machine.

'Mickey, this is your father,' said the most feared heavyweight of all time. 'I'm very disappointed in your message and I want you to change it right now. Being disrespectful in life gets you nowhere.'

Tyson told me that he encouraged the six children he had at the time to make the most of their educational opportunities.

Tyson's then seven-year-old son, Amir, was his constant companion during fight week in Washington. Like his father, Amir had a remarkable memory. He could rattle off all the American presidents and the years they served in the White House – and he was in just his second year at school.

Talk turned to Tyson's first wife, the actress Robin Givens, who was reportedly writing a tell-all book about the couple's turbulent life together. 'I haven't been married to her for 18 years and now she's writing a book about me,' Tyson said. 'I guess she's an actress and at heart they are all egotistical people, and want everyone to hear their voice, their plea, their cry.'

Tyson had an unusual relationship with his second ex-wife, Dr Monica Turner. They divorced in 2003, but in a strange twist, she later left her job as a paediatric resident at Georgetown University Medical Centre to help him manage his life and was one of the key figures in putting together the McBride fight.

He described Dr Turner as a 'wonderful woman' who not only looked after their two children, Rayna and Amir, but also his son Miguel, who he fathered with another woman while still married to Turner. During fight week, well-wishers at his Ritz-Carlton suite disrupted Tyson so often that he went to stay with Dr Turner and their kids at her Washington home. After the fight she even waived her right to US$1.3 million in child support from Tyson's purse.

Tyson, at this stage of the week, was upbeat about his future. He wanted another four or five fights, then to face Vitali Klitschko, the 202-centimetre Ukrainian sports scientist and philosopher, for the WBC title.

'I'm in no hurry but I definitely believe I can be champion again,' Tyson said. He told me he was sorry he bit off part of Evander Holyfield's ear in 1997 and regretted hitting referee John Coyle the night he monstered Lou Savarese in just 38 seconds in 2000.

He became morose when talking about the death of his gangsta rapper friends Biggie Smalls and Tupac Shakur.

The latter died in a welter of bullets just hours after he and Death Row Records boss, Marion 'Suge' Knight, watched Tyson squash Bruce Seldon in Las Vegas in 1996. Tyson said he was the only fighter whose career was interrupted by a long jail term to come back and become heavyweight champion. Tyson had been convicted of raping beauty queen Desiree Washington in 1991.

A writer for a music magazine joined us and confided to Tyson that after meeting him for the first time the previous year, he was so excited he'd used marijuana to prolong the high.

'I know you have partaken in the past,' said the music man. 'Should I stop taking weed?'

'Unless you've got cancer or mental illness you shouldn't be taking it,' Tyson advised. 'But I've got friends who need it because they're so wired.'

Fenech and Tyson had been close for a long while and were world champions at the same time. Fenech's famous 'draw' with WBC super-featherweight champion Azumah Nelson in 1991 was the main preliminary before Tyson launched his title comeback against Donovan 'Razor' Ruddock.

Tyson praised his sparring partners in Washington, Australian Bob Mirovic, Kiwi Shane Cameron and fellow American Corey Sanders, a 195-centimetre, 160-kilogram pizza parlour manager whose left eye was just a grey blur due to a detached retina. As a prank, Sanders would morph into Quasimodo, walking into shops with arms swinging, gummy eye rolling and bellowing, 'Me want ice cream! Me want ice cream!' Tyson waged brutal wars with all three of them in the gym and seemed full of confidence.

Three days before the fight, Tyson arrived shirtless at Washington's Howard University for his last public workout. He had trained with Fenech for ten weeks near his modest ranch home in Phoenix, Arizona. His body looked as powerful as it did in his heyday, the grapefruit-sized biceps sporting tattoos of Arthur Ashe and Chairman Mao, his rock-hard midsection featuring the iconic portrait of Che Guevara. But it was obvious that while Tyson, a couple of weeks from his 39th birthday, looked physically fit, he was mentally flaccid, bored with training and disinclined to suffer too many more blows, despite the imposing debt hanging over his head. His belly looked hard but he no longer had the stomach for fighting.

Tyson told me that when he beat Danish Brian Nielsen in 2001 with a seventh-round technical knockout (TKO), he had trained on Baby Ruth chocolate bars. He spent the week explaining how he had mellowed and was looking to a brighter future as a more humble and caring man, but at the main press conference two days out from the bell, he promised to gut McBride like a fish. The megalomaniacal confidence was back, albeit fleetingly. Tyson added that if the opponent's agent didn't stop talking up the big Irishman's chances there was a chance he'd get McBride killed.

Rock Newman, a businessman best known for guiding the career of heavyweight Riddick Bowe, compared Tyson to Malcolm X, the assassinated black leader who started out as a pimp and drug dealer. He told me he was excited about Tyson's prospects. 'You are going to see a disciplined, in-shape and ferocious Mike Tyson,' he said. 'The eruption, the explosion, the ferocity is going to take place in the ring.'

At the weigh-in on the day before the fight, McBride, nicknamed 'dead man walking' by Tyson's camp, was 17 kilograms heavier than Tyson and 20 centimetres taller.

Tyson was unconcerned: he'd made a career of cutting giants down to bite-size pieces.

On the undercard to the Tyson fight, I helped out in the corner of Hussein Hussein, a great Australian flyweight who that night scored a good points win over a rugged Mexican named Evaristo Primero. Two years earlier, Hussein had captivated the Thai boxing community with his infectious good humour when he was in Bangkok to fight their WBC champ Pongsaklek Wonjongkam.

Hussein had turned up the weigh-in against the pocket-sized southpaw sporting a false set of crooked teeth he'd bought at a novelty store. The teeth were so realistic many Thai fight fans believed Hussein when he said he needed the money from the fight for urgent dental work. Wonjongkam won a 12-round decision.

On the night of the Tyson–McBride fight in a dressing-room normally used by the Washington Wizards basketball team, Muhammad Ali was trying to instil a little magic into Tyson's comeback. As Fenech taped Tyson's fists, Ali placed a shaky hand on the boxer's broad shoulders. He stroked Tyson's neck, rubbed his back and whispered slurred platitudes in his ear.

Once he was in the ring, Tyson was dynamic in ten-second bursts, but that's all.

In Round 6, he made a mockery of his pledge to keep it clean, biting McBride's nipple and trying to break his arm.

Frustrated, he lost two points for ramming his bald, tattooed head into McBride's left eye-socket, opening a wide gash.

After six rounds Tyson was ahead on points, but exhausted.

Rather than see him counted out, Fenech told the referee Joe Cortez his fighter was finished. Tyson simply didn't want to fight. Having promised to gut McBride like a fish, Tyson ended up flopping on the canvas like a beached whale out of his depth as the tide of boxing history turned against him.

Two days before the fight, Tyson had said to me, 'No one's ever had the life that I've had. Regardless of what you might think, that it's been grim and gloomy, I've had a tremendous life.'

After the fight it was a different story. 'My career has been over since 1990,' he said. 'I fought because I liked the lifestyle and the girls. When I look at my fans, they don't love me. They love what I do. I'm an entertainer. I'm a performer. That's what I do. I've wasted my entire life.'

Daniel in the Lion's Den

The cold Tasmanian wind would whistle down the steep hill and rattle the windows along Invermay Road as young Daniel Geale, the future middleweight champion of the world, arrived at the KFC outlet in Mowbray, Launceston, for another shift at the fryer. Every day after school and at all hours on the weekend, the budding young boxer was loading breasts, thighs, wings and drumsticks into the deep fryer.

Fifteen hundred kilometres to the north in Sydney, Anthony Mundine was earning $600,000 a year to wear the red and white uniform of the Dragons rugby league team, telling people he was the greatest player of all time, that the reason he wasn't in the Australian team was that the game was racist, and insulting everyone from Don Bradman to Johnny Raper.

In Launceston, Geale was wearing the red and white uniform of Colonel Sanders and quietly working for the minimum wage while keeping warm beside the cookers. The sizzling chicken smelled finger lickin' good, but the young boxer knew he couldn't afford a solitary bite, not only because his family had never been well off but because Geale had already written down his goals for a successful life, and number one was to become a champion in boxing. Nothing – not even delicious fatty food – was going to stand in his way.

Outwardly, Geale may have had all the menace of Mary Poppins but inside there was a raging fire of determination that had been stoked by hard work and struggle. Unfailingly polite, diligent and resolute, the teenager was proud to be a descendant, through his mother's family, of the Palawa people, the first Tasmanians, a unique race whose full-blooded tribes-people were driven to extinction by the diseases and violence introduced by Europeans. Geale was also proud of his school, Brooks High in working-class Rocherlea, which had just produced a precocious and pugnacious number-three Test batsman named

Ricky Ponting. As Geale read about the exploits of the young cricketer known as 'Punter' he thought often of one day being in the headlines as a champion sportsman, too.

Geale was the son of Wayne and Michelle and brother to Joseph, three years his junior. After watching the movie *Karate Kid* as a nine-year-old, he took up martial arts, but found the training a lot less spectacular than the movie. His interest in boxing would last much longer, much to the surprise of his father, who drove him over to the Lilydale Boxing Club for his first lesson.

'The only boxing I ever did was boxing apples and pears at the orchard,' Wayne said. 'So it was a real shock when the trainer there, Lloyd Poke, said, "You know he can't fight until he's ten?" Daniel was such a nice quiet kid I didn't want him to fight at all.'

But from the age of ten, Geale was fighting all over Tasmania. He loved Aussie rules too, and the way Wayne told it, he kicked the most goals of anyone in his team.

When Mundine walked out of his contract at the Dragons to fight Kiwi Gerard Zohs in a million-dollar promotion at the Sydney Entertainment Centre in 2000, Geale was still fighting for free but now representing his country. The highlight of his amateur career was a gold medal at the 2002 Commonwealth Games in Manchester, along with fellow Aussies Paul Miller and Justin Kane.

In 2004, he came to Sydney to train with his hero, Jeff Fenech, and see if he could make it as a professional. Each morning he'd drive his battered little Hyundai over to Fenech's Marrickville gym and park behind his trainer's Mercedes, or world flyweight champ Vic Darchinyan's BMW, or next to Danny Green's monstrous, rumbling V8 Ford GT.

Before long, Geale and his wife, Sheena, had three kids, Bailey, Ariyelle and Lilyarna, and after Fenech took a break from boxing, the family moved to Sydney's south-west so he could train at the Grange Old School gym near Narellan.

Under trainer Graham Shaw, Geale became one of Australia's best-ever fighters.

But it took time. When Mundine was earning as much as $8 million beating Danny Green at Aussie Stadium in 2006, Geale was still a struggling dad trying to make ends meet from meagre purses at the Campbelltown Catholic Club and Penrith Panthers.

'I used to watch Mundine fight all through those years,' Geale told me. 'I always thought I could beat him but I still had respect for him – his speed, especially.'

The pair eventually clashed in Brisbane in 2009 and Mundine won a close and highly controversial split decision after scoring a flash knockdown in the second round.

In 2011, Geale fulfilled his enormous potential and capitalised on the 20 years of hard work when he travelled to Germany to win the IBF middleweight title from Sebastian Sylvester.

He returned to Germany in 2012 to win the WBA version of the middleweight title from the vastly experienced Felix Sturm.

Sheena and the kids, watching on TV at home, cheered incessantly, though Geale admits the kids probably would have preferred to watch the cartoon channel.

On 30 January 2013 at the Sydney Entertainment Centre, in a rematch with Anthony Mundine, Daniel Geale won a points decision by wide margins to retain his IBF middleweight title.

Several months later he lost his title to the Englishman Darren Barker and the following year put his long-standing mateship with fellow Australian Olympian Jarrod Fletcher aside when they fought at Sydney's Hordern Pavilion.

Geale won by unanimous decision.

Fletcher's greatest moments as a fighter were at the 2006 Commonwealth Games in Melbourne where, on his way to the gold medal, he beat Canada's Adonis Stevenson and England's James DeGale. Both Stevenson and DeGale went on to have long reigns as professional world champs.

Katsidis All Heart after Tragedy

Mexican world champion Juan Manuel Marquez drank his own urine in the lead-up to his world lightweight title defence against Toowoomba's oh-so-tough Michael Katsidis in Las Vegas on 27 November 2010. As disgusting as the practice sounds, the resilient Mexican swore that the amber fluid was full of nutrients and essential for his preparation.

Katsidis had fought some of the world's very best for a decade and held an interim world championship. I was ringside to see his whole-hearted effort against Marquez as he tried to honour his late brother, Stathi, by winning the championship at the MGM Grand.

Star jockey Stathi had died a few weeks earlier, just four days before he was due to ride one of the favourites in the Cox Plate. He was 31.

In Round 3, Marquez missed with a lazy right and Katsidis landed a brutal left hook that spun the Mexican's head and dropped him on his back. Marquez rose on shaky legs and Katsidis came on strong. Suddenly Marquez looked all of his years.

'I didn't protect myself and I got caught,' Marquez told me after the fight. 'Katsidis is a very powerful puncher.'

The 37-year-old warhorse managed to survive the third round and re-establish his brilliant counterpunches. Given his recuperative powers after the heavy knockdown, maybe he'd been right about the urine all along. He probably could have bottled the stuff.

Marquez mounted a relentless assault in his grim fightback. Katsidis's spirit was willing but, as the rounds rolled by, his flesh was weakened in a whirl of brutality.

In Round 9, American referee Kenny Bayless finally jumped between the fighters to save the battered Aussie.

Marquez retained the WBA and WBO titles. Fans of the Australian booed the decision as he had not touched the canvas, but the referee reasoned there was no point Katsidis risking serious injury with his family already reeling from Stathi's death.

It was a cracking fight and Stathi would have been proud of his fearless younger brother.

Thirty-year-old Katsidis had stood up to Marquez's bombs without flinching, but when the subject of Stathi was raised, he finally started to weep.

'Stathi, I love you very much and I miss you mate,' he said between sobs, immediately after the fight.

Katsidis later had his face stitched back together at the University Medical Centre in Las Vegas. He'd found himself in hospital after many of his biggest fights, including his Vegas slugfest with Filipino Czar Amonsot in 2007, when both men ended up lying next to each other in the same emergency room.

Katsidis scored some huge wins in his career, beating 2000 Olympic teammate James Swan in his second pro fight and taking an interim world title in 2007 in a brawl with Englishman Graham Earl. He put on sensational, albeit losing performances against world champs Joel Casamayor and Juan Diaz before coming back to beat top-liners Jesus Chavez, Vicente Escobedo and, in a huge open-air battle at Upton Park in London, the rugged Brit Kevin Mitchell.

While Michael Katsidis was brawling with Marquez, Sydney's Cameroon-born Sakio Bika was in the middle of a battle with Olympic gold medallist Andre Ward in Oakland, California, on the same night.

The undefeated Ward survived Bika's wild swings and occasional headbutt to win a 12-round decision to retain the WBA super middleweight title he'd won from Anthony Mundine's conqueror Mikkel Kessler.

Bika had been working in a glass factory in Douala, Cameroon, when he came to Sydney for the 2000 Olympics. He stayed, got married, had children and went to work every day in the gym, copping heavy punches and landing his own in the toughest sport of all. At various times he was trained by Jeff Fenech, David Birchell, Michael Akkawy and, for much of his career, Mark Pitts, a marvellous fight trainer whose grandfather Arthur Butler was one of the great figures in Australian aviation.

In 2006, Bika had suffered a controversial draw in his first world title shot against Germany's WBC champ Markus Beyer, and then lost world title fights against all-time greats Joe Calzaghe and Andre Ward but gave them both the roughest nights of their careers.

The super-middleweight (76 kg) powerhouse had survived a scorpion bite as a child and years of disappointment in the fight game, but on 22 June 2013 he finally became another of Australia's world champions with a majority decision over previously unbeaten Mexican Marco Antonio Peribán at the Barclays Centre in Brooklyn, New York.

The bout was for the WBC super-middleweight title, and both men fought their way to exhaustion over 12 rounds.

Peribán dominated early, but at the final bell, as they were both throwing wild haymakers, Bika appeared to be moments away from winning by knockout.

Against Peribán, a rangy long-limbed boxer, he refused to be denied, even though the Mexican's speed and left jab had given him problems throughout.

In his first title defence, back in Brooklyn, Bika climbed from the canvas to fight a draw with undefeated American Anthony Dirrell, who took the title a year later with a decision in Carson, California.

In 2015 Bika went 12 furious rounds with the brutal Canadian light-heavyweight world champ Adonis Stevenson and in 2021, at almost 42, he outpointed 47-year-old Sam Soliman to go 2–1 in their series of fights that had started with a Soliman victory almost 20 years earlier.

Lovemore: A Champion by Degrees

One of the greatest experiences I ever had in boxing was being in the corner for my mate Lovemore Ndou when he fought Saul 'Canelo' Alvarez before 10,000 of the Mexican bull's cheering, chanting hometown fans at the Estadio Beto Avila baseball stadium in Veracruz on 4 December 2010.

By then, Lovemore was a 39-year-old former IBF junior-lightweight champion who, while raising a family as a professional boxer, managed to earn multiple law degrees and start a highly successful legal practice in Sydney.

He was at the tail end of a career that had seen him serve as a long-time sparring partner for the great Floyd Mayweather and battle the best in the world for more than a decade including Kell Brook, Matthew Hatton, Paulie Malignaggi, Kermit Cintrón, Sharmba Mitchell and Junior Witter. Long-time world champ Miguel Cotto, of Puerto Rico, said Ndou gave him a tougher fight than anyone, including Mayweather and Manny Pacquiao.

Lovemore was awarded the IBF light-welterweight title after beating 2000 Olympian Naoufel ben Rabah in Sydney in 2007. He lost it a few months later against Paulie Malignaggi in Connecticut.

Three years on, he was now fighting to become the top contender for Pacquiao's WBC light-middleweight title, facing a fiery Mexican redhead who was then 20 and on his way to being proclaimed the best fighter in the world pound for pound.

The Mexicans made it as tough as possible for Lovemore before the fight, putting him in a dressing-room next to an overflowing toilet block, so that the stench almost floored him before Alvarez had thrown a blow.

The huge crowd sang a roaring rendition of the Mexican anthem together and booed Ndou at the start of the bout.

The canvas of the ring floor also had extra thick, spongy padding, meaning Ndou could not use his superior leg speed to its full advantage.

But he still gave the fight a tremendous crack. After the tenth round of some fierce action, Ndou whispered to trainer Harold Volbrecht that his left eardrum had burst and that his balance was off. But wounded, the 'Black Panther' fought even harder and was still going toe to toe at the end of 12 rounds against a bigger man who was almost half his age.

Canelo won a 12-round decision, and the crowd gave Ndou a standing ovation.

Promoter Oscar De La Hoya, the richest boxer in history with a fortune said to be nudging $1 billion, rushed over to Ndou to congratulate him on his mighty effort.

'Oh man, this guy is an absolute beast,' De La Hoya told me. 'Ike Quartey, Azumah Nelson, John Mugabi – they were all great fighters out of Africa. Now you can add the name Lovemore Ndou.'

One of the ringside commentators was Ruben Olivares, the man who beat Lionel Rose for the world bantamweight title in 1969.

As Alvarez celebrated with his fiancée, Marisol Gonzalez, Mexico's 2003 Miss Universe entrant, Ndou was having his bruises tenderly kissed by glamour girl Lauryn Eagle, a champion waterskier who would go on to win an Australian boxing title.

Ndou ended the night hand in hand with the leggy Glamazon, who was dressed in a figure-hugging black mini dress, her mane of long blonde hair blowing in the gentle breeze. So it wasn't such a bad night for Lovemore after all.

Lovemore Ndou was educated in the school of hard knocks and began his journey to fame and freedom in South Africa during the darkest days of apartheid.

He remembers quaking with fear at the age of ten, frail, hungry, alone and thinking it unlikely he'd ever see 11 because he refused to call a white man 'boss'. The white police called him a 'kafir' and threw him into a cell to improve his manners.

Lovemore trembled in fear the whole night, certain that, like many of his friends and neighbours, he would simply vanish or that his parents would be told he'd hung himself in jail.

Despite his fear, though, he wouldn't buckle.

At 21, he was cradling his dying mother in his arms in a godforsaken hospital for blacks only. She was only 42. There was no money for expensive care or treatment. Her name was Emma and she'd raised seven children in a tiny four-room house her husband had fashioned from the red earth in a blacks-only village on the outskirts of a copper town called Musina in Northern Province.

Emma had known poverty all her life, had seldom had a bus fare and helped feed her family by trudging the dusty hot, dangerous roads near the border with Zimbabwe to sell clothes.

She couldn't leave her family much of a legacy but she was leaving her eldest son the gift of an exquisite name – Lovemore. Love more – two words that could solve all the ills, injustices and ignorance that had plagued her people for decades.

Lovemore's father, Freddy, an army mechanic, died young too. He couldn't leave his son much either, except good genes that gave his son a body Michelangelo might have sculpted in bronze: Twiggy's waist and wide-screen shoulders.

In that hospital in Musina, before she closed her eyes for the last time, Lovemore's mother made him promise that he would take care of her other children and give them a better life than the one she was about to lose.

He thought about that promise every day when he was doing his daily 8-kilometre run around Brighton and Dolls Point in Sydney, or when he was in there dodging the bombs of sparring partners Kostya Tszyu and Shannan Taylor.

Ndou had once been in the middle of a black student protest in Johannesburg when police opened fire on the demonstrators. 'I have seen people die all around me. Gunfire and blood and screaming everywhere,' he explained. 'I came to Australia to escape that sort of thing. From the moment I arrived here people treated me just as an individual, just another man. Not a black man – and I knew my children would not suffer because of their colour.'

Every time Ndou fought he would spend time before the bout thinking about the promise he made to his mother and about the life of his greatest hero, Nelson Mandela, a man who spent 27 years in prison, refusing to break or to yield to racism and oppression.

And of another great black man, Martin Luther King Jr, who dreamed of a land where his little children would be judged not by the colour of their skin but by the content of their character.

Where they could be happy.

And free at last.

Lovemore's last pro fight was a 12-round decision against another former world champ, Gairy St Clair, on the Gold Coast in 2012.

Guyana-born St Clair was Johnny Lewis's fifth world titleholder, springing a big upset in 2006 in South Africa to win a points decision over Cassius Baloyi to take the IBO and IBF super-featherweight titles.

Seventeen years later, Ndou represented St Clair in court in January 2023, winning an appeal against a three-month prison sentence that St Clair was facing for allegedly assaulting a security guard after a disagreement over the former world champion not wearing a mask.

At the Downing Centre Courthouse in Sydney, Ndou, with almost as many legal degrees as he had professional fights, successfully argued that St Clair had no previous criminal history and had been a respected member of the community for many years.

The Million-dollar Noby

The story of Noby Clay and Ray Dennis reads like a screenplay: washed-up trainer meets wayward girl with a fighting spirit, and a boxing star is born. The setting was stunning: troubled Palm Island, which I visited for this profile piece in 2011.

Every afternoon he's in his gym, sweating it out with the barefoot kids, holding a punching pad the size of an ottoman in front of his body and getting his fighters to whale away. Ray Dennis's long, skinny white legs and his wiry body shake from the force of every blow. Like a punching production line they come, one after another, and Dennis finishes every session with his shirt soaked with sweat. His old back hurts and the arthritis in his bung hip is murder.

On the wall, photos of history's great Aboriginal boxers peer down in approval at all this frenzied activity – Lionel Rose, Tony Mundine, Hector Thompson, Robbie Peden. And Ron Richards. A national boxing champion and huge drawcard in the 1930s. Richards later spent 17 years detained on Palm Island, 65 kilometres north-east of Townsville. A homeless, penniless alcoholic, he was sent here back when the island was an official dumping ground for Indigenous people – a 'tropical gulag', as one writer put it – for those deemed by the government as 'wayward'.

It's still a deeply troubled place. But it's here that 73-year-old Dennis, his Aboriginal boxing team, and a girl fighter named Noby Clay are reviving Richards's fighting spirit. When Dennis met Noby ('Don't call her Nobby,' he says, 'or she'll belt ya') 11 years ago, she was a wiry teenager bent on smoking marijuana and sniffing paint. Now she's 28, clean, a mother of three and 45 kilograms of sheer ambition, an Australian champion and a strong chance to be in the national team when women's boxing debuts at the London Olympics.

When Noby met Dennis he was a broken man who had lost his family through drinking and gambling. Yet it was this place, with its volatile mix of unemployment, poverty and violence, that became a beacon for Dennis and Noby. Neither was born here, but there was something in the spirit of the island that they believed could refresh their wounded souls. Quite separately, two of life's battlers decided to move to Palm. Here they joined forces, and something magical happened.

Palm Island, or Great Palm as it is sometimes called, is outwardly a majestic destination – turquoise waters, sandy beaches, virgin forests of great gum trees and hoop pine with views across the shimmering waves to other picturesque outcrops in the Coral Sea, islands named Curacoa, Eclipse, Pelorus, Orpheus and Fantome.

Joyful children dive off a concrete pier from which the locals catch what they claim are the tastiest mackerel and coral trout in the world. But there has been trouble in paradise for as long as anyone can remember. Fantome was a leper colony for nearly five decades and Palm an enduring symbol of racial prejudice. From the time the government started sending Indigenous people from all over Australia there in 1918 it was used as a dumping ground for white society, creating a prison of the dispossessed, distressed and disadvantaged.

Palm Island's reputation for violence even made it into the 1999 *Guinness Book of Records* – the same year Ray Dennis decided to move there.

'The book said it was the place in the world where you are most likely to die young,' Noby told me.

Noby's house is also on the same street where Cameron Doomadgee, also known as Mulrunji, took his last steps as a free man before dying in police custody in 2004, a death that left a woeful toll in its aftermath.

Yet it was this volatile environment of violence, poverty, unemployment, overcrowding and suicide that became a lighthouse for Ray and Noby in an ocean of despair. Two of life's losers joined forces as though they had read the script of the Clint Eastwood/Hilary Swank movie *Million Dollar Baby*.

'Funny, hey,' Noby says. 'Me and Ray picked what people say is the worstest place on the whole Earth to start our lives all over again.'

Dennis looks like rugby league coach Wayne Bennett might in another 20 years – tall, wiry, steely-eyed and thin-lipped. He talks slowly and quietly and makes each word count. He walks with a stiff gait, his hip having been broken in 2003 when a horse and rider charging down a Palm street knocked him flying. He's one of the few white men on the island, but after a decade here he reckons he's more black than white. 'I've got more friends here than I ever had anywhere in my whole life,' he says. The locals call him Uncle Ray, and he announces proudly that he has just become a great-grandfather and has rebuilt his relationship with his family after losing contact for years.

Eleven years ago, Dennis was almost down for the count. He was 62, unemployed, divorced and drinking heavily. 'I was destroying myself,' he says. 'I had a flat in Townsville and I used to brew 100 big bottles of my own beer every week and my friends would come over to help me drink 'em. Alcohol wrecked my marriage. That and gambling. My wife divorced me and went to Bundaberg. It broke my heart, really did. My daughters, Carol and Janet, wouldn't talk to me and I had no one left in the world.'

The only thing he had to sustain him into his old age was his love for boxing, a love that had kept him going as a lonely boy on a farm outside Nanango in the South Burnett. Back then Ron Richards, an Aboriginal timber-cutter from Ipswich who'd made it big, was his hero.

Still is. Richards fought before crowds of 14,000 at Sydney Stadium almost every month, waging ten furious battles with his Australian foe, Fred Henneberry, overpowering the great New Yorker Gus Lesnevich and dropping Archie Moore, the 'Ol' Mongoose' from Mississippi. He won the Australian middleweight, light-heavyweight and heavyweight titles, along with the British Empire middleweight title.

Before he lost it all to alcoholism and financial mismanagement, Richards was a rarity for his times, a wealthy Aboriginal man, world famous with four houses in Sydney. Ray's life in Nanango was very different.

'My parents lived so far out of town that I didn't go to school until I was ten,' he says. When he finally made it to class, he was beaten up by older boys who called him an idiot for his lack of education, so he took up boxing to defend himself. An older sparring partner bashed him some more. He left school a day before his 14th birthday and worked for a while on a brother's dairy farm at Mundubbera, then got a job at a drycleaners in Nanango, mixing his boxing training with rugby league, the sport that gave him a broken nose.

Ray studied boxing technique out of a book and competed in the lead-up tournaments to pick the Australian team for the 1956 Melbourne Olympic Games.

Like the rest of Australia, Dennis marvelled at the performances of the young fighters he knew from the nearby Cherbourg Aboriginal Mission – Jeffrey Dynevor, Eddie Barney and Adrian Blair, who in a remarkable feat filled three of the ten places on the Australian boxing team for the 1962 Perth Commonwealth Games, Dynevor winning gold. Barney was the son of the Aboriginal fast bowler Eddie Gilbert, who famously terrorised Don Bradman, dismissing him for a duck.

The three boxers were all trained by a white man, Les Haack, a Murgon butcher who was kept busy coaching fighters and simultaneously managing two families, three children with his white wife Amy and another six, including the actress Leah Purcell, with Les's long-time Aboriginal love Florence.

Ray moved around Australia, working in Bundaberg and Moree, then cutting cane around Ingham and cutting carcasses at the Ross River abattoir in Townsville. From the late 1960s he had a second job in another bloody trade, teaching boxing at Townsville's National Fitness Club for 15 years, moulding national champions Doug Sam and Junior Thompson. A polite lad named Colin Scott, who always called Ray 'Sir', won 21 of 23 amateur fights, before playing State of Origin and Test rugby league.

But Ray says the best fighter he ever trained was young Esrom Geia: 'He knocked out a 21-year-old when he was 11 and he was the North Queensland light-heavyweight champion when he was only 15.'

The good times ended for Dennis at the bottom of his 100 weekly longnecks. In early 1999, half a century after his hero Richards was shipped to Palm Island (Richards died in 1967 after authorities allowed him to return to Sydney), Dennis washed up there, looking for old friends and a second chance. He found Esrom, dying of kidney disease at 42, and Esrom's brother Malcolm, who offered him a spare bed.

And then Dennis began to rekindle the love of his life. He set up a makeshift gym and started teaching the local kids not just left from right but right from wrong. He taught them how to box properly: combination punching, slipping and ducking blows, balance and footwork. Within months his team of a dozen boys and a couple of girls ranging in age from ten to their early 20s had started winning gold medals at the national championships.

'I knew if the young fellas could win some fights they'd build up self-confidence and self-respect,' he says. 'They'd burn up a lot of their energy so they didn't get into strife. They know if they wag school I won't train them. These kids have amazing natural ability, quick reflexes and terrific hand-eye coordination. You just have to show them what to do and they look after the rest. I think a bit of love has come to me because they see what I'm trying to do for them.'

One of the biggest motivators for his team has been the promise of trips to the mainland for tournaments. 'Most of them never get a chance to go anywhere,' Dennis says, 'so to be part of a winning team and to go all over Queensland and then sometimes to Melbourne, Hobart – they're over the moon.'

Noby, who last year was nominated for a Deadly Award honouring Indigenous achievement, wants to go even further – all the way to the 2012 Olympics. But her future might have been very different. Raised on Palm Island by her mother, Sandra Clay, Noby returned to her birthplace, Townsville, as a teenager. 'That's when I started to get into a lot of trouble,' she says. 'At 17, 18, I was an alcoholic and a drug addict. We'd go out stealing bottles of paint. We'd be sniffing the paint, drinking, smoking marijuana. It was a terrible life. If I didn't get away I'd be dead.'

In 2000, Noby returned to Palm Island – it seemed a safer option than Townsville. She had no interest in boxing but partner Robin Nallajar, a rugby league player, had a few amateur fights for Dennis. 'I came down to watch Ray put Robin through his punches and I thought it looked deadly and I said, "Hey, Ray, can I have a go?" Six weeks later I had my first fight.'

At the recently completed Palm Island Police Citizens Youth Club Noby is wearing a pair of white board shorts, a North Queensland Cowboys rugby league jumper and a leather boxing headguard from which her dyed-red hair cascades. Her bare feet caress the canvas stretched across the gymnasium floor as she flits about. Her fists, encased in 16-ounce training gloves among many such pairs donated to the club by the Indigenous rugby league great Steve Renouf, flail ceaselessly against the darting figure of her sparring partner, a 15-year-old junior champion named Albert Gorringe.

'Albert's deadly,' she says as she sucks in her breath in deep gasps after they finish their practice fight. 'He's got so much ability; he's just got to show it when the big bouts are on. If he doesn't box like that at the state titles I'll punch him in the mouth.'

Noby flashes a cheeky, dazzling smile as wide as her ambition, even if her latest addictions to 'Choco-Lattes' and Coca-Cola mean the tiny 45-kilogram boxer had to win her Australian Amateur League Championship light-flyweight title in Geelong last November while high on Nurofen and Panadeine Forte because of a brutal toothache.

Like Ray, Noby has learned to live with pain from the time she can remember. To cope with it, fight it and conquer it.

'When I was very young I was on the beach with my cousin when he accidentally shot me in the head with a slug gun he got for Christmas. He was shooting cans along the beach and I got in the way,' she says.

'I used to get blackouts but they've gone now. I just have to make sure I don't get over-heated or too excited because my heart beats funny.'

She has quit marijuana but still smokes a handful of cigarettes – including one to finish training – every day to calm her nerves.

Noby was born to box. Her father, Dave Sarago ('I've never met him but I spoke to him on the phone a couple of times'), competed at the 1974 Commonwealth Games in Christchurch. Sarago's uncle was Palm Island hero George Bracken, a world-class lightweight in the 1950s, and her mother Sandra's uncle was Alfie Clay, another big crowd-puller in the same era. But when she started competing, Noby was still battling her demons. 'I was on the drink three weeks straight with one day's training and beat the Australian champion who was 11 kilograms heavier than me at Townsville,' she says.

'Another time I went up to Cairns grog-sick and when I saw the sheila I was fightin', I was terrified. I was 18, she was 32 and covered in tatts. But I beat her and gave her a black eye. Then I fought another big girl in Rockhampton, who kept chargin' me so I couldn't use my moves. I was ready to give up, she put so much pressure on me – and then I landed a couple of good ones, I went whack, whack, and once I hurt her I knew I could win.'

Dennis helped Noby give up the drink and dope and think about her future.

She is studying computers at the TAFE on Palm Island and is setting up a website to sell some of her Aboriginal art, including the huge, intricately patterned turtle shells she decorates the way her ancestors did for millennia before her.

'Ray's helped so many people on Palm,' Noby says. 'He's always there for us. When I was in trouble and drinkin', there was no father in my life to help me, and Ray stepped in to help and make me see I had potential.'

As Noby finishes her training session with a smoke, another of Ray's champions, Chris Evers, a raw-boned Indigenous fighter with blond hair, a son named in honour of Ron Richards, and nearly 200 fights on his résumé, is preparing for a turtle hunt with a mate. 'He steers, I spear,' he says.

After taking five years off to raise her children – Robin Cassius, six, Shenzey Alireah, five, and Lorna Jennifer Ann, two – Noby returned to the sport in 2008, and at the Australian Amateur Boxing League titles in Geelong in November 2009 she astounded spectators by outpointing Deanna Schaffer from Mt Isa for the 48-kilogram women's title – in between breastfeeding sessions with Lorna.

Dennis's fighters have shared 41 national titles in the breakaway Amateur League and he has funded his team with his pension money and what he can raise in raffles. He has registered Noby with the establishment body – Boxing Australia Inc – so she has a chance at Olympic selection, and she is likely to compete in the state titles at Caloundra RSL this weekend. No amateur boxing club in Australia has matched Palm Island's success – all the more remarkable considering its isolation, small population and social problems. Dennis took nine boxers to last year's state titles in Mackay in October and came away with ten gold medals, Noby winning both the state 48-kilogram and 54-kilogram crowns. At the Australian amateur titles in Hobart

in November, she was given an honorary gold because there was no one in her weight division to fight and officials wouldn't let her compete at a higher weight.

Most of the kids in the gym are barefoot but they have stars in their eyes.

Ray used to train another eager teenager like them named Eric Doomadgee, but he died in 2006, consumed with grief over the death of his father, Cameron, in police custody 18 months earlier.

'Cameron Doomadgee was a happy-go-lucky bloke,' Ray recalls. 'He was so pleased his son was boxing with me. I trained Eric for two fights. But now they're both gone.'

Noby was one of the last people to see Cameron alive. He died an hour later at the Palm Island police station.

In 2005 Noby told a coronial inquiry on Palm that she saw the 36-year-old walking down her street mid-morning on Friday, 19 November 2004, singing 'Who Let the Dogs Out?', before he was thrown head-first by Senior-Sergeant Chris Hurley into the back of a police paddy wagon.

An autopsy released on 26 November 2004 showed Doomadgee had not only consumed a huge amount of methylated spirits mixed with cordial but he had suffered four broken ribs, a ruptured spleen and his liver had been 'almost cleaved in two'. At least 200 people, many of them school children, went on a rampage, torching Palm Island's courthouse, police station and police barracks.

The Tactical Response Group, wearing body armour and carrying assault rifles, was sent in from Townsville.

Order was finally restored but the wounds continue to fester following the riot and the acquittal of Chris Hurley over charges of manslaughter and assault.

'The government got it all wrong, here,' Noby tells me. 'They brought people from 42 different tribes and stuck them here. They thought the Murri were all the same but a lot of the tribes didn't get on, didn't speak the same language, didn't think the same. There were old hatreds. Lots of old scores. It still goes on.

'I've seen people here run up and king-hit somebody in the main street for something their grandfather did 100 years ago.'

Feral dogs run free around the island and wild horses amble between cars on the narrow streets. Ray Dennis recalls the time a pack of wild dogs tore a newborn foal to pieces in the middle of the township. The last census said there were 2000 people living on the island, overcrowded in 320 houses squeezed into the western corner of Palm, the only part that is inhabited. Ninety per cent of the population was unemployed and the life expectancy was just 50 compared to 80 on the mainland.

It's karaoke night at the Coolgaree Bay Hotel, the only outlet on Palm Island with a liquor licence. The microphone is being shared by Noby, her mother and Milton Thaiday, a distant cousin of Bronco Sam and a former top-line rugby league and union player. Nallajar shoots some pool and Dennis sinks a couple of cans of mid-strength. He still has a drink, but not like the bad old days.

Nallajar says he worries about Noby's health and safety every time she fights – but his admiration for her only grows. 'I ask the Lord to watch over her,' he says. 'I know she loves boxing and she's building a future for us.' The pair plan to marry this year. And despite the problems on Palm, Nallajar says it's a wonderful place to live. The blue weatherboard cottage where Noby lives with Nallajar and their children is on the same street where Cameron Doomadgee took his last steps as a free man. Right in front of their house is the old single man's quarters where Ron Richards did his time. Nallajar helped build the new government offices on the site of the police station that was burned after Doomadgee's death, and some of Noby's artwork is displayed there. Despite the problems on Palm, Nallajar says it's still a grand home with its natural beauty and abundant fresh food. Often he'll forgo the woomera and spear preferred by Chris Evers, grab a .22 rifle and head for Curacao island to bring home fresh goat to supplement Noby's toasted sandwiches and pizza.

Later, back at her cottage, Noby savours a smoke and a cup of tea on the porch and talks about the ghosts of Palm Island. While she says it is important to honour Palm's heritage, she says: 'We should try to move on and forget all the bad stuff that's happened here. If you stay looking back all the time, you'll never go forward.' Then she considers her chance to fight at the Olympics and what that would mean for the island and her people. Dennis tells her that if she wins gold, she'll be a multi-million-dollar baby.

Noby ponders the delicate taste of the moment and says it's far sweeter than the taste of paint she once knew so well.

Noby drinks in the moment. 'A little girl from Palm Island going to the Olympic Games,' she says. 'Jeez, that'd be deadly.'

Postscript: *Noby Clay missed out on boxing at the Olympics. Ultimately, her weight division was not included in the competition. But to the people of Palm Island she will always be a great champion.*

Alex in the Land of the Giants

In 2014 I travelled to Oberhausen, Germany, with Alex Leapai as he challenged Wladimir Klitschko for the world heavyweight title. Before that I wrote about his extraordinary life.

It's a heavenly Sunday morning and inside an assembly room at the Springwood State High School, Alex Leapai, a boulder-shaped boxer with arms thicker than most men's thighs, is singing his heart out.

He and about 50 other members of the Logan Central congregation of the London Missionary Society use the school hall for their church services, and Leapai says his faith has transformed a life careering out of control. He says that in the Samoan community, God and family come first, but sport is a very close second.

Leapai, 34, is the number-one contender for the world heavyweight title held by Ukrainian Olympic gold medallist Wladimir Klitschko, one of the best heavyweight boxers of all time.

But at this church service, Leapai is just another 108-kilogram man who is not worried so much about the mighty Klitschko as the Almighty above. Like the other Samoan men in church, he is wearing the traditional white lava-lava skirt and he sports a pristine white shirt and red tie. The women all wear long white dresses and wide-brimmed white hats.

Behind Leapai sits his father Faataui Elisaia Leapai, a Samoan chief and former heavyweight boxer, and nearby are his brother Leroy and various uncles and aunts. Also, there are the younger members of the Leapai clan, Alex's wife, Theresa, and their six children he is fighting to support.

When the music stops, the congregation listens with rapt attention to a sermon in the Samoan language. Leapai holds the hands of his children and sometimes pats them on the head, sharing his hymn book.

Then the quietly spoken truck driver from Slacks Creek closes his eyes, bows his shaved head and whispers a silent prayer, thanking God for a second chance at life.

The dramatic conversion of world boxing's Cinderella Man began in 2006 when a metal door clanged behind him in the maximum-security wing at the Woodford Correctional Centre, north of Brisbane. It was his first lonely night in jail of what would be a six-month lag for assault.

Leapai could trust no one and was deathly afraid of a knife in his back. 'When I went to jail my wife was pregnant with our first boy. I was so ashamed,' he says bashfully. 'My mum and dad had worked so hard to give me chances in life and I'd wasted all of them. My dad worked two jobs welding and labouring to put food on the table. I knew how much my going to jail hurt the Samoan community. I had acted like an idiot. I didn't appreciate what Australia had done for us.'

Leapai spent his first night as a convict drowning in tears, staring at four walls, a wash basin and a prison bed. His loneliness and deprivation gave way to contemplation about his wife and children and his community. He threw himself onto the concrete floor and prayed to God for forgiveness. And help. Then he opened his heart and prayed that God would make the Samoan people proud of him.

Now, eight years later, he is on a crusade to shock the world with the power of his faith and dedication.

In two weeks, Leapai will receive at least $1.5 million to fight the towering Klitschko for the heavyweight championship of the world, the same title once held by Muhammad Ali, Mike Tyson and Joe Louis. If he defies the odds and slays the giant, Leapai will receive more than $3 million for a rematch.

Australia has never had a world heavyweight champion. The bout will take place in Oberhausen, Germany, on the morning of 27 April 2014 and will be beamed live to 150 countries.

Leapai is at his church every Sunday but three days a week he is at his other temple – an old farm shed in the backyard of his trainer Noel Thornberry – on a dirt road between Gatton and Grantham, west of Brisbane. He hits other gyms in Brisbane, too, but it is out here, in the Queensland bush, that Leapai has been doing most of his preparation beside fields of lucerne and pumpkins, and the occasional brown snake.

Thornberry's shed is filled with tattered punching bags and rusting exercise equipment. A battered skateboard rests in the middle of a boxing ring on a faded canvas floor as Leapai waits to begin training. His smile is punctuated by gaps from the times he forgot to duck, and his schoolgirl handshake belies

Thornberry's opinion he is the hardest punching boxer in the world.

It's more than 40 years since Noel Thornberry's father, Trevor 'The Iceman', weakened by a virus, melted in the tenth round against Englishman Jackson McQuade at Brisbane's Festival Hall on 28 May 1971. Now, here in the shed, Trevor's lean, hard and weathered face scrunches up as he attempts to recall that fight, but he can remember nothing of the night he suffered severe brain damage and almost died.

There is no memory of that final bout, nor of the weeks he spent in hospital, nor of the way his family nurtured him back to life, teaching the once-feared fighter to walk again.

Trevor has been an invalid pensioner ever since.

His wife, Carol and her kids – Noel, then four, Rick, three, and Leah, six months – were left destitute. Australia's *Fighter* magazine started an appeal and boxing identities from around the world tossed in donations for a deposit on a small house at Gatton, where Carol and Trevor had happy times picking spuds.

The only thing Trevor knows about his 14 consecutive wins and 13 knockouts is what his wife and children have told him in the years since.

Yet, despite what happened to the old pug, Leapai is all ears as The Iceman, now 70 and still fit enough to jog every day, tells him: 'Mate, you rip this big bloke up the guts with some body shots and you'll cut him down to size. Don't matter how big they are, you've got the power to bowl him over.'

The 'big bloke' is the 198-centimetre Klitschko, who has a 15-centimetre height advantage over Leapai, has been unbeaten for ten years and has loomed over world boxing like a colossus since winning the 1996 Olympic super-heavyweight gold medal.

Klitschko is the son of a Soviet air force general and the brother of former boxing champ Vitali Klitschko, now one of Ukraine's major political leaders.

While Leapai has until recently boxed in anonymous penury, Klitschko has made $100 million and owns several luxury homes. The champion is finishing his fight preparations at a plush ski resort in the Austrian Alps and says victory is crucial for the morale of all Ukrainians facing a fight with Russia.

Leapai, meanwhile, is out here in the bush in a place synonymous with hard times. Noel Thornberry, 47, a father of five, went to many funerals after the recent Grantham floods, and all around his shed are the remnants of nature's more recent violence, a mighty wind that ripped walls apart, toppled great water tanks and sent his kids' trampoline cartwheeling.

Thornberry has lived and breathed boxing since before he could walk. He learned to read from studying fight magazines, mesmerised by the photos of his father. Trevor was an itinerant fruit picker from Orange, New South Wales, when he took to boxing while working in the potato fields around Gatton in the late 1960s. Reg Layton, the craggy-faced boxing promoter, found Trevor a job at the Woolloongabba iceworks. A caravan in the Brisbane suburb of Carina became the first permanent home for the wild Thornberrys.

Despite the damage to his father, Noel remained fascinated by boxing. He had his first professional fight in 1984 and three years later, at Gatton, won the Queensland middleweight title.

When brother Rick started boxing, Noel was his trainer, mum Carol sold tickets and sister Leah was the round card girl.

'It makes us sound like a bunch of country hicks,' Noel says, 'but from Gatton we were able to get Rick world title fights against Sven Ottke and Joe Calzaghe.'

Rick's success and Noel's reputation as an honest manager in an otherwise cut-throat sport prompted Samoan boxer Maselino Masoe to join Thornberry's team.

Masoe won a world middleweight title in Miami in 2004. That same year, unbeknown to Thornberry, Leapai had his first professional fight at Brisbane's Broncos Leagues Club.

Born in Samoa, Leapai had moved with his parents to Auckland at the age of four and then to Brisbane when he was 12. His parents saw Australia as a land of opportunity, but Leapai was a wild child. He finished Year 12 at Woodridge High but when he wasn't playing Samoan-style cricket and developing a huge overhand right punch he calls 'The Samoan Bowler', he was fighting in the park or on the streets. He was banned from rugby league for attacking a referee.

Leapai married Theresa, his high-school sweetheart, and found a job in Slacks Creek delivering office partitions. But he also smoked dope and drank heavily. He and Theresa had three children and another on the way when Leapai went to jail for beating up bouncers at a nightclub in Brisbane's Caxton Street, a deed that still makes him hang his head. His son Alex Jr was born while he was in jail.

Leapai had a professional record of one win and one draw when Thornberry first laid eyes on him. It was ten years ago at the Mansfield Tavern and Leapai, training occasionally in Brisbane on a diet of hamburgers and pies, lumbered to a points loss against Russian journeyman Yan Kulkov.

'Alex lost but I saw raw power in him that I knew could be developed,' Thornberry says. 'I also knew that deep down he was a good person. Dedicated, and with the right training and a proper diet, I thought he could be a world champion.'

After Leapai was finally released from jail, he would drive two hours to Gatton and two hours back, three times a week, an eight-year journey up Darren Lockyer Way and down boxing's hard road. It was always a struggle. When he got to the shed, he would train like a man possessed, refining his explosive power as he waited year after year for the opportunity to unload on the world stage.

Thornberry promoted most of his fights and almost always lost money. He opened a real estate business in Gatton to make ends meet but floods came and property prices sank.

Leapai's old Holden broke down nine times on his drives from Slacks Creek to the shed. But in 2008, while kneeling to pray in his corner before a fight at the Brisbane Convention Centre, he caught the eye of the deeply religious property developer Phil Murphy.

Murphy's Oxmar Properties became Leapai's sponsor, and his car troubles were over.

Slowly but surely, more and more supporters came on board, not so much with financial backing but with a wave of emotional encouragement.

Even though he was losing money hand over fist, Thornberry spent most nights and mornings at the farm, on the phone and in battles with overseas promoters in New York and Berlin, trying to jag one big opportunity.

It finally came when Leapai was matched with Russian Denis Boytsov, who, like Klitschko, hadn't lost a fight in ten years.

Leapai was supposed to be the patsy in the Denis Boytsov story but in November 2013 in Germany, the massive truck driver defied a torn calf muscle to drop the Russian twice.

As he was declared the winner, Leapai cried like he'd done that first night in jail, knowing that his harrowing odyssey of redemption was nearing its climax.

Leapai will be a huge underdog against Klitschko but that only spurs him on.

'I know what it's like to hit rock bottom,' Leapai says, 'and I know what it's like to fight your way back. I want the world to see what you can achieve if you dedicate yourself to something and try with everything you've got.'

Theresa Leapai still can't watch her husband fight and shudders at the thought of him being punched in the face.

But 12-year-old Maria sums up the hopes and prayers of his family: 'I hope my Dad wins. He's worked so hard, for so long.'

When he closes his eyes to thank God, Leapai knows the

world heavyweight title will not be won in the sporting stadium as much as in the silent chambers of his heart, deep inside his own resolve.

Whether he emerges triumphant or not on 27 April, Leapai has already made an astounding comeback. He credits his salvation to his unwavering belief in God.

But just as important has been Noel Thornberry's unwavering belief in Alex Leapai. And Leapai's belief in himself.

Postscript: *Wladimir Klitschko's massive advantages in height and reach proved too much for Alex. Leapai picked up Klitschko in the first round and hurled him into the ropes but New Jersey referee Eddie Cotton, who would die from COVID a few years later, put a count on Leapai for what looked like a slip rather than a knockdown.*

The point was academic in the end, as Klitschko outboxed Leapai from long range, peppering him with crunching straight lefts and the kind of right hands that earned him the nickname Dr Steel Hammer.

A left hook staggered Klitschko in the fifth but that only caused him to hit back harder until the referee called a halt at 2 minutes, 5 seconds of the round after Leapai was sent sprawling by huge head shots.

Seven years later, Wladimir and his cornerman, Vitali, also a world heavyweight champion and the mayor of Kyiv, would combine as figureheads in a show of strength against Russia's invasion of their homeland.

Lucas Browne's Fleeting Glory

The most decisive blow of Lucas Browne's career came out of nowhere, a split second of sweet clarity amid chaotic turbulence.

Brown's astonishing fightback to win the WBA heavyweight title from Ruslan Chagaev in Grozny on 5 March 2016 brought home to Australia a trophy that had eluded our best for more than a century.

The manner of his victory and the surroundings of his achievement made it all that more remarkable. Browne climbed from the canvas to stop Chagaev – the first time an Aussie won a world heavyweight crown. He defied the 3–1 odds against him and the vast experience of the champ to overwhelm Chagaev in Round 10.

Browne was once shot at while working as a bouncer at a club at Revesby, and he survived cannon blasts from Chagaev to notch his 24th win from 24 pro fights and his 21st by knockout.

Browne didn't take up boxing until he was in his late 20s after his marriage dissolved, and he was fighting in enemy territory in more ways than one. In a heavily militarised region of Russia, the bout had been prefaced by a choreographed display of weaponry by fierce-looking men in fur hats brandishing assault rifles. In Chagaev's corner was Chechnya's hard-line pro-Russian president Ramzan Kadyrov, a close ally of Russian leader Vladimir Putin.

At the time, Chechnya was one of the world's worst trouble spots, and Chagaev, who represented Uzbekistan at the 2000 Olympics, had become a cult hero there. In the lead-up to the fight, he was surrounded wherever he went by machine gun–toting security guards.

The world champ also had one of the best records in heavyweight boxing. His only two losses from 37 fights had been against Olympic gold medallists Wladimir Klitschko and Alexander Povetkin, yet neither of them beat Chagaev as brutally as the relatively unknown Aussie bouncer.

The 196-centimetre Australian came into the fight at 113.1 kilograms, the lightest of his seven-year professional career and a credit to his trainer Rodney Williams. The 36-year-old former cage fighter and kickboxer had been 10 kilograms heavier in 2014 when he became Australia's first Commonwealth heavyweight champion since the West Indian-born Peter Jackson in 1892.

Chagaev, a chunky 180-centimetre southpaw, weighed in at 112.7 kilograms. The 37-year-old had rarely been heavier, but he showed great speed of foot and explosive hand speed.

In the early rounds, the big Australian used his greater height and reach to stay away from the fast-punching champion. Browne was defying the odds that suggested he'd be humiliated.

Then BANG. In Round 6, Chagaev landed a hard right to the body and big left to the chin that dumped Browne on his backside. He was badly hurt, and while he climbed back into the fray, it seemed only a matter of time before the local hero's hand would be raised in triumph and machine gun bullets fired into the air to celebrate.

Then a glimmer of hope presented itself to the big Aussie battler. With less than a minute to go in Round 10, Chagaev threw a southpaw left hook and instinctively Browne fired a right-hand counter that carried every ounce of effort, hope and desire. It landed flush on Chagaev's chin, and he went down as though he'd been hit with a baseball bat.

The Uzbekistani slowly staggered to his feet but he was a sitting duck for more of Browne's heavy ammunition, and the former bouncer unloaded with both hands.

With Chagaev staggering and sagging, South African referee Stanley Christodoulou stopped the fight with seconds left in the round.

For the first time ever, a ring announcer said: 'And the new heavyweight champion of the world ... from Australia.'

When Browne arrived back at Sydney airport with the world championship belt, I'd never seen anyone happier than his mum, Leonie. 'She was just so happy that things have worked out for me,' Browne told me. 'My father Graeme died suddenly about five years ago so he didn't get to see my success, but Mum is very proud for him too.'

There was a twist in the tale of Browne's success, though. Following his world title win, Browne was suspended for six months after a positive test for a banned substance. There had been previously suspicious test results out of the Russian trouble spot, and the WBA accepted Browne's claim that he did not willingly take the small amount of Clenbuterol that was detected in the test.

Six months after the Chagaev fight, Browne was allowed to box again.

While victory over Chagaev had been the biggest win of his seven-year boxing career, Lucas Browne was not too proud to admit that he won the biggest fight of his life by a good 100 metres when he was working as a doorman at the Revesby Workers Club in Sydney and a patron shot at him five times. Before taking on the brutal world of boxing, Browne had spent 13 years as a bouncer at different clubs and had tackled opponents carrying guns, knives, bats and knuckledusters.

Browne grew up in the western Sydney suburb of Granville and his first sporting success came in rugby league. In the Parramatta juniors he played alongside Eric Grothe Jr, Nathan Hindmarsh and Nathan Cayless.

He started cage fighting in 2009, scoring six knockouts in his first six fights. For a while, he put his best foot forward as a kickboxer before deciding his best chance to make it in sport was through boxing.

One of Browne's best recent victories came in 2019 against former rugby league 'bad boy' John Hopoate, who made his professional boxing debut on the first Green–Mundine card in 2006. The heavy-punching Hopoate survived a savage knockout loss to Ben Edwards early in his boxing career. He went on to win the Australian heavyweight title against veteran Bob Mirovic on the Gold Coast in 2008, but the following year, he lasted only until the second round against former world champ Oliver McCall.

Bob Mirovic was a fighter I had a lot to do with over the years: first in 2003, when I was in Bob's corner as he faced the biggest-ever world champ, the 213-centimetre (7 feet) Russian Nikolai Valuev on the undercard of the first Danny Green–Markus Beyer fight at the Nurburgring motor-racing track near Cologne; and two years later, when he served as Mike Tyson's sparring partner.

Bob stands 196 centimetres, and for the fight he weighed about 120 kilograms, but the massive Russian dwarfed him.

Valuev was surprisingly mobile for such a huge human and with 150 kilograms behind his punches, he hit like a bulldozer. Bob was always going to struggle against the giant, who became world champ two years later, but with his live-wire coach Angelo Hyder geeing him up in the corner, Bob gave it everything he had and was still on his feet at the final bell after eight rounds of pure heart. Bob was always a courageous boxer.

Two years after going the distance with Valuev, Bob faced American veteran Rob Calloway on the Gold Coast. Bob fought the last nine rounds of his epic battle with a broken jaw before losing on points.

Settling the Score at Adelaide Oval

For 17 years, Danny Green had dreamt of beating Anthony Mundine. Since their first fight 11 years earlier, which Mundine won over 12 rounds at Sydney Football Stadium, Green had insisted that he was the better fighter, and that the first bout had been the result of having to drain weight to box at the 76-kilogram limit.

In February 2017, at the age of 43, Danny Green finally got his opportunity to prove he wasn't all talk.

Just before the fight, Australia's legendary trainer Johnny Lewis called me to say he was praying that the increasingly fragile Mundine didn't get badly hurt. The 41-year-old had been battered in two of his previous three fights against 70-kilogram fighters, and Johnny feared that he wouldn't be able to cope with a powerhouse who had competed at the elite level at 90 kilograms.

At the cavernous Adelaide Oval, Danny Green came into the fight wearing 'Grant' brand gloves, which are favoured by heavy punchers. Led in by a team of Aboriginal dancers, Anthony Mundine wore 'Winning' brand gloves, which were indicative of a fighter with fragile hands.

Mundine showed his old moves early, clipping Green with a cheap shot that left him badly concussed halfway through the opening round.

After referee Frank Garza called break, Mundine nailed Green with a big punch behind the ear, sending Green spinning across the ring. Mundine was showing glimpses of the scintillating speed and the magical movement that he'd used to embarrass Green in their first fight.

Fighting at 83 kilograms, Green's strength and power was palpable for the huge crowd and perilous for Mundine. But Mundine, who was a muscular 80 kilograms, made him miss a lot. (In an extraordinary move the following year, he sweated back down to a scrawny 70 kilograms and was a walking cadaver as Jeff Horn knocked him out at Suncorp Stadium in front of 25,000 people.)

In what would be his last fight, and in front of a crowd of 27,860, Green eventually handed Mundine his eighth defeat in 55 fights. Scores were 94–94, 96–94 and 98–90 but the fight was close, and Mundine's corner exploded with anger at the decision.

Green not only retained his Australian cruiserweight title but, more importantly to him, he settled an old score.

Billy has Dibs on Courage

One of the bravest and most inspirational people I've met in boxing is the remarkable Billy Dib.

I was ringside for Billy's first professional fight, a stoppage of Chad Roy Naidu at Homebush in 2004, and for his last fight 18 years later, a disqualification win over the flamboyant Jacob Ng on the Gold Coast.

Billy won the IBO featherweight title in 2008 and the IBF featherweight title in 2011. In 2018 he went 12 rounds for the world junior-lightweight title against American Tevin Farmer on a card promoted by Paul Nasari, one of the best blokes in boxing.

Then, late in 2022, The 37-year-old announced that he was locked in the toughest fight of his life. He was battling cancer.

Billy's diagnosis came just six years after he'd lost his first wife, Sara, due to complications stemming from treatment for leukaemia. The pair had brought forward their wedding to two weeks after her diagnosis, but she died just six weeks later.

Billy later remarried, and he and wife, Berry, had announced the birth of Laith Bilal Dib in 2019.

Now Billy had been found to suffer from an aggressive and rare form of non-Hodgkin's lymphoma. He'd been experiencing intense stomach pain and doctors had removed a 5-centimetre tumour.

'Despite sharing the ring with some dangerous opponents in my career, this is one of the most frightening situations I have found myself in,' Billy said not long after his surgery.

'At the moment, I am recovering from the surgery, and it has been tough. I have been unable to eat for the last nine days and am contemplating a return to the featherweight division (jokes).'

In an emotional video posted to Facebook on 22 January 2023, Billy told his supporters: 'Through the mercy and the grace of God I have now made it out of Round 3 of my chemo treatment. It's been quite a difficult and daunting journey, one that I wouldn't wish on my worst enemy.

'Although I don't know what is going on with my sickness and I'm not sure what is in store for me, my will is to survive and to be around for my wife and son for many years to come.

'I'm grateful that God is giving me time because I've been able to rectify all my life issues. Every single thing that has been bothering me has now been rectified and that is only through God's mercy. I have been able to tell all those around me how much I love them and that's the most important thing to me because, God willing, I will get through this cancer and survive. But I do know that if I don't make it through this cancer, then my wife and son know how much I love them. My family – my father, my mother, my siblings – know how much I love them.

'I believe I am going to make it through this sickness and through faith, through love, through believing that I will beat this sickness I am here today.

'I choose to use my time now to shed light upon people, to put a smile on people's faces. We're all checking out of this world at some stage and I want to be remembered as someone who made an impact on people's lives and inspired people to be better.

'God bless you all.'

Manny Pacquiao: Running with the Bull

The cloying heat mixed with the thick smog that envelops everything in Manila when I caught Manny Pacquiao cold.

The world welterweight champion had been running away from me when, red-faced and sweating, I went after him with the same intensity I'd shown a couple of hours earlier chasing down an omelette at the hotel's breakfast buffet.

When I lunged at him, his head spun around and his little legs clicked up another gear as he tried to get some distance from me. The fighting senator was shocked and chagrined.

Our showdown took place in May 2017 when I was in Manila covering the Pacman's preparations for his world title defence against 'The Fighting Schoolteacher' in Brisbane on 2 July.

Fifteen minutes earlier, we'd set off, along with some other journalists, cameramen and a security detail, for Pacquiao's regular 5-kilometre run past the multi-million-dollar homes that neighbour his mansion on Cambridge Circle. Running with the bulls in Pamplona is dangerous; running with a raging bull in Manila, equally so.

My 55-year-old legs had struggled to keep pace with his but in the pursuit of a good story, I kept running, then doubled back to catch Pacquiao on his second loop of the 2.5-kilometre circuit.

When he'd left the media pack well behind and with only his mate Benjamin Garcia on a pushbike for company, I seized my chance and leapt out at him from behind some trees.

Bewildered at my apparent turn of speed and the fact I looked likely to collapse at any time, Pacquiao could only ask in broken English: 'Where you come?'

'Shortcut,' I replied.

'Where short?' he spluttered, nonplussed and perhaps worried that Horn could ambush him with a sneaky move of his own.

We ran together for a few hundred metres more, Pacquiao probably thinking about Jeff Horn's big right hand and me thinking about cardiac arrest.

The world champ even affected an Aussie accent to keep me upright. 'Come on, mate,' he said, a couple of times turning around to run backwards as I lumbered after him. 'Come on, mate.'

The world welterweight champion, who up to that point had earned more than A$600 million from boxing, had been practising his Aussie accent over the previous few weeks almost as much as he'd been practising slipping Horn's power-punches to land his own.

Pacquiao told me he loved running in the heat. I told him I didn't. He said that being 38 and having been a professional boxer for 22 years had taught him all the tricks about fitness and maintaining his speed as he got older.

I survived the run to make it back to his house and watch him go through speed drills and 2000 sit-ups.

I asked him why he thought he could beat Jeff Horn. Pacquiao said it was like going for a run. Speed and experience.

We chatted about great Australian boxers and Pacquiao and his brother, Bobby, said they were both big fans of Jeff Fenech, whose record Australian crowd of 38,000 for his 1992 rematch with Azumah Nelson in Melbourne was about to be toppled by the crowd for the Horn–Pacquiao fight.

Pacquiao had already beaten three Australians – Todd Makelim, Arnel Barotillo and Nedal 'Skinny' Hussein, a Fenech-trained fighter who decked the Filipino great in the fourth round in 2000 before being stopped late on cuts in what now seems like a rort.

'Hussein was a tough, dirty fighter,' Pacquiao told me. 'He hit me with headbutts and elbows all night.'

I told Pacquiao that he did the same to Hussein and he just laughed, a little embarrassed.

Covering Pacquiao's preparations for the Horn fight in Manila was an eye opener. He was already one of the greatest boxers of all time, but as a senator with presidential ambitions, he'd also become a leading political figure in his nation of 111 million people.

Going to dinner with the Philippines' most celebrated hero was an adventure in itself. Horns blared and tyres screeched in a screaming tangle of weaving cars and near misses on Ayala Avenue in the capital of Manila.

Three skinny, wild-eyed youngsters were perched precariously on the back running board of an overflowing purple 'Jeepney' bus as it scooted through the traffic, their matted hair billowing in the breeze as the gaudy vehicle, festooned with ribbons and flowers, raced along at breakneck speed. The Jeepney screeched to a temporary halt as the traffic stalled. The children, jolted by the sudden stop, struggled to stay upright but then leapt off the bus and ran to the windows of paused cars, tapping frantically on the windshields, begging for money and food, desperation in their sad faces. Every day, hungry, homeless children risk their lives begging amid the chaotic traffic on the busy road outside the five-star Shangri-La Hotel.

Once Pacquiao lived among these lost children on the edge of oblivion, dirty, despondent and bedraggled, a thousand miles from home and a million miles from hope. Pacquiao was once just another barefoot kid trying to survive on Manila's mean streets but promoters claimed that half a billion people in 159 countries would watch the telecast of his fight with Jeff Horn. Pacquiao was taking no chances with his life in the lead-up. As children darted through the busy traffic, he arrived at the Shangri-La in an armoured car for dinner with a dozen Australian journalists. The windscreen of his vehicle was as thick as glass bricks and on the front passenger seat beside the driver was a Turkish-made 9mm pistol.

Guns abound in Manila, with armed guards in almost every shop. Two weeks after Pacquiao hosted the media dinner, 39 people were killed 6 kilometres away as a gunman attacked the Resorts World Manila casino.

Pacquiao told me he was cautious wherever he travelled. He is one of the richest men in his country and was a key supporter of the controversial president of the day, Rodrigo Duterte, whose war on drug pushers had resulted in an estimated 7000 people being gunned down.

In 2016, government agents foiled a plot to kidnap Pacquiao by the terrorist group Abu Sayyaf, an organisation blamed for the beheading of two Canadian hostages.

Pacquiao looked relaxed, even a little bashful, as he sauntered into the Shangri-La's Japanese restaurant with a bodyguard and two friends. He was dressed casually in jeans and jacket and slipped into the seat next to mine. He ate in the restaurant several times a week, and on this night picked up the A$5400 restaurant tab with not so much a blink of an eye as a nod to his bodyguard.

His driver told me later that Pacquiao had more than 100 people maintaining his four mansions in the Philippines and sometimes, when he treated different groups of them to a night out, the bill would hit $30,000. He was not too concerned about money. Even when he lost a fight against Floyd Mayweather in 2015 in Las Vegas he made what *Forbes* magazine estimated was more than A$160 million.

Yet this very rich man remained a child at heart. Over a dinner of sea cucumber, tempura prawns and other delicacies, he laughed uproariously and often, and found Australian accents hilarious, mimicking the voices around him with a 'G'day, mate' or 'How's it goin', mate?'

At one stage, the 38-year-old, who speaks in broken English, suddenly morphed into Mel Gibson portraying the Scottish folk hero from the movie *Braveheart*.

'Ma name is William Wallace,' Pacquiao said, sounding very much like Sean Connery. 'They can take away our lives but they will never take our freedom.' He giggled, and it was impossible not to be infected with his good humour.

Pacquiao had three phones with him – one for his work as a senator, one for boxing contacts and one for his wife and five children. That was the only phone he answered at the dinner table and the one he used to show me the 'Real Boxing Manny Pacquiao' Android app in which he beats up challengers from around the world.

I'd just spent three days watching Pacquiao train for the Horn fight and all along he seemed to be taking things easy, punching in rapid-fire bursts only occasionally and spending much of his gym time signing autographs, posing for pictures or chatting with friends. I asked him if he was underestimating the Brisbane boxer who, despite being unbeaten in 17 professional fights, was a rank outsider. For a while Pacquiao didn't answer. He was concentrating on his phone as his thumbs worked his boxing game with machine-gun speed. On the face of the phone, the head of Pacquiao's opponent was being knocked in all directions.

'I win,' he said finally, with the look of a small boy delighted at a new toy. His expression then got serious. 'No, I never underestimate anyone. This is Jeff Horn's big chance. I remember when I was starting out. I would lie awake at night and dream of winning a big fight. I will be 100 per cent ready.'

Pacquiao closed his soft brown eyes for a moment. 'I fight to inspire poor people everywhere,' he told me, 'to give poor people hope. They know the life I come from. They know if they try hard anything is possible.'

Then he laughed loudly again and reprised the role of William Wallace. 'I can speak Scotland [sic],' he said proudly. 'Call me Braveheart.'

At the time, Pacquiao's promoter was Bob Arum, then an 85-year-old Harvard-trained lawyer who began promoting fights for Muhammad Ali in 1966 and became the most successful boxing entrepreneur of all time, outlasting his great rival Don King while showcasing the likes of Joe Frazier, Sugar Ray Leonard, Marvin Hagler, Thomas Hearns and Roberto Durán.

Arum said there had never been a boxer like the Filipino whirlwind, whose frenetic all-action style, sizzling hand speed and savage power made him a global phenomenon.

'Manny has won world titles across eight weight divisions from flyweight (51 kg) to junior-middleweight (70 kg),' Arum told me in Melbourne during Pacquiao's promotional tour to Australia in April 2017. 'No one in boxing history has come close to what Manny has done. But the truly great things he does are not in the boxing ring but for the poor people of the Philippines.'

In 2016 Pacquiao announced that out of his own pocket he had paid for 1000 homes to be built for the poor in General Santos City, where he was raised.

Senator Emmanuel Dapidran Pacquiao came into this world on 17 December 1978, in a remote corner of Kibawe, a jungle town of 35,000 on the southern Philippines island of Mindanao. He was delivered by a midwife in a thatched hut with a dirt floor.

His mother, Dionisia, hoped that one day he would become a Catholic priest. Pacquiao's father, Rosalio, was a farm labourer climbing trees to harvest coconuts for 14 hours a day to make $1.50. Rosalio eventually left home to take up with another woman, only coming back for a short stay during which – in a fit of anger – he killed and cooked Pacquiao's pet dog.

Pacquiao says he learned to fight as a small boy watching roosters scratch and peck each other to death in cockfights, which are still popular in the Philippines.

At 12, now living with his mother and five siblings in General Santos City, a metropolis of half a million people, Pacquiao left school to sell peanuts, donuts and cigarettes on street corners to help his family. But he envisioned a different future in 1990 when he watched a boxing match on television between Mike Tyson and the underdog James 'Buster' Douglas.

As Douglas climbed from the canvas to drive Tyson to the floor with a series of huge blows, Pacquiao recalled: 'This was my first hope in life that I could be something or someone. I was the underdog, and maybe not even big enough to be a fighter. I wasn't from anywhere in the world that mattered. I had nothing to lose.'

Pacquiao became an amateur boxer at 13 and at only 40 kilograms hit hard enough to break the ribs of other boys. By 15, and still sleeping at home on a mattress of cardboard, he was a local hero.

He yearned to make money to help his mother, and at 16 he and a friend, Eugene Barutag, stowed away on a freighter bound for the boxing arenas of Manila, 1600 kilometres to the north.

'When I was on the boat I was crying,' Pacquiao recalled. 'I didn't know if I would ever see my family again.'

With its towering skyscrapers and endless traffic, Manila

terrified him. The two boys slept in a park, and Pacquiao made $5 a day when he could find work, first scraping off rust at a scrap metal yard, then toiling as a gardener, construction worker, waiter and tailor. He washed dishes so he could eat restaurant leftovers.

Pacquiao began training in the first real boxing gym he had seen and even though it was up four flights of steep stairs in a dilapidated building in a Manila slum, Pacquiao felt at home with the threadbare equipment, dusty floors and the ever-present pong of body odour. The gym owner let him sleep in a tiny room little bigger than a cupboard.

In December 1995, he and Barutag appeared on the same fight card together, against different opponents, at a small Manila hall. Barutag was winning his fight but faded badly in the later rounds and took one heavy punch after another before collapsing in his corner, unconscious.

Pacquiao's eyes welled with tears when he recalled how he held Barutag in his arms backstage. 'He was my close friend. I feel so bad,' Pacquiao said. 'I was saying to him, "Come on, you can make it," but his eyes looked straight ahead and he was not breathing anymore.' Pacquiao's friend was dead at 16.

Incredibly, minutes after that numbing tragedy, the baby-faced Pacquiao, now weighing 50 kilograms, climbed into the same ring to beat his opponent by a points decision. Pacquiao spent the next three days sitting by Barutag's open coffin and he paid for the funeral from the little money he had saved.

Three years later, in Thailand, Pacquiao won the WBC flyweight (51 kg) title, the first of 12 world championships he would eventually hold.

Horn and Rushton, a Dynamic Duo

The first time Jeff Horn laid eyes on Manny Pacquiao, the Filipino was beating up one of the biggest names in the sport on TV. It was 6 December 2008, and Horn had just started getting serious about boxing. In the biggest fight that year, the rank underdog Pacquiao overwhelmed Oscar De La Hoya, Olympic gold medallist and hero of American boxing. Pacquiao had been a world champ at lighter weights for a decade but no one outside his own stable knew he was that good. Pacquiao tormented De La Hoya for eight rounds.

Horn, then a boxing novice, remembered being 'wowed' by the Filipino's astonishing speed and power and could hardly believe that 11 years after being beaten up at high school he would be facing that same fighter before the biggest crowd ever seen for an Australian boxing match.

Pacquiao's win over De La Hoya catapulted him into the stratosphere of boxing earnings and he was soon collecting multimillion-dollar paydays and the scalps of other major stars Ricky Hatton, Miguel Cotto, Antonio Margarito and Shane Mosley.

By his own admission, Pacquiao was once an uncontrollable wild man. While he became a member of the Philippines government that advocated the death penalty for drug dealers, he admits he has used cocaine, methamphetamine and marijuana. As a rich young sports idol, he also ran a casino and owned a strip club employing 100 women.

In 2011, just as his wife, Jinkee, was planning to divorce him, Pacquiao had what he calls 'a spiritual reawakening' and became a non-denominational Christian. He said he experienced dreams and visions and heard the voice of God 'so powerful' that he felt he was trembling and melting. In the years since, he said Jinkee had helped him become not just a better fighter but a better man.

Horn thought I was kidding when I rang him six months before the fight to say there was a definite chance he could be fighting Pacquiao at Suncorp Stadium and that a deal was in the works.

Horn had never drawn more than 1800 people for a fight in Brisbane and the thought of him somehow drawing what potentially could be a bigger crowd than the State of Origin matches at Suncorp seemed absurd. But the fight proved to be a huge hit, the audience drawn by the story of the mild-mannered victim of bullies standing up for himself against one of the great figures in boxing history.

Trainer Glenn Rushton was the man who turned Jeff Horn from a timid teenager into a world champion boxer.

It started on a Thursday night, 20 April 2006, when Horn, then an 18-year-old nerd, chugged down Compton Road in Stretton, a suburb in Brisbane's south. He had a little acne and no confidence. He was with his cousin, Mat Symons, and was driving his old Volvo 240GL rattler.

The boxy vehicle looked out of place among a row of massive homes that remind some visitors of Canberra's embassy precinct. It was the grandest boulevard Horn had ever driven down and, nervously, he parked in front of the biggest house he'd ever seen. He'd heard that inside this palace there was a karate expert who ran self-defence classes, but it all looked a bit too fantastic to be true.

As Horn and Symons warily approached a high mauve and cream concrete fence, they suspected they'd written down the wrong address. Behind the fence was a vast tiled courtyard complete with a massive fountain with what looked like four stone dolphins bursting free. The building looked like a Las Vegas hotel.

'I'm looking at Mat and saying, "what the ...', Horn recalled. 'I was sure we must have taken a wrong turn.'

Horn would later learn that inside this palace were seven bedrooms with ensuites, nine bathrooms, an indoor squash court, a tennis court, recording studio, indoor cinema, a giant *Star Wars* mural, a lap pool and a swim-up bar. But the mansion also contained a massive indoor gymnasium. Martial arts whiz Rushton had built the house in 1998 and used the home gym to conduct self-defence classes.

Rushton's opulent property was less than a 20-minute drive from Horn's home in Pallara but, without realising it, the tentative teenager had started a long, arduous journey that would take him to places, experiences and emotions he never thought possible. As he stood in front of Rushton's house, Horn had turned the corner towards a future that was beyond his wildest imagination.

When Horn nervously lined up with 20 other karate students in martial arts attire for his first self-defence lesson, Rushton remembered the new boy as a 'soft, wimpy sort of a kid'.

'He looked like a mummy's boy,' Rushton said.

When Horn told the karate expert that he'd been picked on a lot at school, Rushton said he could understand why.

'One of the things Glenn always told me,' Horn said, 'is that you might get knocked down in life but you have to keep getting up. He reckons that maybe one of the reasons we have so much depression in society is that people aren't taught resilience. In life you get bullied and in business you can get hurt, but he says you have to roll with the punches and press on. That's what I did against Pacquiao and look how it turned out.'

The wily, wiry trainer saw a spark of talent in his young student and knew he could fan that spark into something monumental. Almost nine years before the Pacquiao fight, Rushton gave Horn, then a novice amateur fighter, a pair of boxing gloves as a gift for his 21st birthday. The gloves came with an inscription that read: 'All it takes to reach the stars is a leap of faith'.

Soon after Horn started boxing he was joined in the gym by Joe Goodall, a meek 193-centimeter, 105-kilogram giant who wanted to stay fit after being injured playing Aussie rules. Rushton made him a believer, too.

Goodall, 25, won a silver medal at the 2014 Commonwealth Games and a bronze medal in the super-heavyweight division at the World Amateur Championships.

Rushton says he always taught Horn to be confident but never arrogant. 'When he first came to my gym he didn't even know how to throw a punch, but he was naturally quick and physically tough.

'Jeff was a pretty good soccer player and he had terrific footwork and he picked up what I was teaching him very quickly. He trained with me one day a week for about a year and a half and in 2008 told me he wanted to take up boxing seriously. I said, "Jeff, give me four years and you'll go to the Olympics."'

Despite two losses in the amateurs to the brilliant Beijing Olympian Todd Kidd, Horn qualified for the 2012 London Olympics, where he made the quarter-finals.

'Five years later, I told him he could beat Manny Pacquiao,' Rushton said. 'Jeff is more than just a brilliant boxer. He is one of the finest young men you would ever know. The courage and strength of character he showed against Pacquiao will never be forgotten.'

'All along I predicted that Manny Pacquiao would face the most punishing fight of his life against Jeff,' Rushton told me with the enthusiasm of a sharebroker whose stock picks have gone through the roof. 'I know Jeff inside out. I know what he's made of and what's inside him. He's a very placid, lovely young man but, like Clark Kent, he has a Superman alter ego. He just needed someone to make him believe.'

Rushton is a cross between Chuck Norris and Anthony Robbins, mixing martial arts with motivational messages. For Horn he is a miracle worker, a dream-weaver, a guru whose prophecies have all come true.

Horn's father, Jeff Snr, describes Rushton as 'the master motivator'.

'You don't have to spend much time in his company for his enthusiasm to become infectious,' he says. 'Glenn filled Jeff with a belief that he could beat anyone in the world. He was right every step of the way.'

* * *

Glenn Rushton had all sorts of jobs before becoming the trainer of a world boxing champion. He's been a cabinetmaker, fruit picker, bricklayer, construction boss, karate instructor, insurance salesman, fight promoter, photographer, property developer and investment adviser. He sold health products through multi-level marketing and in his 20s he ironed out more than a few troublemakers as a pub bouncer.

These days he describes himself as a 'teacher' and he has learned from the best, devouring self-help books for decades. Like Napoleon Hill he thought and grew rich, and like Dale Carnegie he won friends and influenced people. Horn still addresses Rushton by the nickname 'Renshi', a martial arts term for an expert instructor.

When he was nine, Rushton moved with his two brothers to live with their father in Townsville. Three years later, at Townsville's Rising Sun picture theatre one night, an usher rammed Rushton's head into a brick wall. He had mistaken him for another kid who had thrown rocks on the roof. 'I promised myself that it would be the last time I got beaten up by anyone,' he says.

Rushton took boxing lessons at Townsville's National Fitness Centre with Neil Pattel, a classmate in Year 7 at Currajong State School. Pattel eventually became an Australian boxing champion and, two weeks after Horn beat Pacquiao, Rushton inducted Pattel into the Queensland Boxing Hall of Fame.

Rushton says his dad never really got over the breakup of his marriage, and their home in Townsville was no place for a teenager who believed he was a rich man born in a poor man's body and just bursting to break free. When Rushton was 14 his father gave him $20 and Rushton hit the road to go fruit-picking in Shepparton, Victoria, 2500 kilometres to the south.

'I stayed down there for 18 months working 12 hours a day, seven days a week,' he said. 'Once I worked 83 days straight. I tell all the boxers I train that the only time money comes before success is in the dictionary, and it's important to always do your best at whatever you're doing.'

Eleven-and-a-half years after Jeff Horn started training with Glenn Rushton, he and his mentor were in Rushton's home cinema, perched on a sofa in front of a movie screen so fantastically humungous that it could grace a drive-in picture theatre.

Horn and Rushton were watching a replay of Horn's victory over Pacquiao at Suncorp Stadium on 2 July 2017. It was the day that a Disneyesque fairytale came true, when a former bullied schoolboy morphed into a superhero and – with a massive worldwide audience watching – beat one of history's greatest champions.

The experience was still so surreal for Horn that the new world welterweight champion sometimes wondered if one of the most electrifying afternoons in Queensland sports history really happened, though he had a scar over his right eye and – in the street where he once parked the old Volvo – a bright yellow $230,000 Lexus to prove that it did.

On the big screen in Rushton's house, Horn watched himself become dazed and confused by a barrage of punches from the left-handed Filipino in the ninth round. Horn's chopped-up face looked like raw meat and as he sat in the corner between rounds, the American referee Mark Nelson threatened to stop the fight and declare Pacquiao the winner by knockout.

But, in the great crisis of their lives, Rushton told his fighter to 'hold the dream', to maintain the vision of a glorious future as a world champion. Horn could make millions by beating Pacquiao or he could go back to fighting for $15,000 a bout. Which did he want?

In the final three rounds, Horn fought back to create boxing history. He was subsequently voted the most inspirational sportsperson in Australia when he took out the 2017 Don Award in Melbourne, beating the likes of Olympic gold medallist Sally Pearson and State of Origin hero Johnathan Thurston.

In his acceptance speech, Horn paid tribute to Rushton, who was seated nearby with his wife, Lillian, for daring to think big and believing in the potential of a teenager who, when he first stepped into his gym, didn't even know how to throw a punch.

Dundee Kim: My Brilliant Korea

Watching Dundee Kim, the Korean trainer who helped Jeff Horn become world welterweight champion, was always an education.

While Glenn Rushton was Horn's trainer and manager, the boxer would work out with his Korean-born coach two days a week at one of Kim's three gyms in Brisbane.

Until a month before a fight, Kim would also supervise an extra hour of weight training exercises as Horn dripped sweat like a leaking tap, pushing dumbbells skyward like pistons and smashing a weighted medicine ball into the floor as though trying to crack the concrete.

At primary school, Kim's teacher told him that he was dumber than a dog. In the decades since, though, Kim has proved to be smarter than a fox.

Born Deuk-Rae Kim on a farm outside Gangneung, a city of 200,000 three hours' drive south of the North Korean border, he always wanted to be somewhere else. His family grew rice, corn, potatoes, beans, watermelons and had a few cows. 'The soil is very rich,' Kim says, 'but we were very poor.'

The natural beauty of the area, from the spectacular beaches to the snow-capped mountains of nearby Pyeong-Chang – host city for the 2018 Winter Olympics – drew waves of tourists from Japan and China. They made Kim think a lot about the world beyond subsistence farming.

School bullies made him think about learning self-defence.

He left school at 15. Rigorous physical training, starting with long runs at 5.30 a.m., became a staple of his life in between labouring on farms and running a street stall selling food. At 19 he enlisted in the South Korean Army and spent two years doing compulsory military service.

In 1990 he went to Japan on a working visa, learning the language and helping train a 51-kilogram world boxing champion named Hiroki Ioka. He worked on construction sites too, and at night memorised pages of Japanese books, practising the language by chatting with strangers on buses and trains. He followed that with four years in China studying international business at the Beijing University of Technology and back in Korea worked as a waiter for eight months near Seoul's Incheon Airport. The tips were good and he saved enough money to pay for his wedding to his primary school classmate, Kyung Yun Park.

The couple arrived in Brisbane in 1998 with only a few thousand dollars to make a new home.

A friend suggested the new arrivals should use common Australian names to better blend into their new community so Dundee Kim named himself after the movie character Crocodile Dundee and Mrs Kim became 'Kylie'.

University tuition was expensive but Kim found an economy rate at the Kenmore Christian College and embarked on two years of study for a diploma in theology.

Before long he put his faith in his own life experiences and began knocking on doors in Brisbane looking for a job as a marketing officer for a university.

Over six years Dundee helped build up the number of international students at Central Queensland University from 50 to 1100.

He became regional director of international relations at James Cook University's Brisbane campus, where he also received his MBA. Then he decided to make his passion for boxing and physical fitness a full-time career. He opened his gym at West End and in 2013 was reading a newspaper article I wrote when he saw a great action photograph by Annette Dew of Jeff Horn punching Anthony Mundine in the face during a sparring session. Knowing that Horn was a humble young hero, Kim thought he would be a good fit for his gym and offered the aspiring boxer his services as a conditioning expert. Kim trained Horn twice a week, supplementing Glenn Rushton's work, and he was a key figure in Horn's great win over Pacquiao.

Slim Pickings for 'Skinny'

In 2023 Skinny Hussein was exploring his legal options after Carlos 'Sonny' Padilla, the referee of his 2000 fight with Manny Pacquiao, admitted that he had helped the badly hurt Filipino win.

Padilla, a well-known Filipino actor who also refereed the famous Muhammad Ali–Joe Frazier 'Thrilla in Manila' in 1975, admitted to giving Pacquiao a slow ten-count after Hussein dropped him in Round 4.

Pacquiao was on the canvas for 18 seconds, which under normal rules should have resulted in Hussein winning by knockout. Padilla also ruled a Pacquiao headbutt that caused bleeding over Hussein's eye as a 'legal punch', so when the ringside doctor stopped the fight in Round 10, it was ruled as a technical knockout win for the Filipino.

At the time Hussein was undefeated with a 19–0 record. The fight, held in Antipolo, east of Manila in 2000, was for the WBC International super-bantamweight title. A win over Pacquiao would have been a huge career boost for Hussein, who went on to lose two world title bouts by decision.

In an interview posted on the WBC's YouTube channel, Padilla, 88, said: 'I am a Filipino and everybody is Filipino watching the fight, so I prolong the count. I know how to do it.' Padilla was grinning when he said it.

Combat Veteran Fights for a Cause

Justin Frost spent seven years in the Australian Army and saw combat and death in the hellhole of Kabul. He says the most dangerous place for an Australian soldier, though, is not in the bloody war zones of the world but right back home in suburbia.

Frost, 27, won the Australian light-welterweight title by outpointing Tasmanian Olympian Jackson Woods at the Eatons Hill Hotel in November 2019. Frost was using the big bout as a platform to highlight the terrible toll suffered by ex-service men and women, including his mate Joel Clifton, an aspiring heavyweight and combat veteran. Clifton overcame crippling war injuries to fight for the Australian heavyweight title in 2016 but was found dead in a Manila hotel room during a holiday in the Philippines two years later.

Frost said the army was a 'massive network of mates' and he wanted to promote the message that those mates were the best defence in fighting back against attacks of despair.

Statistics show that, between 2001 and 2016, an Australian service man or woman was almost seven times more likely to die from suicide than in deployment, and Frost hoped his title fight drew more attention to the clear and present danger facing them.

Huni Turns up the Heat on our Best Heavyweights

It was a red-hot day at a backyard gym in Brisbane and Justis Huni, Australia's new world boxing champion, was telling me about the cold chill that went through him in the land of the giants.

A shiver went down his spine, and not just because the temperature in St Petersburg, Russia, hit -12°C as he made sporting history in November 2016.

'When I saw all the big guys I had to fight – guys up to two metres tall and 130 kilograms, I had some doubts that I could do it,' the softly spoken 17-year-old told me.

'But once I started winning, my confidence grew. I felt like I was on top of the world when my hand was raised after the final. I will never forget that moment.'

Huni became Australia's first-ever world youth (under 19) boxing champ when he mowed down five of the best young amateur boxers in the world to take the super-heavyweight gold medal at the world titles.

He'd trained in a backyard gym at Bethania in Queensland with his dad, Rocki, and his coach, Mark Wilson, who celebrated his 60th birthday with the gold medal success.

The 190-centimetre, 92-kilogram Huni had the draw from Hell at the 7000-seat Sibur Arena, facing fighters from Olympic boxing powerhouses Kazakhstan, Uzbekistan and Armenia, before nailing American Richard Torrez in the semi-final, and outclassing Giorgi Tchigladze of Georgia to win gold.

Huni was the lightest boxer in his division but used the speed and angles that he and his coaches had been working on since he followed his brother Lopeti to the Bethania gym eight years earlier.

'He's still developing a big punch, but the speed is his big winner,' Mark Wilson told me. 'For a super-heavyweight, Justis is incredibly quick – as fast as a middleweight.'

Wilson has coached other star fighters such as Chris McCullen, Tyrone Tongia and his own son Brendon Wilson, as well as the brilliant Clay Waterman, who won Australia's first world junior (under-17) title in 2011. In 2022 he guided Jai Opetaia to the world cruiserweight title. He told me that Huni was the next big thing in Australian boxing and not just because he expected him to grow by another 5 centimetres and 15 kilograms as he built towards the 2020 Olympics.

Huni has uncles nudging 210 centimetres and is a mix of Tongan, Swedish, Samoan and Dutch heritage. Three years after winning that world title, he took home a bronze medal at the world amateur championships in Ekaterinburg, Russia. A bout of gastric forced him out of the event after he'd made the semi-finals.

In February 2020 he and Demsey McKean slugged it out at Huni's Bethania gym in sparring as McKean prepared to beat the slick American Jonathan Rice at The Star, on the Gold Coast. Huni's flashy boxing style – hit and not be hit – is based on fast footwork, head movement and lightning counters.

The biggest win of Huni's early pro career came in June 2021, when he handed former rugby league star Paul Gallen his first defeat. At the time, the shorter, thickset Gallen was unbeaten in 12 pro fights, but he had no answer to Huni's speed and movement.

While Gallen copped a beating from the opening bell, he lasted until a minute into the 10th and final round when referee John Cauchi saved the former Cronulla Sharks skipper from Huni's incessant punches.

Gallen was never in the fight but world boxing icon Tyson Fury, who watched a telecast, said: 'May I say, Paul Gallen's very gutsy. He's got some balls on him.'

Gallen beat some tough footballers during his eight years as a professional boxer, including Justin Hodges, Ben Hannant, Anthony Watt, Darcy Lussick and Junior Paulo. As well, he beat legitimate Aussie boxing contenders Herman Ene-Purcell, Randall Rayment and John Hopoate, a former rugby league player and ex-Australian heavyweight champion.

He also out-punched mixed martial arts veteran Mark Hunt, who would later hand football great Sonny Bill Williams his first loss as a professional.

Gallen had two cracks at the national boxing title but came up short against Huni and, in May 2022, Kris Terzievski.

Gallen's biggest win was a stunning stoppage of former world heavyweight champion Lucas 'Big Daddy' Browne.

His much-hyped fights in the last three years of his career reportedly grossed $25 million, of which he pocketed $9 million, more than he made from 16 years at the top of rugby league.

Rugby league players have had a notable presence in boxing in recent years and among the best of them was Solomon Haumono, who won the Australian heavyweight title in 2012 and fought world champions Joseph Parker and Tomasz Adamek.

Joey Williams won 12 of 16 pro fights, and in 2014 won the WBF super-lightweight title. Joey also became a best-selling author as an advocate for greater awareness around mental health.

Garth Wood played for the Rabbitohs and Tigers but his greatest sporting moment came when he knocked out Anthony Mundine in a huge upset in 2010. He also won the television boxing contest *The Contender*, beating Olympian Kariz Kariuki and heavy-hitting former Russian amateur star Victor Oganov.

Probably the best rugby league player to take up boxing was Herb Narvo, who was a star forward on the 1937 Kangaroo tour before winning the Australian heavyweight title in 1943, taking only 25 seconds to ice Billy Britt. After his final fight at Sydney Stadium in 1946, Narvo went on to captain-coach St George to the grand final.

Tayla Kicks on with Gloves

Tayla Harris was the first of the women's football stars to make it as a professional boxer. She became a star forward for Brisbane, Carlton and Melbourne in AFL Women's, and won the Australian women's middleweight title over Margarite Butcher in 2019, before winning the junior-middleweight title against Janay Harding in the same year.

A decade earlier, when she was 12, Tayla Harris's father, Warren, took her to the Arana Hills PCYC in Brisbane's north to learn self-defence. Tayla started kickboxing and loved it.

'My coach had an eye patch, and he was really tough,' she told me during a break at Shaggy King's Corporate Box Gym in the Brisbane suburb of Lutwyche. 'I was scared. If you did anything wrong, you had to do 100 push-ups. Or 100 kicks. I loved the training but then footy took over when I started making representative teams.

'When I got my driver's licence in year 12, I would drive past the Corporate Box Gym ... and they had a big sign out the front for boxing. I started working for AFL Queensland in Yeronga and I kept driving past the sign to and from work. I walked in one day and asked if I could start training.

'When I started, I couldn't even skip but my coach back then, Aaron Smith, started me on 10 skips a day and then 20. I got better pretty quickly. I got so obsessed with boxing training that I'd train all morning, then go to a friends' house for lunch and come back to do more. One day [former Australian champ] Shaggy King, who runs the gym, said, "Do you want to have a real fight?" And it started a whole second career for me.

'Boxing gives me explosive fitness and I attribute a lot of my development in footy to boxing training, especially the mental side of it. After experiencing the last round of an Australian title fight you know you can push through anything on the footy field.'

The Moloney Brothers: Little Champions

Andrew Moloney became Australia's latest world boxing champion in Melbourne in 2019 but said the victory wouldn't be complete until his twin brother, Jason, older by a minute, joined him with a title, too.

The brothers didn't have such a good start in the sport, and Andrew lost his first seven amateur fights before remaining undefeated in Australia for years.

Andrew, a 2014 Commonwealth Games gold medallist, stopped Brooklyn's Elton Dharry after eight savage rounds at the

Margaret Court Arena to win the Interim WBA super-flyweight (52 kg) title.

The fight was actually the main event on the Code War promotion, though the earlier battle between Paul Gallen and former Aussie rules star Barry Hall, which ended in a draw after six rounds, stole most of the media attention.

Moloney's firefight lived up to the main event status, as Guyana-born Dharry made the unbeaten Kingscliff fighter battle desperately to retain his unbeaten status and capture his first world crown.

Moloney, 28, who came into the bout unbeaten in 20 starts, was rocked badly in Round 5 by a big right uppercut, but he managed to hold on to his senses.

In the sixth round, Moloney's fast accurate jab began to close Dharry's right eye, and the wound became steadily worse.

In the break after Round 8, ringside doctor John O'Neill had seen enough and Moloney was declared the winner.

Earlier, Jason, who represented Australia with Andrew at the 2010 Delhi Commonwealth Games, stopped world number-ten bantamweight Dixon Flores of Nicaragua in Round 2.

At the time, the Moloneys, both young fathers, lived within a few hundred metres of each other at Kingscliff in northern New South Wales, after moving north from Melbourne to train with Danny Green's coach Angelo Hyder.

Jason came close to winning the world bantamweight title in Florida in 2018, losing a close decision to Emmanuel Rodríguez. In 2020, Japanese juggernaut Naoya Inoue halted him in seven.

Andrew lost his world title to Texan Joshua Franco, but both brothers remain high in the world ratings.

The Beautiful Brutality

One of the most brutal and yet beautiful fights I ever saw was on the eve of the publication of this book – an IBO world cruiserweight title bout between rugged Kiwi-born Brisbane slugger Floyd Masson and Italy's former European champ Fabio Turchi.

It was a bloody battle promoted by my mate Angelo Di Carlo at the Eatons Hill Hotel on Brisbane's northside on 1 April 2023.

After 11 rounds of trying to rip each other apart, the two tough southpaws embraced in centre ring before the start of Round 12. It was a symbol of mutual respect for the courage, strength, tenacity and fitness fighters need at the highest level.

In the end both men left the arena in ambulances after the 36-minute slugfest that saw Masson win a unanimous points decision. Masson and Turchi were taken to Brisbane's Mater Hospital urinating blood.

With his heavily pregnant wife Hannah ringside, and with IBF champ Jai Opetaia providing television commentary, Masson refused to buckle no matter what Turchi threw at him.

'Words can't describe how I feel,' Masson told the crowd after the fight. 'I have to thank Fabio; he was a warrior.'

Liam Paro: Fighting for a Mate

They were the best of friends. A pair of live-wire eight-year-olds with a zest for life who would play rugby league for the North Mackay Magpies and dream of conquering the world together.

They would share their ambitions whenever they laced on their boots. They were little kids but they had big dreams and it became the mantra for Liam Paro and Regan Grieve that they were going to 'conquer the world'.

Regan grew into a hard-running, big-tackling second-rower who was signed by the North Queensland Cowboys and captained the Queensland under-18 team. At 185 centimetres and 107 kilograms he became one of the best rugby league prospects in the country.

Liam was much smaller, a tough fullback or hooker. At 22 the slick southpaw became a world junior boxing champion at

63 kilograms under the guidance of promoter Angelo Di Carlo and his son Alfie, Paro's trainer.

The Di Carlos, prominent property developers in Brisbane, have been mainstays in Brisbane boxing for decades. Angelo's younger son Nathan boxed at the 2006 Commonwealth Games and together the family has given hundreds of Australians their big chance in boxing. They also guided another North Queenslander, Mark Flanagan, to a pair of world cruiserweight title shots.

Liam has the words 'Conquer the World' tattooed on his rib cage. He had the painful artwork done after carrying his boyhood mate's coffin at their old footy ground. Despite what seemed a brilliant rugby league career ahead of him, Regan Grieve took his own life on Australia Day 2015, aged just 18, only hours after laughing with his friends and telling them 'I'm feeling great'.

Liam has the dates of Grieve's birth and death tattooed on his ribs as well, and still plans to conquer the world in memory of his mate. 'Regan's death devastated me,' Liam said. 'We played for the Magpies together, went to Mackay North State High together and we ended up moving to Townsville together to pursue sport.

'Regan was signed by the Cowboys, and I went up there to train in boxing with Mark Flanagan and Dennis Clancy.

'I can't tell you how much it hurt when I had to carry my best friend's coffin and help bury him, especially when he was just 18 and had so much going for him. I hope the message on my ribs reminds people of his life and how important it was, and how we all have to fight to prevent youth suicide.'

On 15 October 2022, at the South Bank Piazza in South Brisbane, Paro faced the toughest test of his career in the lean and lanky Brock Jarvis, a mauler and brawler in the manner of his coach Jeff Fenech.

As a young tearaway on the streets of Sydney's inner-west, Fenech had been steered towards boxing by Brock's uncle Pat Jarvis, an Australian representative in rugby league and a policeman in charge of the Newtown Police Youth Club.

Almost 40 years later Fenech began steering Brock towards a world championship.

After 13 amateur fights, Brock made his professional debut in Bangkok in 2015 and had his second pro fight in Mexico.

Then unbeaten in 20 pro fights, he promised to be a nightmare all night for Paro. The fight, however, lasted just 149 seconds as the cagey Paro unloaded with devastating counter-punches for the most spectacular win of his career.

Promise to his Dying Dad

Liam Wilson's slugfest with Mexico's world champ Emanuel Navarrete in Arizona on 3 February 2023 was a nine-round thrill ride that saw both men on the canvas.

Wilson is well used to thrill rides.

His earliest memories are of a police chase near Kingaroy, Queensland, sirens blaring, lights flashing, eyeballs bulging as his father, Pete Wilson, made a run for it, pedal to the metal with three small children in his XR Falcon.

Three-year-old Liam and his twin sister Sharni watched on helpless as the oldest of the kids, seven-year-old Ethan, tried to help his dad's getaway by throwing XXXX beer cans at the pursuit vehicle on their tail.

As they roared along in the car on a bush backroad and then smashed through household fences, the kids were experiencing just one of the many wild times they had growing up with a father who poured himself a brandy for breakfast every morning almost until the day his relatives poured his ashes under a tree at Stanthorpe.

Pete Wilson did 18 months in the Arthur Gorrie Correctional Centre after that car chase.

Liam then watched his father drown in a sea of booze, and was at his bedside at a hospital in Toowoomba in 2012 as he went under for the last time.

Liam promised his dying father that he would one day win a world title.

And against the free-swinging Navarrete at the Desert Diamond Arena in Glendale, Arizona, in a fight for the World Boxing Organisation's super-featherweight (59-kilogram) title, he almost did it.

Liam was a huge underdog against the Mexican who was unbeaten for 10 years and had already won world championships in two lighter weight divisions.

But the raw-boned Queensland father of two was not overawed.

A day after Wilson inexplicably weighed four pounds under the weight limit for the fight at the official weigh-in – and claimed that the scales had been tampered with to give Navarrete an advantage – he went right after the heavy-hitting Mexican at the opening bell.

In Round 4 Wilson landed his 'left hook from hell', and a series of big rights that dropped Navarrete for the first time in his 38-fight career.

Navarrete's mouthguard was also dislodged and by the time referee Chris Flores replaced it properly, Navarrete had been given 27 vital seconds of recovery time to clear his spinning head.

The Mexican made the most of the opportunity, and while Wilson kept the pressure on, Navarrete's experience told heavily. In Round 9 he dropped Wilson and then battered him to a standstill as the referee stopped the fight.

A shattered Wilson told reporters that the fight should have been halted in Round 4 with Navarrete out on his feet.

Wilson said his promise to win a world title for his father would have to wait.

'Dad was 52 when he died,' Liam told me. 'He was a panel beater and did a bit at the meatworks.'

It was heartbreaking for him to see Pete's sad decline.

Liam received a phone call just before his sixteenth birthday that his father had been flown to a hospital in Toowoomba after falling off his veranda in Kingaroy.

'His liver had shut down and pneumonia came on,' he told me.

'I spent a week up at the hospital watching him die but I promised him that I would win a world title one day in his memory. And I will.'

Random Thoughts on some Great Champs

Reg Layton was as tough as he looked and a man who commanded great respect. His wife called him a cuddly old bear, and he was famous for being kind to animals and old boxers. Animals were not always kind to him though; during his lifetime he survived attacks from a death adder and a sea snake.

When I first started writing about boxing for the Brisbane *Telegraph*, an afternoon newspaper, in 1980, Reg was the city's major promoter.

He was born in Perth in 1920 and during tough times in the Great Depression finished his schooling at age 12 to work on a farm. Reg first showed his boxing talent way back in 1938 when he came out the worse for wear in a 30-man street brawl in the West Australian port of Geraldton. One of the onlookers was the American former world champ Tod Morgan, who was plying his trade in Australian rings. 'I wasn't going too well out there,' Layton said. 'No,' Morgan replied, 'but you kept getting up.'

Brisbane's 'House of Stoush', Festival Hall, was too small to accommodate the 1971 fight between rising Queensland star Jeff White and former world champion Lionel Rose. So promoters Reg Layton and Wally Taylor sold 10,000 tickets at the Milton Tennis Stadium. White had just outpointed the brilliant Brisbane pug Alan Moore, while Rose had upset Japanese sensation Guts Ishimatsu.

Rose was the overwhelming favourite after some dynamic sparring sessions in South Brisbane with Wayne Doherty and Con Russell in front of a giant electric fan, a feeble defence against Brisbane's summer swelter. But the Brisbane boxer gradually overcame Rose's speed and outmuscled him at close range to win a 15-round decision.

It was one of the biggest nights ever in Brisbane boxing.

As the pair embraced at the end of a marathon battle, Rose, the beaten favourite, patted White on the chest and said simply, 'Good fight, kid'.

It was 40 years since Muhammad Ali had won an Olympic gold medal but even with the ravages of Parkinson's disease making him walk in slow motion, he remained the biggest show-stopper in sport.

When Paul Thompson, competition manager of the Sydney Olympics, ushered Ali into the boxing arena for the 2000 Games, the fighting in the ring actually stopped. 'It's the first and only time I'd ever seen it happen,' said Thompson, a former Australian champion, who was inducted into the Queensland Boxing Hall of Fame for more than half a century of service to the sport.

'The fighting stopped until Ali was seated. He was still that much of a hit with fans and fighters. He worked miracles in the boxing ring when he was fighting and he did it at our games as well.'

In a major coup, Thompson secured Ali and another former world champ Evander Holyfield as guests for the Sydney boxing competition, an event which produced such champions as Miguel Cotto, Jermain Taylor, Guillermo Rigondeaux, Danny Green and Michael Katsidis.

Even though Thompson won the Australian amateur light-heavyweight title, he counts his greatest achievement in the sport as guiding Grahame 'Spike' Cheney to an Olympic silver medal in 1988 when Thompson was the Australian team's trainer/manager.

Thompson sparred with the great pro fighter Bobby Dunlop in Sydney and while working as a bricklayer in New Guinea represented that country at the 1974 Commonwealth Games.

He retired from competition in 1975 and became one of the most respected trainers and administrators in the sport.

Merv Williams, the former boxing champ who was behind the microphone for so many *TV Ringside* epics, made his name more for his quick quips than his fast fists.

Some of his more famous sayings included: 'He couldn't go two rounds with a revolving door', 'He's like a boarding house cup of tea – big and weak' and 'He 'its 'em so far they have to take a packed lunch!'

There have been some almighty comebacks in boxing but none more stunning than that by Wollongong fighter Shannan Taylor, who fought Shane Mosley for the world welterweight title in 2001 and Arthur Abraham for the world middleweight title five years later.

Shannan lived fast and hard during his career. In 2011 he was at a party when he snorted a nose full of what he thought was cocaine. It was actually heroin and he spent a week in hospital in an induced coma as rumours circulated around the boxing world that he had actually passed away. Obituaries appeared on some boxing websites.

Happily Shannan recovered, and turned his back on the party lifestyle. He and his wife and children were on hand to cheer him when he was inducted into the Australian Boxing Hall of Fame in Melbourne in 2018.

Few Aussie fighters have been as persistent and patient as Brisbane's Dennis Hogan.

He was born in Dublin and grew up in the village of Carnalway, outside Kilcullen. His grandfather Paddy Burke was a local hero, the highly respected coach at the St David's Boxing Club in Naas, housed inside an old army barracks.

'As soon as I could run fast, from the age of five or six,' Hogan told me, 'all the other fighters in the gym used to call me "Rocky" because my little legs would be going like crazy as we did laps in the old barracks.'

Hogan became an Irish international amateur representative, but it wasn't until he moved to Brisbane to work as a builder that he turned professional. He had three world title cracks that ended in defeat, including a desperately close battle with the unbeaten Jaime Munguia that I watched from ringside in Monterrey, Mexico in 2019.

Hogan was 37 and thought to be well past his best when, with Stephen Edwards as his trainer, he finally beat Britain's Sam Eggington in 2022 for the IBO super-welterweight title.

One of the best fight trainers I ever met was Bruce Farthing, who spent more than three decades turning out fighters from the City of Sydney Police Boys Club in Woolloomooloo.

Bruce was a world class light-heavyweight in the 1950s when he scored a win over the great Tongan Johnny Halafihi. Among the top fighters he coached were Jamien Wright, Brian Williams, Simon Paterson Steve Dack and Paul and Michael Isgro.

Jeff Fenech: Heart of a Champion

On 4 October 2019, Jeff Fenech suffered a heart infection while training his team of Australian boxers during a short break in Thailand.

Although feeling desperately ill for days, Jeff insisted he was okay, but his fighters knew something was terribly amiss and rang local paramedics, a move that probably saved his life.

The fighter who showed so much ticker throughout his

fighting career was rushed to intensive care in Bangkok after he began coughing up blood.

The illness required five hours of open-heart surgery, as the boxing great hovered close to death. Fenech's own father, Paul, died young with heart complications, so Jeff's crisis in Thailand was an agonising time for the boxer and his family.

Fenech was set to miss his eldest daughter Jessica's wedding at St Mary's Cathedral in Sydney that month as he recovered from the emergency surgery in Bangkok.

So Jess and her groom Carmello did the next best thing, surprising Fenech with an intimate wedding ceremony by his bedside in intensive care.

Fenech had tears in his eyes as the happy couple exchanged vows and later told *A Current Affair*: 'For them to think of me was pretty special. I was really proud that they did that for me ... it made me want to fight even harder to get back to Australia for them.'

Having been in Fenech's corner for all of his world title wins, I know he is a hard man to keep down. Fenech ignored his doctors' advice and jumped on a red-eye flight back to Sydney just ten days after his life-saving operation.

After touching down, he was put straight onto a stretcher and taken to hospital for a medical assessment. Then, with just an hour to spare, he was discharged from hospital and made it to the wedding.

'Of course your dad's going to walk you down the aisle,' a tearful Fenech said as he surprised Jess outside the church and then walked her to the St Mary's altar in front of 300 guests.

Fenech later said it was the best day of his life, better than winning all his world titles.

His last-minute dash to his daughter's wedding was just another chapter in the extraordinary thrill ride of this amazing fighting machine who did so much to help me and many others during his life.

No fighter anywhere ever had more ticker than Jeff Fenech.

I knew his dad, Paul, very well. Paul grew up in Malta during World War II and blamed the damp, dank ruins of the intense bombing campaigns for his poor health and faulty heart.

Many times as a boy, Paul would hear trapped people wailing under tons of rubble as the Germans tried to blow his tiny island home out of the sea. It felt as though there were earthquakes every day.

'I remember people lying on top of each other in the catacombs,' he once told me, 'huddled together, and the sounds of dripping water, the pom-pom guns, the bombing and the screams.'

Paul was immensely proud of how his son rose through the ranks of boxing, representing his country at the Olympics and becoming Australia's most successful fighter. The great driving force of Fenech's career was immense pride and massive courage.

Shortly before he died, Paul told me: 'My son is so brave – perhaps when he was born God took some of my heart and gave it to Jeff.'